MONEY DOCTORS

the experts in personal finance

JOHN LOWE

THE O'BRIEN PRESS
DUBLIN

First Published 2019 by
The O'Brien Press
12 Terenure Road East, Rathgar,
Dublin 6, D06 HD27, Ireland.
Tel: +353 1 4923333; Fa x +353 1 4922777
E-mail: books@obrien.ie. Website: www.obrien.ie
The O'Brien Press is a member of Publishing Ireland.

ISBN: 978-1-78849-163-1

1 3 5 7 8 6 4 2
19 21 23 22 20

Published in:

DUBLIN
UNESCO
City of Literature

Printed and bound by Scandbook AB, Sweden.
The paper in this book is produced using pulp from managed forests.

The publisher would like to acknowledge the following for the use of their logos: Life
Insurance Association, Brokers Ireland, Financial Services & Pensions Ombudsman, AIB,
Bank of Ireland, Permanent TSB, National Irish Bank, Ulster Bank, the Credit Union, VHI
Healthcare, Laya Healthcare, Irish Life and GoldCore Ltd. The author and publisher have made
every effort to trace all copyright holders, but if any have been inadvertently overlooked we
would be pleased to make the necessary arrangement at the first opportunity.

CONTENTS

ACKNOWLEDGEMENTS

There are many people who deserve a special mention for their personal help and support and who have guided me throughout my career. Included are family, friends, mentors and colleagues. Special mention and special thanks go to the following for their great assistance in the production of this edition of the finance guide:

My family, who continue to support and love me. My sincere thanks also to Jonathan Self (writer, novelist and mentor), George Butler and Stephanie Cahill (longstanding friends and colleagues in Money Doctors), John P Carlin (friend and accountant), Michael and Ivan O'Brien and all in the O'Brien Press, not forgetting Fergal Tobin my original publisher and the person who introduced me to Fergal, novelist Monica McInerney.

Special thanks to the myriad of radio stations, presenters and listeners across the country that regularly take my commentary, including RTÉ Radio, Newstalk, East Coast FM (Declan Meehan), Clare FM, LMFM (Gerry Kelly), Highland Radio, Waterford Local Radio FM, Midlands 103FM, Limerick's Live 95FM (my friend Joe Nash), TodayFM, Sunshine Radio, Ocean FM, Cork 96FM, RedFM, C103 FM, MidWest Radio, South East Radio and, last but not least, the editors and all the team at the Irish Daily Star (Thursdays) and Sinann & Charlotte in RTE.ie/LifeStyle for publishing my weekly article.

PREFACE

Welcome to 2020 and the fifteenth edition of *Money Doctors* – Ireland's bestselling and most comprehensive finance guide, now published for the first time by the O'Brien Press (thank you Michael and Ivan).

The year 2019 was one of stunning growth and great successes for Ireland. We have achieved practically full employment – 2.3 million people working, growth in excess of 8% (where the EU average is 1.6%) and a very buoyant economy. Poverty and deprivation rates have fallen for the fourth year in a row, while wages were up 3% – well ahead of inflation, which has stayed at a low level. We continue to enjoy comparatively low interest rates, though there are some mortgage holders who would prefer the EU average for their standard variable interest rate. There is still a sizeable difference.

We relished the successes of our sports stars in 2019, particularly Shane Lowry's epic first Open victory in Portrush last July, and are excited at the prospect of another Ryder Cup in Ireland in 2026 at Europe's number one hotel and resort, Adare Manor in County Limerick – well done the team there. The Dublin football team hit the magic 5 in a row All Ireland championships, while Tipperary won the 132nd and their 28th All Ireland hurling final against Kilkenny in August.

The only blots on the landscape are the continuing crises in housing and healthcare, with soaring rents and the danger of a new property bubble continuing to develop. House prices in the major urban areas, though levelled off in 2019, are increasingly outside the reach of the average earner. Homelessness has reached record levels, and there is little evidence to date that the government's Rebuilding Ireland initiative has had any tangible effects, other than running out of funds after year one of a three-year plan, though Budget 2020 did earmark further monies for this programme.

Climate change was very much on the agenda both for world leaders and the Irish electorate. The latter's views were evidenced at the European and local elections last May.

Boris Johnson took over the role of Prime Minister in the UK last July, though not without his detractors, while Ursula Von der Leyen became the first female President of the European Commission.

More than ever, this is a time for taking a step back and having a long, hard look at your finances. With a 'bear' (falling) market still on the horizon, your money needs to be carefully managed. *Money Doctors 2020* has been streamlined, amended and updated to include Budget 2020, and a major new chapter to help the ever-growing immigrant population in Ireland entitled 'Non-Nationals – a guide to living in Ireland' plus an updated '100 Ways to Save Cash'. Also included in the appendices are 'Tips for the Top' – 5 innovative or market-leading products or services that deserve special mention and have my endorsement. The Jargon Buster appendix has moved from this book to my website (www.moneydoctors. ie) and you can access it on the home page from all devices. I am, as always, grateful to Jim Power, one of Ireland's best known independent economists, who gives his take on the global and Irish economy for 2020.

I am deeply grateful to my readers for buying and reading this book, and for constant questions, suggestions and helpful comments. If there are topics you feel I should cover in future years or areas where you think greater expansion would be beneficial, please feel free to contact me at my Stillorgan, County Dublin, office: (+353 1) 278 5555 or jlowe@ moneydoctors.ie.

Dealing with money should not be a chore but a pleasure. Whether you read this book from cover to cover or dip in and out, I hope it will inspire you in all your future financial dealings. While it's not about waiting for the storm to pass, as we have been dancing in the rain of late, we must prepare in case the storm comes back. Remember, finances need constant review. Have a great year and many thanks again for your support.

John Lowe, Dublin, December 2019

IS THIS BOOK FOR YOU?

This book is for everyone living in Ireland who wants to better manage and structure their personal finances.

- You will find this book relevant regardless of your financial position, age or gender.
- This guide concentrates on 'how to' information: how to manage your mortgage, how to get rid of your debts, how to build up savings, how to save tax and how to protect your family.
- If there is a particular subject you want to learn about, then check the detailed contents page or the index.
- The book is written in plain English and contains plenty of:
    - case histories;
    - real-life examples;
    - checklists; and
    - action-orientated advice.
- The book is divided into nine sections plus Appendices, covering every aspect of personal finance. It is an annual handbook, so the information it contains will be up to date and includes the latest budgetary and legislative changes.
- Each chapter begins with a summary and ends with a list of action points.

Look out for the symbols used throughout the book:

Money Doctors Wealth Warning This symbol is used to warn you about something that may have an adverse affect on your financial wealth!

Money Doctors Wealth Check This symbol is used to highlight something that could really improve your financial fitness.

GETTING THE MOST OUT OF THIS BOOK

John Lowe of Money Doctors says this book will be relevant to you if:
- you have money questions and don't know whom to turn to for honest, accurate, unbiased answers;
- you want the latest financial information;
- you want to reduce your tax bill;
- you worry about money;
- you have, or plan to get, a mortgage
- you have credit cards, store cards, hire-purchase agreements, an overdraft, personal loans, a mortgage or any other borrowings;
- you have money on deposit or save money on a regular basis;
- you want to build up your capital worth and guarantee yourself a comfortable (and possibly an early) retirement;
- you have capital and don't know how to invest it;
- you have dependants and you are worried about their well-being;
- you have (or think you should have) any sort of life or critical illness cover/income protection;
- you worry about the quality of financial advice you are receiving; or
- you are separating, or thinking of it.

MONEY DOCTORS WEBSITE

Money Doctors 2020 is not just a book: it is a complete service. Visit the free Money Doctors website at www.moneydoctors.ie, where you will find:
- extra articles and checklists covering a huge range of personal finance topics;
- the latest personal finance tips, advice and information, via our blogs;
- online mortgage applications and other financial services;
- special calculators, allowing you to see at the press of a button what your mortgage or other loan will cost you, and how much your savings will earn you;
- timely information, such as current tax rates and allowances, via subscription to the Money Doctors monthly ezine;
- the chance to arrange a consultation with John Lowe, the Money Doctor;
- podcasts on a variety of financial subjects; and
- an opportunity to join us on Twitter (@themoneydoc) LinkedIn, Pinterest and Facebook.

CONSUMER PROTECTION

You should only ever deal with an **authorised adviser** for insurance, investment and pension advice and credit services, including mortgage and debt advice.

An individual or firm that is authorised will not only have had to pass stringent tests to qualify, but their performance will be strictly monitored on an ongoing basis by the Central Bank of Ireland.

You should be aware that there are a number of professional bodies covering the financial services industry. My own belief is that you should only deal with members of these bodies. These are:

- Brokers Ireland

- Life Insurance Association

- Institute of Banking in Ireland

Your financial adviser should ideally be a Qualified Financial Adviser (QFA) as well as having substantial financial experience. Individual membership of other professional bodies, such as the Institute of Bankers in Ireland, is also desirable.

Finally, if you are looking for advice on buying company shares, then you should deal with intermediaries who are members of (or affiliated members of) the Irish Stock Exchange or an authorised agent.

Don't allow yourself to be talked into accepting advice from someone who isn't both independent and qualified. If in doubt visit my website, www.moneydoctors.ie.

It all comes down to belief patterns

I am far too practical a person to be taken in by 'psycho-babble'. However, I do believe that if you want to be financially better off than you are at the moment, then you simply must come to grips with your own belief patterns as they relate to money. Here are some things people have said to me about money:

'I would always shop around for a better deal on most things – but not on financial products.'

'I hate talking about money. I find it embarrassing.'

'Money seems to slip through my fingers.'

'I worry about money all the time but I don't do anything about it, because I am not sure what to do.'

'Money is boring. We have enough. Why think about it?'

In my experience, almost everyone has deeply held beliefs in relation to money – usually negative beliefs. Most can be attributed to one or more of the following factors:

Formative experiences: For instance, in the case of someone whose family suffered financial hardship when they were growing up. Naturally, this would influence their attitude to money.

Parental influence: Some parents talk about money, while others don't – either way, children can end up being worried about there not being enough. By the same token, some parents are spendthrift, while others are positively tight-fisted – again influencing their children's beliefs.

Lack of education: Though there have been recent moves to change the national curriculum, 'personal finance' is still not really taught properly in our schools.

The mystification of money: Financial institutions seem to conspire to make money as mysterious a subject as possible.

Lack of trust in personal finance professionals: Bank managers are viewed as 'fair-weather friends' and the institutions they work for as impersonal and greedy. Insurance and pensions salespeople are hardly revered in society. People are suspicious of the experts they rely on to give them advice.

Society's attitude to money: There are some societies where money is discussed openly. In Ireland, however, it is considered rude to talk about money and crass to spend too much time managing it.

The link between belief and behaviour

There is no doubt in my mind that there is a direct link between (a) what you believe about money, (b) your behaviour in relation to money and (c) how much money you end up having. The fact is that **if you view money in a negative way, you are reducing your chances of a financially stable life**. You aren't giving yourself a proper chance.

What's more, if you think that sorting out your personal finances will take more time and effort than *not* sorting them out, think again. Not paying attention to money is likely to result in you:

- wasting a vast amount of energy worrying;
- wasting a vast amount of cash;

- putting yourself and your dependants at risk;
- reducing your standard of living;
- increasing the number of years you have to work; and
- suffering a shortfall in your pension fund when you reach retirement age.

If you start to *think* more positively about money, I guarantee that you will begin to *behave* more positively about money. And if you behave more positively about money, I guarantee that you will find yourself able to build up much greater wealth.

What are your financial dreams?

- To own your own home without a mortgage?
- To have enough money to retire early?
- To be wealthy enough to pay for all the things you want – such as an education for your children or a second home – without going into debt?

Whatever your dreams, unless you are very, very lucky, the only way to make them come true is to make a proper plan. Such a plan – **a financial plan** – will help ensure that you get from where you are to where you want to be. Creating one is a lot simpler and quicker than you may imagine, as I explain in the first section of this book. Furthermore, I guarantee that the process of writing a plan will – in itself – make you substantially better off. Why? Read on and you'll find out.

MONEY DOCTORS WEALTH CHECK

The section on financial planning explains:

- what a financial plan is;
- why you need a financial plan;
- the stages involved in writing a financial plan;
- practical tips on writing your own plan; and
- where to get professional financial planning help you can trust.

It also includes sample financial plans, and more besides.

Everything, in fact, you need to make financial planning easy.

PART 1

HOW TO BECOME FINANCIALLY FIT IN 2020

1

ALL IT TAKES IS A LITTLE PLANNING

HOW YOUR FINANCIAL PLAN WILL MAKE YOU BETTER OFF

Many people are under the impression that financial planning is a complex process requiring great expertise. In fact, creating a financial plan is a remarkably straightforward activity. It involves three easy steps:

1. Decide what your financial or money objectives are, and prioritise them.
2. Assess what resources you have available to you now, and consider what resources you may have in the future.
3. Work out what actions you need to take to make your financial objectives come true.

This short chapter explains the 'ins and outs' of writing a first-class financial plan. The next chapter explains, in greater detail, how to write your own.

WHY YOU NEED A FINANCIAL PLAN

Your financial plan should have the same qualities as a road map. That is to say, it should help you to reach your destination; to make your journey as fast as possible; and to prevent you wasting time or energy.

MONEY DOCTORS WEALTH CHECK

A little planning brings big rewards

Having a financial plan will bring both material and emotional rewards. From a material perspective a financial plan will make it possible for you to meet your financial objectives. These might include some or all of the following:

- wiping out all your personal debts;
- paying off your mortgage years earlier;
- never having to borrow again;
- having enough money to afford the things that are important to you, such as an education for your children or a second home;

> • having enough money to retire early;
>
> • knowing that you and your dependants are protected against financial hardships; and
>
> • being wealthy enough never to have to worry about the future – whatever it may bring.
>
> And the emotional benefits? You'll feel a tangible peace of mind once you have your financial affairs in order. In addition, a well-considered financial plan guarantees that you will never need to waste energy worrying about money again.
>
> Some people's circumstances, of course, may be such that they will not manage to achieve any or all of these objectives. For these people, financial planning is crucial to getting the maximum advantage from limited resources even with insolvency.

SUPPOSING YOU *DON'T* PLAN?

Suppose you don't bother with a financial plan at all? Leaving something as important as your financial future to chance is risky. True, we live in a country with a relatively generous State benefit system. But would you really want to rely on it? You probably wouldn't starve, but you wouldn't have an easy time of it.

Incidentally, many people assume that the worst thing anyone can do is ignore financial planning completely. In fact, in my experience the people who are worst off are those who *compartmentalise* their money decisions. Let me give you just three examples:

1. When you want to buy a home, you look for a mortgage.
2. When you begin to think about retirement, you start a pension.
3. When you have a young family, you take out life insurance.

This compartmentalised approach to money is both wasteful and risky, because you may:

- end up spending more than you have to on borrowing money;
- by default, pay more tax than you need to;
- end up with inferior and expensive financial products;
- risk your capital, your income, and the standard of living of you and your dependants;
- miss opportunities; and
- make yourself unhappy worrying about your financial security.

A symptom of this approach is responding to ad hoc situations in a knee-jerk manner – for example, subscribing for newly issued shares on a whim, or paying for education fees when you hadn't expected to do so.

INSTANT SAVINGS AND MORE

One key benefit of creating a financial plan is that it will involve a review of your existing financial products. Such a review is bound to result in all sorts of savings as you identify products that are either over-priced or unnecessary. Let me give you just one real-life example:

> One of the Money Doctors' 'patients', Tony, an ex-banker, told me that he'd spent more time choosing his last car than choosing his mortgage. As a result he was, without realising it, paying 1% above the home loan market rate. He'd also allowed himself to be sold a very expensive life insurance plan. I calculated that, over the 25-year term of Tony's €210,000 mortgage, these two products alone would cost him a staggering additional €38,000 in unnecessary payments.

Frankly, because people pay less attention to their finances than to other areas of their lives, they tend to get 'ripped off'. With a financial plan in place, you'll know that you aren't:

- accepting lower rates of return on your savings;
- paying more tax than you have to;
- paying more to borrow than you have to;
- taking out insurance policies that you don't need, or that don't provide you with the protection that you want, and that may well be over-priced;
- making poor investment decisions;
- failing to plan properly for your retirement; or
- putting your money at risk.

WHAT DOES A FINANCIAL PLAN LOOK LIKE?

Your financial plan may be no more than a single piece of paper on which you've jotted down some notes. You might think of it in the same way that you think of a career plan, or any other sort of life plan. It is to guide you, save you time, and ensure that none of your effort is wasted. Or, if you are comfortable using spreadsheet software, you could also do it electronically. Whatever way you choose to complete a financial plan, remember it is essential for giving you a map of your financial road to the future.

HOW LONG SHOULD A FINANCIAL PLAN LAST FOR?

Obviously, there is no set period for a financial plan. My general advice is to write it so that it covers the **current** and **next phase** of your life.

For instance, if you've just left university and you're starting your first job, then you might write a financial plan designed to take you through to when you own your home. Bear in mind that financial plans need to be *flexible*. You may change your ideas about what you want, or circumstances may intervene and require a change of direction.

A financial plan that only covers a specific, short-term requirement (for instance, saving for your retirement) isn't going to bring you lasting financial success.

IF YOU THINK YOU NEED HELP

You will find everything you need to write your own financial plan in this book. However, you may decide you'd like some professional help. There are any number of people who would like to help you with your personal finances, from bank managers to life insurance salespeople, from credit brokers to pension specialists.

The golden rule is: the fewer options the 'experts' can offer you, the less you should trust them.

Let me give you one pertinent example: If you go to your bank and express an interest in taking out a pension, whoever you speak to is duty-bound to offer you something from the bank's own range of products, even if he or she knows that you would get a better deal elsewhere. If, on the other hand, you go to an independent financial adviser, he or she should recommend the best and most competitively priced product for your needs.

For more tips on getting professional help, see [p.29].

THE MONEY DOCTOR SAYS ...

• There is nothing in the least bit complicated about writing a financial plan. It is simply a matter of working out what your money ambitions are, how far you have got to date, and what action you need to take to get to where you want to go.

• Unless you are very, very lucky, the only way you are going to make your financial dreams come true is by planning.

• Your plan may be a single piece of paper with a few notes.

• The process of writing a plan is likely to bring big savings, as you identify financial products you have already bought that are either (a) over-priced or (b) not really necessary.

• Everything you need to write a financial plan is in this book. But if you want help, use an experienced, independent and authorised financial adviser, and be prepared to pay for that advice.

2
WRITING A FINANCIAL PLAN

If you've put off writing a financial plan because you thought it would be time-consuming and tedious, then this chapter will reassure you. Not only is it possible to produce a detailed financial plan in a matter of hours, but as you get involved in the process you may find it considerably more interesting than you imagined.

HOW DO YOU DECIDE WHAT YOUR FINANCIAL OBJECTIVES SHOULD BE?

My advice is to start by **dreaming**. Consider what you'd like to be doing in, say, five years' time, ten years' time and twenty years' time. Consider what work (if any) you'll be doing, where you'll be living, and how you'll be spending your leisure time. What will your family situation be? Once you have a clear picture of the future life you'd like to have, start expressing it in financial terms.

Your financial objectives might include:
- owning your own home, outright, without a mortgage;
- making sure you have sufficient income to retire (possibly early) and live in comfort;
- ensuring that you and your dependants will not suffer financial hardship regardless of any misfortunes that may befall you;

- having sufficient wealth to pay for things that you consider important, whether it's charitable donations, an education for your children, or some other item such as a second home or a caravan; and
- having sufficient wealth to allow you to spend your time as you wish – for instance, having the money to start your own business.

PRIORITISING YOUR FINANCIAL OBJECTIVES

Having produced a list of financial objectives, your next task should be to put them in order of priority.

What you consider important will be determined to a great extent by your personal circumstances. For instance, if you're in third-level education, you'll have a very different view of money to someone five years away from retirement. Someone with a lot of debts will have different concerns to someone with a lump sum to invest.

Nevertheless, regardless of your age, existing wealth, health, number of dependants, or any other factor, I would recommend that you keep the following principles in mind when deciding what your financial priorities should be:

1 For most people, their greatest asset is their **income**. Unless you are fortunate enough to receive a windfall, it is almost certainly your income which you will use to achieve your financial objectives. Under these circumstances, you don't want to risk it and you don't want to waste it. There are all sorts of relatively inexpensive insurance policies designed to protect your income. And by making sure that you don't waste a single cent (especially when buying financial services) you can ensure that it's used to optimum purpose.

2 **Personal debt** – by which I mean everything from store cards to mortgages – will be the biggest drain on your income. If you've borrowed money (and, obviously, there are many circumstances under which this makes excellent sense) then you should make it a priority to repay your loans as quickly as possible. This is easily achievable, as I explain in Part 3.

3 It is vital to have a safety net or **emergency fund** to deal with all the little trials, tribulations and extra expenses that life throws our way. In Part 6, I suggest how much this fund should be, and the best way to build it up.

4 If you've got a good, secure income, it doesn't actually matter what other assets you own. Emotionally, it's nice to have the security of

owning your own home. Financially, it certainly makes sense. But, actually, the best investment that most people can make is in a really decent **pension plan**. With a good pension plan you can leave work early and – if you live to 100 or more – never have to worry about money again. One of the best things about modern pension plans is that they are both flexible and diverse.

5   It is not inconceivable that we will live to a very old age, and in some cases suffer a reduction in our mental ability to handle money matters. Before this may arise it is worth considering setting up an **enduring power of attorney**. This is a document providing for the management of a person's affairs in the event of their becoming mentally incapacitated. The appointed person (the 'attorney') may be allowed to take a wide range of actions on your behalf in relation to property, business and social affairs. He or she may make payments from specified accounts, make appropriate provision for your needs and make appropriate gifts to the donor's relations or friends. You can appoint anyone you wish to be your attorney, such as a spouse, family member, friend or colleague.

6   Know thyself! There is no point in setting financial objectives that you're going to find impossible to attain. Your financial objectives may involve modest changes to your behaviour, but they shouldn't require a complete change in your personality!

TEN UNIVERSAL NEEDS

Ultimately, financial planning is about tailoring a solution to meet your precise requirements. There are, however, a number of 'universal' needs that most of us face. To my mind they are:

1. Having an emergency fund to cover unexpected expenses.
2. Paying off any expensive personal loans and credit card debt.
3. Short-term saving for cars, holidays and so forth.
4. Income protection, in case you are unable to work for any reason.
5. Life assurance (for you and, if relevant, your partner).
6. Starting a pension plan (in my opinion it is never too early).
7. Buying a home with the help of a mortgage.
8. Saving for major purchases.
9. Planning for education fees (if you have children), whether for private school or university.
10. Building up your personal investments.

To this, I suppose I might add long-term care planning if you're worried that your pension and/or the State may not provide for you sufficiently in retirement.

SETTING REALISTIC AIMS

If you had unlimited funds, you could achieve all your financial ambitions without difficulty and you wouldn't need a financial plan. As it is, for most of us life is more complicated. Since we can't have everything we want instantly, we need to set realistic targets and work towards them in easy stages. To make sure we have realistic targets we must test them. Let me give you an example:

David is 40 and self-employed. His objective is to be financially independent by the age of 55. At that point he wants to be able to live comfortably without working. His current income is €40,000 a year and he feels that he'll be able to manage on much less, say €25,000 a year, once he retires. To achieve this, he'll need capital resources of between €500,000 and €600,000. At this point in time he has a pension fund worth €100,000 which, if it grows in real terms (i.e. after the effects of inflation) by 5% a year, will be worth some €208,000 in 15 years. He also has €25,000 of stocks and shares, which he expects to grow at a slightly faster rate, say 7% a year, which would mean an extra €74,000 in 15 years.

In other words, David has a shortfall of between €212,000 and €312,000. To fill this shortfall, he would have to save at least €600 a month (assuming a growth rate of at least 7%) until he reaches 55. However, €600 a month, or more, is a lot of cash to find, so he may have to adjust his expectations. Perhaps he could live on less? Or postpone his retirement an extra five years? Or earn additional money?

Note: this example is just to give you a feel for what I'm talking about. Inflation would need to be taken into account when deciding what to do. I have ignored current pension returns and low growth rates. Everything is cyclical.

Once you settle on your overall objectives, you'll have to decide what is most important to you. For instance, would you rather pay off your mortgage ten years early, or take an annual holiday overseas? Is being able to retire early more important than putting your children through private school?

You must also weigh up other priorities. I always recommend that those with dependants take out income protection insurance before they take out life cover. Why? Anyone under retirement age is 20 times more likely to be unable to work for a prolonged period due to sickness than they are to die. Another recommendation I often make is that people with high personal debt pay it off or consolidate it before they start saving money. This is because it costs more to borrow than you can hope to earn from most forms of low-risk investment.

The two key points here are:

1. Keep your financial expectations realistic.
2. Test them to make sure.

HOW FAR HAVE YOU GOT?

If the first stage of a financial plan involves deciding what you want, then the second stage is working out where you've got to so far. You need to produce an honest and realistic assessment of:

- what resources you have;
- what demands there are on your resources; and
- what action you are already taking to meet your targets.

Once you have this information you'll know what surplus is available to you, or whether you have a shortfall that needs to be made up.

If you visit my website – www.moneydoctor.ie – you'll find several aids to help you reach your goals. Email info@moneydoctors.ie for a Word document budget plan. Or you can use the questionnaire that follows.

YOUR MONTHLY INCOME AND OUTGOINGS

I usually suggest that people start with their income and – if relevant –
their spouse/partner's income. The best way to calculate it is as follows:

Monthly income – gross	You €	Spouse/partner €
Salary or wages	_____	_____
Profits from business	_____	_____
Investment income	_____	_____
State benefits	_____	_____
Pensions	_____	_____
Other earnings	_____	_____
Anything else	_____	_____
Subtotal A	_____	_____
Less tax (PRSI and income tax)	_____	_____
Subtotal B	_____	_____

The resulting figure (Subtotal B) is your disposable income. You now
need to consider how you spend it.

Monthly outgoings	You €	Spouse/partner €
Rent/mortgage	_____	_____
Utilities (gas, electricity, telephone, etc.)	_____	_____
Food	_____	_____
Household items	_____	_____
Drink	_____	_____
Car(s)	_____	_____
Home insurance	_____	_____
Life insurance	_____	_____
Other insurance	_____	_____
Clothes	_____	_____
Child-related expenses	_____	_____
Credit cards	_____	_____

	You	Spouse/partner
Other loan repayments	_____	_____
Spending money	_____	_____
Pension contribution	_____	_____
Regular saving plans	_____	_____
Anything else	_____	_____
Subtotal C	_____	_____

By subtracting your monthly outgoings (Subtotal C) from your disposable income (Subtotal B), you will arrive at your available surplus. Don't despair if this is a 'minus' figure. That's why you are reading this book – and, together, we are going to do something about it!

YOUR ASSETS

Working out what assets you have involves the same process as working out what your surplus income is. You need to tot up the value of everything you own and subtract any debts or other liabilities you may have.

Start with a list of the assets themselves:

Assets	You	Spouse/partner
	€	€
Home	_____	_____
Personal belongings	_____	_____
Furniture and contents of home	_____	_____
Car(s)	_____	_____
Other property	_____	_____
Other valuables	_____	_____
Cash	_____	_____
Savings	_____	_____
Shares	_____	_____
Other investments	_____	_____
Subtotal D	_____	_____

With regard to any investments you have – savings plans or a pension, for instance – you may want to work out what they will be worth at whatever point in the future you intend to cash them in. This can be a complex business. A pension fund, for instance, may grow by more or less than the predicted amount. Therefore, it could be well worth your while to get professional assistance with your calculations.

YOUR LIABILITIES

Liabilities	You €	Spouse/partner €
Mortgage	_____	_____
Credit card debts	_____	_____
Personal loans	_____	_____
Hire-purchase	_____	_____
Overdraft	_____	_____
Other loans	_____	_____
Tax	_____	_____
Other liabilities	_____	_____
Subtotal E	_____	_____

By subtracting your total liabilities (Subtotal E) from the value of your assets (Subtotal D) you will arrive at what financial experts call your 'net worth'. While it is not good if this is a 'minus' figure, once again you shouldn't despair. The whole purpose of a money plan is to strengthen your finances.

THE IMPORTANCE OF MAKING ASSUMPTIONS

All financial planning requires 'assumptions'. Some of these assumptions will be personal to you, such as how much income you expect to earn in the future or how many children you anticipate supporting. Other assumptions will be related to factors only partly within your control, such as the return you can expect to receive from a particular investment. You'll also need to allow for financial factors beyond your control, such as the state of the economy.

The longer the period you're planning for, the less accurate your assumptions will be. It's very hard to predict exactly what you'll be earning in, say, five or ten years, let alone what you'll be earning in twenty years.

In order to improve the quality of their assumptions, many people use historic figures for guidance. Here are some statistics that you may find helpful:

Inflation: There was a time when inflation had the single greatest influence on the economy and thus on financial planning. Although inflation has been quite low for the last few years, it still has a marked effect on the cost of borrowing and on the value of investments. An inflation rate is the general rise in prices as measured against a standard level of purchasing power. The best-known measures of inflation are the Consumer Price Index (CPI), which measures consumer prices, and the Gross Domestic Product (GDP) deflator, which measures inflation across the whole of the domestic economy. The inflation rate in Ireland was recorded at -0.10% in June 2015. It averaged 4.92% from 1976 to 2015, reaching an all-time high of 23.15% in October 1981 and a record low of -6.56% in October 2009. Inflation for the 12-month period to May 2019 was 0.4%.

Interest rates: Interest rates vary enormously, especially when you are borrowing. For instance, in 2019, when a typical mortgage cost 3.5% per year, you could pay up to 21% on a typical store card. Over the last ten years, the average mortgage rate has been about 4.5% a year.

Investments: Not only do the returns on different types of investment vary dramatically, so do the returns within each investment type. So, while investing in the stock market could bring a better average return than investing in property, one individual investor might do substantially better or worse than another. In general, it is best to spread your money between different types of investment, and to assume an average return of between 4% and 7% a year in real terms. For instance, between 1997 and 2007, the average return from government bonds was 4.7% a year, while the average return on the stock market was 10.1%. In 2019, pension returns averaged 9%.

MONEY DOCTORS WEALTH CHECK

How much capital will you need?

One of the hardest calculations to make is how much capital you will need to provide a sufficient income for your needs. Many factors affect this, such as inflation, tax and investment performance.

On the whole, my advice is to assume a 2.5% return after inflation and tax. This means that for every €1,000 of annual income you require, you'll need €40,000 of capital. Put another way, if you want an annual income of €20,000 a year you'll need at least €800,000 worth of capital.

MONEY DOCTORS WEALTH WARNING

An important reminder

Do you have a will? If you do, when did you last update it? Are you taking full advantage of all the tax allowances and exemptions to make sure that your beneficiaries don't have to pay unnecessary inheritance tax?

If you are over 18 (or if you are younger, but married) you should draw up a will, because if you don't, your money will be distributed in accordance with the Succession Act of 1965. This means that your estate could end up not going to your chosen beneficiary or beneficiaries and could even end up filling the government's coffers.

If you need advice on capital acquisitions tax, you should arrange a consultation with the Money Doctor (info@moneydoctors. ie). Don't forget, both you and your partner should draw up a will, and you should also consider:

• giving an enduring power of attorney to someone you trust should you become physically incapacitated; and

• creating a living will, explaining anything you would like done should you become so unwell as to be unable to communicate.

WHERE DO YOU NEED TO TAKE ACTION?

Answer the questions below with a 'yes', 'no' or 'maybe'. Every question you answer with a 'no' or 'maybe' suggests an area where you need to take action.

- Do you spend less than you earn each month?
- Are you satisfied with your standard of living?
- Do you pay your credit card and charge card bills in full, on time, every month?
- Have you taken out sufficient life cover to ensure that your family's lifestyle won't be adversely affected if you die?
- Are you happy with where you live? Can you afford it?
- If you had to manage without an income, would you be able to support yourself for at least three months using money you have saved?
- Do you have a clear sense of financial goals? Have you spent any time thinking about how you're going to achieve them?

- Do you have a pension? Will it be sufficient to support you in reasonable comfort?
- Do you have a will?
- Do you have other investments designed to bring you long-term capital growth?

THE MONEY DOCTOR SAYS ...

- If you are not sure where to begin, begin at the beginning. Work out what you want from your money – what your priorities are.
- Although everyone's circumstances are different, we all have the same basic needs – to secure our future regardless of what happens. This is done through a combination of saving, investment and insurance.
- Take a little time to work out where you are financially – it may be the most profitable half-hour you ever spend.
- Don't be shy about asking for help. If you know you want to sort out your finances, but find it difficult, call in expert help.

3

MONEY IS A FAMILY AFFAIR

HOW A FAMILY CAN WORK TOGETHER TO ACHIEVE LONG-TERM FINANCIAL SECURITY

Anyone who has been in a settled relationship will know that money and love can be a potent combination – both good and bad. If you and your partner share the same attitude to money, you'll be able to build a secure future for yourselves faster, more efficiently and more enjoyably than if you are in conflict.

However, it would be ridiculous not to acknowledge that many relationships are blighted by arguments about money, and that reaching a compromise isn't always easy. In this chapter we look at how couples – and families – can work together to reach their financial goals. We also look at the importance of educating children about money.

PROBLEM? WHAT PROBLEM?

All relationship money problems tend to boil down to one or more of the following issues:

- how the money is earned and who is earning it;
- how the money is spent and who is spending it;
- how the money is being managed and who is managing it;
- how the money is being saved (if it is being saved at all) and who is doing the saving;
- how the money is being invested (if it is being invested at all) and who is handling the investment decisions; and
- what debts you have – both individually and jointly – and why they were incurred.

Of all the subjects that couples argue about – from the choice of holiday destination to who should do the washing up – money arguments are the hardest to resolve. This is because our money beliefs tend to be (a) firmly held, (b) unconscious and (c) non-negotiable.

Couples who want to build a financially secure future need to keep an open mind regarding each other's viewpoint. One of you may be a saver and the other a spender, but that doesn't mean compromise isn't possible.

ARE YOU AND YOUR PARTNER FINANCIALLY COMPATIBLE?

When a couple disagrees about money, it is almost always because they each hold different money beliefs. Which of the following categories best describes you and your partner?

Worry warts: People who worry so much that they never really enjoy money – even when they have plenty.

Big spenders: People who spend money whether or not they have it. They don't mind going into debt to fund their lifestyle.

Careful savers: People who are committed to saving. Sometimes they can be obsessive about it to the point of miserliness, however.

Optimistic dreamers: People who believe that through some miracle – perhaps an unexpected legacy or a lottery win – all their financial worries will be solved overnight.

Outright fools: People – sorry to be harsh – whose spending and borrowing is reckless.

Clever planners: People who plan for a secure financial future but still manage to enjoy a good lifestyle now.

Where a couple consists of two 'clever planners' you tend to get minimum friction. Otherwise, sooner or later, disagreements are bound to arise.

In an ideal world, one would discuss money with a future partner before making any sort of commitment, as this would allow you to check that you are financially compatible. However, we don't live in an ideal world, and most couples will find themselves tackling financial issues after they have been together for some time. Looking on the bright side, maybe this is preferable. After all, you now know and understand each other better.

OPENING A DIALOGUE

The first and most important step for anyone in a relationship is to **open a dialogue** with their partner. If you don't communicate you won't know what they are thinking, and they won't know what you are thinking. My advice is to have a gentle discussion in which you discuss some or all of the following topics:

- Your individual values in relation to money. What do each of you think is important?
- Any assumptions either of you may have. For example, one of you may assume that finances should always be joint; the other may have fixed ideas about keeping them separate.
- Your dreams and desires and your partner's dreams and desires. How do you each envisage the future?

- Your fears and your partner's fears. What are you each most worried about? Each of you will have ingrained attitudes, and you need to recognise what these are before any sort of agreement can be reached.

ANYTHING TO DECLARE?

There are several tricky areas when it comes to discussing personal finance with your partner. One subject that never fails to cause problems is 'secret debts' and 'secret savings'. By this I mean:

- One or both partners have borrowed money without telling the other one.
- One or both partners have tucked money away without telling the other one.

Other 'secrets' that couples keep from each other include:

- How much one or the other really earns.
- Money that one or the other has given away or promised (this often arises where one or the other has been married before).

If you are harbouring a money secret from your partner, my advice is to come clean. The longer you leave it, the worse it will be when it is discovered. Also, it is much harder (and sometimes impossible) to analyse your joint financial position if one of you is holding out.

MONEY DOCTORS WEALTH CHECK

The gentle art of confession

You have a money secret that you need to tell your partner. How can you do it without risking a break-up? Here are some tips:

- Pick your moment. No one likes to receive bad news just when they have to go to work or do something else. Better to raise the topic when you are alone and there is time to talk about it.
- If appropriate, don't forget to say 'sorry'.
- A medical doctor once told me that he always prepares family members for news about the death of a loved one a day or two before it is likely to happen with the words 'I am afraid you should expect the worst' – this gives them time to get used to the idea. If you start by saying you have a confession to make and that it may shock or anger them, the conversation is likely to be less acrimonious.
- Don't fool yourself that – say – borrowing or spending money without telling your partner won't upset them. But, equally, remember that it is only money. The important thing is that there should be honesty in your relationship.

BUILDING A JOINT APPROACH TO MONEY

Disagreements about personal finance can be very divisive – I have seen figures suggesting that half of all couples that break up do so because of disagreements about money. So when I say that you need to agree a joint financial strategy with your partner, I don't say it lightly. This is an approach that I have found works well:

- **Look for common ground:** It is likely, for instance, that you both want the same thing – to be free of debt and have plenty of spare cash.
- **Communicate freely and honestly:** Assess where you are and how each of you have contributed to the current state of affairs. Be honest. Discuss each of your strengths and weaknesses – the things you are doing right, and the things you are doing wrong.
- **Compromise:** Don't allow past behaviour and events poison your chance of success. Put grievances behind you. Start afresh and, in doing so, accept that you will both have to agree to do things differently in the future.

SHARING OUT THE CHORES

There are certain basic money chores that have to be done. One of the most useful things any couple can do in relation to personal finances is to agree who is going to take on which responsibilities. I recommend that all major decisions be made jointly, and that each partner keep the other informed about what they are doing. The tasks that need to be divided up include:

- paying household bills;
- filing and organising financial paperwork;
- doing the household shopping;
- checking the bank accounts and reconciling the balances;
- looking after spending money and accessing cash;
- shopping for larger purchases;
- saving money and arranging any loans;
- investment decisions;
- keeping an eye on investments; and
- dealing with financial institutions – banks, insurance companies and so forth.

In many relationships, one or other partner will take over management of the financial affairs. Even where this works without a hitch, I feel it is not entirely a good idea. Supposing one of you should die unexpectedly – how would the other cope? Also, what happens if you go your separate ways at some point? I can't overstress how important it is to share information and decisions.

MONEY DOCTORS WEALTH CHECK

How to make yourself financially compatible

Here are some valuable tips on handling joint finances – whether with your partner or with someone else, such as a flatmate or friend.

- Maintain your independence. A joint account is perfect for joint responsibilities, but it is a good idea to keep an account for yourself so that you have money available to spend as you want. Decide which areas are joint expenditure and which you are each going to handle alone.

- If one half of a partnership takes over all the money management, it can lead to big trouble. The person 'in charge' may end up resenting the fact that he or she is doing all the work, and he or she may also become controlling. The person not involved is leaving himself or herself vulnerable, adopting an essentially childlike position. Both of you should take decisions together – even if one of you does the day-to-day accounting.

- Be honest about how you each feel. If one of you wants to save and the other wants to spend, admit it and work out a strategy that allows each of you to do as you please. Compromise!

- Plan for a future that isn't completely dependent on staying together. I realise that this may seem pessimistic, but I frequently find myself counselling people who unexpectedly find themselves having to deal with money for the first time.

THE IMPORTANCE OF INVOLVING AND EDUCATING YOUR CHILDREN

How did your parents' approach to money influence you? Now, consider how your attitude will influence your own children. Regardless of your level of wealth, everything you say or do in relation to money will have an effect:

- If you don't discuss money in front of them, they won't learn anything about it.
- Whatever emotions you display – such as fear, worry or indifference – will colour their own relationship with money.

- If you are mean with money or overly generous; if you never waste a penny, or if you spend like there's no tomorrow; your children will be watching and learning.

Given that they are unlikely to learn much about money from any other quarter, and given the way debt is spreading through society like some super-virus, it is clearly important that you educate your children about personal finance. You need to teach them the key principles, including how to:

- save for a specific purpose;
- stick to a budget;
- choose competitive products;
- shop around; and
- spend money wisely.

THE MONEY DOCTOR SAYS...

My upbringing was fairly typical for Ireland in the 1970s. There were six of us squeezed into a three-bedroomed house. My father was the only income earner and, although we never went without, money was always tight. I am reminded of the comedian Les Dawson's visit to the butcher with his mother: She asked for 'a few bones for the dog', to which Les said, 'But we don't have a dog, Mum!'

Of course, we didn't have the luxuries that today's generation have come to expect. In Ireland today, our children really do not appreciate the hardship their parents went through and, in some respects, this is a pity, because parents' values are so much different to their children's. However, the last recession has refocused the core values of parents and their children.

Clearly, what you *don't* want to do is worry your children about money. Still, I believe there is a lot to be said for showing them where your income comes from, and what you then do with it.

When your children realise how well you manage money they can't fail to be proud of you. Naturally, they will grow up not just wanting to be debt-free and rich enough to retire young, but actually understanding how this can be achieved. What better legacy could you leave?

If your financial circumstances radically change, it is far better to keep your children in the loop and ask them to help with economising. This way, the shock of change will be far less pronounced.

THE MONEY DOCTOR SAYS...

- If you are in a relationship, it is vital that you discuss your financial objectives together, sort out your differences and formulate a joint plan.
- Honesty is vital! You have to work together, not against each other.
- Two heads are better than one. If you are working together you'll reach your objectives sooner – and it will be more fun, too.
- It is important to educate your children about finance. Don't let them leave home without good money habits and a genuine understanding of how money works.

4

GETTING HELP

Should you adopt a DIY approach to your financial planning, or should you get professional help? If you do seek help, who can you trust to give the best advice?

Are you the sort of person who relishes the challenge of managing their own finances? Or are you the sort of person who would feel happier passing the whole task on to someone else?

HOW FAR SHOULD YOU GO?

You want to make the most of your money. In practical terms this means:
- keeping the cost of your borrowing (including your mortgage) to a bare minimum, and making sure that you have the most suitable mortgage for your needs;
- earning the highest possible return from your savings and investments, without taking undue risk or paying unnecessary fees or commission;
- obtaining the best possible pension plan;
- taking out only the most appropriate insurance, at the lowest possible price;
- not paying a cent more in tax than you have to;
- not paying a cent more for any other financial services or products than you have to; and
- not being caught by any unscrupulous operators.

With the help of this book (and by visiting www.moneydoctors.ie), you will certainly be able to achieve all of the above by yourself. However, does the DIY approach make sense for you? The following questions may help you to decide:

Have you got the right temperament? Financial planning can be stressful and time-consuming. If you hate figure work, don't like making decisions and worry about taking risks, then maybe you would be better off seeking professional assistance.

Have you got the time? Are you willing to give up a few hours a
month to make sure you are optimising your finances? Do you see
this as being quite good fun? If not, then maybe the DIY approach
isn't best for you.

Can you access the information you need? Financial planning requires
access to information. If you can't gain access to the internet, and
if you aren't near a good library, then it is possible you should let
someone else do the legwork for you.

How to find someone you can trust

Whenever I do a radio phone-in as the Money Doctor, the question I get
asked most is: 'Who can I turn to for help with my money problems?'

Consumers, understandably, want independent and expert advice. The
trouble is that most people offering advice work for financial institutions,
which have their own products to promote. Bluntly, if you talk to a life
assurance salesperson about your retirement planning, you know she or he
isn't going to recommend anything except the life assurance products her
or his own company sells.

The best place to get advice is from someone who isn't under any
pressure to *sell* anything, but is in a position to do what is best for you.

This book is designed to give you all the information you need to
organise your finances, save you tax and find the most appropriate
products for your needs. However, if you want to discuss your situation
with someone, face to face, make sure you talk to a professional who is
experienced in all financial areas. In other words, contact an independent
financial adviser and be prepared to pay for their advice.

What can you expect from your independent professional financial adviser?

A key advantage to appointing an authorised adviser (someone who
is independent, professional, qualified and stringently regulated) for
insurances and investments is that they owe their allegiance to you and
not to any financial institution or investment house. *Your needs* will
be paramount. Therefore, you can expect them to provide you with the
following services:

Strategic planning: They will look at your complete financial position,
agree your financial objectives with you, and advise you on how
to reach your money targets. They should also assess your existing

position, and review any financial products you have in place to make sure they meet your requirements.

Competitive analysis: Having decided what products you need, your adviser should search the market for the best product offering the best value for money.

Negotiation services: When an insurance company quotes a rate, it isn't necessarily fixed in stone. In fact, it is possible to negotiate discounts on a huge range of financial products. Your adviser will know what else is available in the market and should negotiate to get you the best possible deal.

Background information: Your adviser should provide you with background information on any products or companies they recommend.

Administration: Your adviser should deal with all the paperwork on your behalf and assist with the filling out of any forms.

Regular reviews: Your adviser should monitor your needs without being asked. They should constantly be thinking about your situation and making sure that whatever they have recommended is performing in the desired manner.

Your adviser should be able to look after all your financial needs, including:

- mortgages;
- re-finance;
- commercial loans;
- personal loans;
- asset finance and leasing;
- life cover;
- income protection and other insurance;
- health cover;
- all savings and investments;
- pensions; and
- property and other general insurance.

Where more specialised advice is needed (say, in the selection of shares to build a portfolio, or specific tax planning), your adviser should be able to recommend other impartial professionals.

Saving tax

A first-class financial adviser will be able to advise you on tax-saving products. **For specialist tax advice, however, you should always go to an accountant or qualified tax consultant.** If the size of your tax bill doesn't warrant appointing an accountant, however, your financial adviser should be able to assist you. Tax is a big part of financial planning. After all, what's the point of making a better return on your investments only to lose it through poor tax advice? *Always* check that your adviser is taking your tax position into account and is properly qualified to assist you.

A very short history lesson

Prior to November 2001, there were over 9,000 'insurance brokers' offering financial advice. At that point, the Central Bank took over regulation and forced them to register. Six thousand dropped out immediately, mainly because the scale of their operations meant they did not have the time or resources to provide the level of product research required.

Of the two authorisations available, there are currently around 400 authorised advisers, who must give 'best advice' irrespective of agencies held. The balance of about 2,500 are **multi-agency intermediaries** (originally called RAIPIs, then 'restricted intermediaries'). They can only give advice on the insurance and investment appointments held.

Then, in 2003, in order to ensure that consumers receive reliable and independent advice, the government set up the Irish Financial Services Regulatory Authority (IFSRA, then changed to the 'Financial Regulator'), an independent agency that took over the regulatory role previously filled by the Central Bank. Regulation is now entrusted again to the Central Bank of Ireland.

When considering any professional adviser, you should check:
- that they are regulated by the Central Bank of Ireland; and
- what services they are authorised to provide, and at what cost.

Financial advisers must now give you a **Terms of Business** booklet, outlining their terms of business, fees chargeable, appointments with product providers, Central Bank of Ireland authorisation and notification of the Investors' Compensation Act.

MONEY DOCTORS WEALTH WARNING

Some things are best not delegated

There is an enormous amount to be said for getting a really good professional adviser to sort out everything for you. You'll save money. You'll save time. And you will end up with the best possible products for your needs. But no matter how good your adviser, you should always take time to:

- understand what he or she is proposing, and why;
- learn about the products you are committing to; and
- check up on the financial institutions that will be supplying those products.

THE MONEY DOCTOR SAYS ...

- It is possible to handle all your financial decisions without reference to anyone else. However, it requires time and commitment.
- If you do decide to use a professional adviser, make sure that they are fully authorised and don't be shy about asking them questions.
- Remember, it is important to have clear financial objectives.

PART 2

YOUR FINANCIAL RIGHTS

Are you entitled to claim any government benefits? How does the law protect you as an employee? What do you do if you buy something and are unhappy with the way you have been treated?

This section of the book will answer all of your questions with regard to your financial rights. In Chapter 5 you'll discover how the social welfare system works and how to assess what you may be entitled to. In Chapter 6 you'll learn about your rights as an employee. And in Chapter 7 you'll find out what your rights are as a consumer. I've also included useful sources of additional information and important contact information.

5

YOUR RIGHT TO SOCIAL WELFARE

HOW THE SYSTEM WORKS AND HOW TO MAKE SURE YOU RECEIVE YOUR ENTITLEMENTS

The Irish state provides its citizens with one of the most advanced, generous and comprehensive social welfare systems in the world. It isn't, however, what you would call a simple system, being made up of a bewildering array of:

- assistance payments;
- benefits;
- supplements;
- allowances;
- grants; and
- pensions.

Many of the financial benefits available are 'contributory', meaning that you are only entitled to them if you have made **PRSI** (Pay-Related Social Insurance) contributions in the past. Others are available to everyone, including people who have moved here from abroad.

As one would expect, the state only provides social welfare when certain conditions are met. Sometimes these conditions are very straightforward. For instance, with very few exceptions, a special grant of €6,000 is paid to widows or widowers with dependent children following the death of their spouse. In other instances, you have to meet stringent requirements, often related to the size and number of your PRSI contributions. A good example of this is the invalidity pension, which is payable if you have been 'incapable of work for at least twelve months and are likely to be incapable of work for a further twelve months, or you are permanently incapable'. To qualify for this benefit you must also have paid PRSI at Class A, E or H for at least 260 weeks, and you must have had at least 48 weeks' PRSI paid or credited in the last tax year!

I am afraid the system is made even more confusing by frequent changes to the nature, values, names and conditions attached to the various benefits available.

So, how can you discover exactly what you are entitled to?
This chapter will outline, in broad terms, the various forms of social welfare that are available, along with the more important conditions that must be met in order to claim them. Using this, you should be able to ascertain what benefits you might be entitled to.

Your next step should be to contact your local Social Welfare Office or Citizens Information Centre for further assistance. You'll find both listed in your local phone book.

Another approach is to write directly to:
The Information Service,
Department of Social Protection
Áras Mhic Dhiarmada, Store Street, Dublin 1
Tel: (01) 704 3000.
       or
Retirement/Old Age Contributory & Non-Contributory Pensions
College Road, Sligo, County Sligo
Tel: (071) 915 7100/LoCall: 1890 50 00 00.
Or, if you have access to the internet, you can go to www.welfare.ie.

THE DIFFERENCE BETWEEN CONTRIBUTORY AND NON-CONTRIBUTORY PAYMENTS

The terms 'contributory' and 'non-contributory' are bandied about a good deal in relation to social welfare benefits. The terms are slightly misleading, because they imply that you have to have contributed personally to be eligible for certain payments, and this contribution is generally assumed to be PRSI payments. However, a completely different system operated prior to 1974; another system was in place until 1953; and both may entitle you to contributory benefits.

The word 'contributory' is confusing in another respect, too. You may well be eligible to receive a contributory benefit if you are married to someone who has made contributions, or if you are the child or dependant of someone who has made contributions.

Another point to bear in mind is that you may have been in regular employment but earning so little that you were not liable to make any PRSI payments. If you are a public servant, your entitlements will be linked to when you joined. If you are self-employed, a completely different set of regulations applies.

My advice, therefore, is never to assume that you won't be entitled to a particular form of social welfare until you have fully investigated each and every one of the conditions attached to it. Don't ever assume that because something is 'contributory' or 'non-contributory' it won't apply to you.

THE DIFFERENT TYPES OF SOCIAL WELFARE

At the start of this chapter, I listed the categories of social welfare payments. But what do these various terms mean?

On the whole, social welfare **benefits** tend to be available only to those who have made PRSI contributions. Furthermore, though there are a few exceptions, social welfare benefits are not affected by your level of wealth.

Social welfare **assistance**, on the other hand, is given only to those who satisfy a 'means test'.

A good example of the difference is jobseeker's benefit, which has PRSI conditions attached to it but for which there is no means test, and the non-contributory old age pension, which is classified as social assistance and is subject to means testing.

SO, WHAT IS MEANS TESTING?

In order that financial assistance only goes to those who are most needy, the government checks each claimant's financial circumstances first. This check is called a 'means test'.

Your means are considered to be:

- any cash income you have;
- the value of your assets (your home is excluded up to a certain value, but if you own a farm it is included); and
- your savings and investments.

In some cases, your residential situation will be relevant. For instance, if you are unemployed but live at home with your parents and you are under the age of 24, this could reduce your entitlement.

When you apply for a means-tested form of social assistance, a 'means test officer' will consider your case. The criteria used to assess your entitlement will, of course, vary according to the form of social assistance you are applying to receive. You should expect, however, to be asked about your entire financial situation. This could include:

- your income;
- your spouse's income;
- your partner's income (if co-habiting);
- farm income (if relevant);

- any savings, investments or other assets you may own, such as property;
- your general circumstances, such as where you live, whom you live with, who is dependent on you, and so forth;
- any debts you may have;
- your weekly outgoings, including rent; and
- any other benefits you may be receiving.

Naturally, any information you provide will be treated in the strictest confidence.

There will, of course, be other conditions as well. For instance, you have to be genuinely unemployed to claim jobseeker's allowance. But your means will be the deciding point. Note that even if you're not eligible for the maximum amount of assistance, you could still be entitled to a reduced amount.

WHAT ARE YOU ENTITLED TO? SOCIAL WELFARE PAYMENTS IN DETAIL

Below is a summary of all the main social welfare payments. You'll also find an explanation of what they could be worth to you, together with some of the more notable conditions.

Remember, the Department of Social Protection is there to help you. You shouldn't hesitate to ask their advice about what you are entitled to.

Social welfare pensions

The state makes available two different types of social welfare pension:

Contributory pension: So-called because your entitlement is linked to the amount and class of PRSI you have paid during your working life.

Non-contributory pension: Means-tested and available to those who haven't made any contributions during their working lives.

Contributory pensions are paid to those who have reached the age of 66 and are not means-tested. The qualifying age will rise to 67 in 2021, and 68 in 2028.

The maximum standard amount for a contributory pension is €248.30 per week, but the actual sum you receive will be determined by the number and value of contributions you made during your working life – and your age. Additional sums are payable if you have dependent children and live alone.

The maximum standard amount payable as an old age non-contributory pension is currently €237 per week, or €247 per week for those aged over 80. Again, you may be able to claim more if you have dependent children or live alone.

Regardless of whether you have made contributions or not, additional amounts may be available if you are blind, or if you live on certain offshore islands.

Pensions for widows and widowers

If you are – or become – a widow or widower, then you will also have pension entitlements. These are:

The contributory widow(er)'s pension: As its name implies, this is available to widows or widowers where sufficient PRSI contributions have been made, and is worth up to €208.50 per week for those under 66, €248.30 for those aged 66 to 80, and €258.30 for those aged over 80.

The non-contributory widow(er)'s pension: This is means-tested and could be worth as much as €203 a week.

In both instances if you have a dependent child, live alone and/or are resident on certain offshore islands, you may be entitled to receive an additional sum.

Free travel

You may be entitled to free travel if you are permanently living in the State and:

- you are aged 66 or over; or
- you are getting disability allowance, blind person's pension, carer's allowance or an invalidity pension from the Department of Social Protection.

Household Benefits Package

This is a package of allowances to help with the cost of running a household. The package is available to everyone aged over 70, and to people under 70 in certain circumstances. There are two allowances in the Household Benefits Package:

- The electricity or natural gas allowance; and
- The free TV licence allowance.

MONEY DOCTORS WEALTH CHECK

You don't have to be retired to claim free electricity and other benefits

The Household Benefits Package is also available to those entitled to other payments, such as an invalidity pension or a carer's allowance (see below). Under these circumstances your age will not be relevant to your eligibility.

Supplementary welfare allowance

This provides a basic weekly allowance as a right to eligible people who have little or no income. If you have a low income, you may also qualify for a weekly supplement under the scheme to meet certain special needs. In addition, payments can be made in cases of urgent or exceptional needs.

There are four types of payments: **basic** payments, **supplements**, **exceptional needs** payments and **urgent needs** payments. To find out more, contact the Department of Social Welfare's community welfare service at your local office.

One-parent family payment

This is a payment for men and women under 66 who are bringing up children without the support of a partner. To qualify for this payment, you must meet certain conditions and you must satisfy a means test.

You can earn up to €110 per week and qualify for the one-parent family payment. Half of the remainder of your gross earnings up to €425 per week is assessed as means. The age limit for an eligible child is 7 years, and you must have at least one child below the relevant age limit.

Guardian's payment (contributory)

This allowance is payable where both parents have died, or one parent has died and the other has abandoned the child. Being a contributory allowance, one or other of the parents must have made sufficient PRSI contributions. The payment is made up to the age of 18, or 22 if the child is in full-time education. It can be as much as €186 a week.

Guardian's payment (non-contributory)

If a child does not qualify for the contributory guardian's benefit, he or she may instead be eligible for the **non-contributory guardian's payment**. This pension is means-tested. It can be as much as €186 a week.

Invalidity pension

This is a contributory pension, so it is only available to those who meet the PRSI payment qualifications. It is payable instead of a disability benefit if you've been incapable of work for at least 12 months and are likely to be incapable of work for a further 12 months, or if you're permanently incapable of work.

As with many other pensions, the amount you receive will increase if you have dependent children, live alone, or live on certain offshore islands. If you are eligible for an invalidity pension you may also be able to claim an additional sum if you support someone else. It can be as much as €208.50 a week up to age 66 for a single individual.

Medical cards

Medical cards entitle you to a range of free medical care. Eligibility is means-tested, but there are a number of exceptions, including for some people aged 70 or over, and anyone drawing a state pension from another EU country.

Different income limits exist for those aged under 70 and those aged over 70 and vary depending on the number of children or dependants and whether they are aged over 16 and in full-time education. Although your circumstances may not entitle you to a medical card, you could still be eligible for a **doctor visit card**, which would allow you to receive free care from your GP. There are special, separately means-tested cards for over-70s. In addition, from August 2015, all over-70s who do not qualify for a medical card are entitled to free GP visits. Since June 2015, all children under the age of 6 are entitled to free GP visits, and it is proposed to extend this to all children under 12 in the near future. If this section is relevant to you, you should seek assistance from the Department of Social Protection – see contact details on p. 35.

Treatment benefits

The state provides a range of contributory **treatment benefits** covering dental care, eye testing, glasses, contact lenses and hearing aids. In some instances, the benefits are entirely free and in others you must pay a part of the cost. There may also be upper limits on the amounts which can be claimed.

Maternity benefit

A contributory **maternity benefit** is payable to women in current employment or self-employment who have been paying PRSI. It is only payable where the mother has been making contributions – the father's contributions have no bearing on eligibility. The standard rate is €245 per week, which is taxable but not subject to PRSI or USC and is paid for 26 weeks. A new two-week paternity benefit was introduced from September 2016 with the same eligibility conditions and rate as maternity benefit.

Adoptive benefit

If you adopt a child you may still be eligible for a payment equivalent in value to the maternity benefit. This is a contributory benefit. It can be as much as €245 a week for a continuous period of 24 weeks from the date of placement of your child and it is taxable.

Asylum seekers

If you are applying for refugee status, you can obtain rent-free accommodation at a regional centre. Each adult is entitled to a personal allowance of €21.60 per week and €21.60 for each child. More information can be obtained from:

Reception and Integration Agency
PO Box 11487
Dublin 2
Tel: (01) 418 3200

MONEY DOCTORS WEALTH WARNING

A tightening-up of the rules: Habitual Resident's Test

Since 2004, the government has introduced a new **Habitual Resident's Test**, meaning that in order to receive a whole range of payments you must be able to prove that you are 'habitually resident in Ireland'. However, the rules do allow you to be resident of the UK, Channel Islands or the Isle of Man. Payments affected by this rule include unemployment assistance, old age contributory pension, one-parent family payment and supplementary welfare allowance.

Child benefit

Child benefit is not means-tested, nor do you have to make any contribution in order to receive it. It is paid each month, and the amount you receive depends on the number of qualifying children living with you and their ages. In some instances the payment may be made until the children reach the age of 18. The current rate is €140 per month for each child under 16 years old. It also pays to have multiple births – one and a half times the usual rate is payable for twins (each), and double for triplets or greater (each).

Early Childhood Care and Education scheme (ECCE)

This scheme provides two years of early childhood care and education for children of pre-school age. Children are eligible for the scheme if they are aged over three years and not older than five and a half years. The State pays a capitation fee to participating playschools and daycare centres.

Jobseeker's benefit

Jobseeker's benefit is only paid to those who satisfy the PRSI conditions. The amount you receive will be linked to your age and the amount of PRSI paid. It can be as much as €203 a week.

The duration of jobseeker's benefit was reduced in April 2013. For people with 260 contributions, the benefit period was reduced from 12 to nine months; for those with fewer than 260 contributions, it was reduced from nine to six months.

Jobseeker's allowance

This was previously known as unemployment assistance, and is a means-tested payment available to those who are unemployed and have not made sufficient PRSI contributions or have used up their entitlement to jobseeker's benefit.

It can be as much as €203 per week for those aged over 26, with proportionate increases for qualified adult or child dependants.

Back-to-work enterprise allowance

This scheme encourages people getting certain social welfare payments to become self-employed. If you take part in this scheme, you can keep a percentage of your social welfare payment for up to two years. In addition to your weekly payment, you may also get help with setting up your business under a scheme called the Enterprise Support Grant.

If you live in an area covered by a Local Development Company (LDC), you should apply to the Enterprise Officer in your local office; otherwise, you should apply to the Case Officer in your social welfare office.

Carer's benefit

If you leave work in order to look after someone in need of full-time care and attention, then you may well be eligible for the contributory carer's benefit. Additionally, you may be entitled to an **annual carer support grant**, which would be paid to you in June each year. This grant is available to all carers providing full-time care, subject to certain conditions. The carer support grant is currently worth €1,700 per person cared for. The carer's benefit can be as much as €330 a week if you are caring for more than one person.

Disability and injury benefits

A range of disability and injury benefits – all contributory – is available to those unable to work due to a disability or injury. If you are disabled or suffer an injury you may also be eligible, without means testing, for a range of other benefits including **medical care**, and a **constant attendant's allowance**. If you are a public servant and have to give up work due to ill health, you will be eligible for an **early retirement pension**. These benefits have a maximum personal rate of €203 a week.

Widowed parent's grant

A special grant of €6,000 is available to widows or widowers with dependent children following the death of their spouse. This is not means-tested and only minimal conditions are attached to it.

Working family payment

Formerly known as family income supplement, the purpose of this scheme is to help families on low incomes. To be eligible, at least one member of the family must be working at least part-time, and the family income must be below a certain level. Although the working family payment is based on the family's weekly income, once it has been set it doesn't normally fluctuate. However, if your circumstances change (for instance, if you have another child), you can apply to have it increased. The supplement is based on 60% of the difference between your net family income and the income limit that applies to your family circumstances (see Department of Social Protection leaflet **FISI**).

Drugs payment scheme

Even if you are not eligible for a medical card, you could well be eligible to receive support under the drugs payment scheme. Once you are registered, no individual or family is expected to pay more than €124 a month for prescription drugs included on the list of 'essential medicines'. To register, you should get the relevant form from your pharmacy or local health office.

The nursing homes support scheme

The nursing homes support scheme, also known as 'fair deal', provides financial support to people who need long-term nursing home care. The scheme is operated by the Health Service Executive (HSE), and replaced the Nursing Home Subvention on 27 October 2009.

Under this scheme, you make a contribution towards the cost of your care and the State pays the balance. The scheme covers approved private nursing homes, as well as voluntary and public nursing homes. Anyone who is ordinarily resident in the State and is assessed as needing long-term nursing home care can apply for the scheme.

Disabled persons

A host of grants and allowances exist for disabled and incapacitated persons. These include the blind welfare allowance, blind person's pension, carer's allowance, disability allowance, motorised transport grant, domiciliary care allowance and many more. Various tax credits and allowances are also available to disabled people.

Free travel

Free travel on public transport is available to everyone aged 66 or over. It is also available to anyone receiving an invalidity pension, a disability allowance, a blind person's pension or a carer's allowance. Note that if you are entitled to free travel, and you're married or cohabiting with someone, they may travel with you, also free of charge.

If you have been turned down for a benefit, or considered ineligible, you can contact:

Social Welfare Appeals Office
D'Olier House
D'Olier Street, Dublin 2
Tel: (01) 673 2800
Lo Call: 1890 747434

MONEY DOCTORS WEALTH CHECK

What you're entitled to elsewhere in the EU

As Ireland is part of the European Union, you are entitled to a wide range of benefits in other EU member states. However, since EU member states each have their own social welfare system, claiming entitlements in other countries can be fraught with problems. Keep in mind too that contributions made in one member state do not necessarily qualify you for benefits in another. For instance, if you have been working overseas and return home to Ireland, you will not automatically be eligible for unemployment benefit. However, if you have been registered as unemployed for four weeks in Ireland, you are then entitled to move to another EU country to look for work and still receive the benefit for up to three months.

If you are thinking of living or working in another EU member state, then you should ask at your local social welfare office for their leaflet describing the benefits available to you.

Incidentally, not only are you legally entitled to look for work in any EU member state without a work permit, but you can also take advantage of each member state's national placement service. To do this, contact your local Intreo employment services office. Details of your application will be sent overseas through the SEDOC system free of charge.

MONEY DOCTORS WEALTH WARNING

Social welfare benefits are not necessarily tax-free

Social welfare benefits are not automatically tax-free. Whether they are taxable will largely depend on the income level of the recipient. Although tax will not be deducted by the Department of Social Protection on any payments made to you, the Revenue Commissioners will often take the tax directly from some other source of income that may be payable to the recipient. However, on the plus side, some of the 'taxable benefits' you may be entitled to will also qualify you for the PAYE tax credit. These are:

- state pension (contributory);
- contributory survivor's pension; and
- guardian's payment.

A number of other benefits may also be liable to income tax. These are:

- invalidity pension;
- one-parent family payment;
- carer's allowance;
- jobseeker's benefit;
- jobseeker's allowance;
- blind person's pension;
- non-contributory widow(er)'s pension;
- non-contributory guardian's pension; and
- social assistance allowance for deserted or prisoners' wives.

The Revenue Commissioners do, however, make some useful concessions:

- If you are receiving a disability benefit, the first six days will not be subject to tax.

- If you are receiving social welfare payments, child-dependent additions are not taxed (except for invalidity pensions).
- If you are a 'short-term worker' (that it is to say, you work in a trade where short-term employment is the norm), then any jobseeker's allowance you receive will not be taxed.

MONEY DOCTORS WEALTH CHECK

Don't forget to apply for a European Health Insurance Card

If you're travelling or staying temporarily in another EU member state (excluding the UK), then you should apply for a European Health Insurance Card. This will ensure that you are eligible for free health care if you become ill or have an accident when overseas. You can do this through your HSE local centre.

THE MONEY DOCTOR SAYS ...

- You may be entitled to all sorts of social welfare payments that you weren't aware of.
- Check through all the allowances, benefits and grants summarised in this chapter to see which might apply to you.
- Contact your local Department of Social Protection to find out more and to make a claim. Remember, they are there to help you.

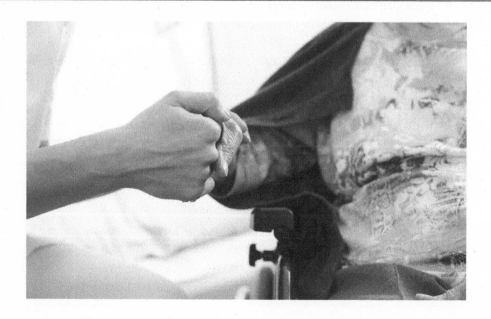

6

YOUR EMPLOYMENT RIGHTS

When people think of 'employee rights', they usually think of legal rights relating to things like discrimination and redundancy. But if you are an employee you have financial rights, too. For instance, you have the right to be paid a **minimum wage** and the right to **holiday pay**. This chapter explains these rights in plain English.

YOU MAY BE MORE PROTECTED THAN YOU IMAGINE

In the last few years the Irish government has enacted a considerable amount of new legislation to protect employees. One reason for this was that many employers were seeking to get around the existing employment legislation by putting their workers on 'contract'. Seasonal and part-time workers were also at a disadvantage. Since 2003, however, workers on fixed-term contracts must be treated just as well as full-time employees. Furthermore, an employee cannot be expected to work on a fixed-term contract for more than four years.

MINIMUM WAGE

Since 1 April 2000, all but a tiny minority of workers over the age of 18 are entitled to be paid a minimum amount of money per hour, known as the **national minimum wage**. In July 2011, the national minimum wage was set at €8.65 per hour. In Budget 2019 it was increased to €9.80 per hour. However, you should note that:

- If you're in a new job you are only entitled to 80% of the minimum wage for your first year, and 90% in your second year.
- There are various age categories – if you're under 18, the hourly rate is €6.86; aged 18 it is €7.84; aged 19 it is €8.82; and aged 20+ it is €9.80.

ANNUAL LEAVE ENTITLEMENT

You are entitled to a minimum of four weeks' annual leave, plus public holidays, of which there are nine per year.

HOLIDAY PAY

If you are in paid employment, then you are legally entitled to paid holidays. The holiday year usually runs from 1 April to 31 March. However, your employer is entitled to use an alternative 12-month period. Broadly speaking, if you're working full time, you should be entitled to a minimum of four working weeks over the year. Of course, if you switch jobs, this may reduce your entitlement.

YOUR WORKING WEEK

Under the Organisation of Working Time Act, employees cannot be expected to work more than 48 hours a week. However, there are innumerable exceptions to this. For instance, the Act does not apply to junior hospital doctors, transport employees, fishermen, family members working on a farm or in a private house, or the Gardaí.

There are also rules regarding rest periods. You're legally entitled to an 11-hour rest period every 24 hours; one period of 24 hours' rest per week preceded by a daily rest period – in other words a total of 35 hours in a single block; and rest breaks of 15 minutes where up to four-and-a-half hours have been worked, or 30 minutes where up to six hours have been worked. Slightly different arrangements apply to night workers.

ON-CALL WORKERS

If you are expected to be on call for work, then you should be paid for it. The rule is that you are entitled to receive pay for at least a quarter of your on-call hours even if you don't end up working. The maximum amount your employer has to pay you for is 15 on-call hours a week.

DISMISSAL RIGHTS

Your employer can only dismiss you if he or she can prove that you aren't capable, competent or qualified to do the work you were employed to do. Alternatively, your employer must show that your conduct was in some way unacceptable; or that by continuing to employ you, he or she would contravene another statutory requirement. The only other reason an employer may dismiss you is if he or she is making you redundant [(see p. 52)]. This said, unfair dismissal normally only applies to those who have been employed for at least a year's continuous service with the same employer. Furthermore, there are many exclusions, including those who are aged 65 and over.

If you feel that you've been unfairly dismissed then you must make your complaint within six months.

Note that once you've completed at least 13 weeks with the same employer, you are entitled to pre-set periods of notice of dismissal. These range from one week's notice if you've been working for between 13 weeks and two years; to eight weeks' notice if you've been working for over 15 years.

TIME OFF WORK

There are various other reasons why you can legitimately claim time off work. For instance, you can take:

- **Emergency time** off in order to deal with family emergencies resulting from an accident or illness. You are entitled to up to five days over a period of 36 months, and such leave is paid.
- Up to 26 weeks' **maternity leave** if you become pregnant, during which time you can claim maternity benefit. Your employer is not obliged to give you any additional income over and above this maternity benefit. When the maternity benefit period ends, you're entitled to take up to a further 16 weeks of unpaid leave.
- Time off if you are an **expectant mother**, **parent** or **carer** with a special need. For instance, expectant mothers can take time off without loss of pay to go to medical examinations.

WHAT TO DO IF YOU ARE UNHAPPY WITH YOUR EMPLOYER

If you feel that your employment rights are being abused, you can obtain further information from:
Workplace Relations Commission
O'Brien Road, Carlow
LoCall: 1890 80 80 90
Tel: (059) 917 8990

REDUNDANCY

If you have worked for the same employer for at least two years – even if it is part-time – and you are made redundant, then you may well be eligible for a **redundancy payment**. Various conditions apply. For instance, you must be aged between 16 and 66, and you must normally have worked at least eight hours a week. Also, 'redundancy' only covers the situation where you've been dismissed because – essentially – your employer no longer needs your services. This could be for a variety of reasons, including a change in location, or a decision by the employer to carry on the business with fewer employees.

The amount you receive will be based on the number of years you've worked. You should receive two weeks' pay for every year of service to a maximum of €600 a week, topped up with one additional week's pay. If you receive a large lump-sum redundancy payment then you may be liable to pay tax on it. For further information about this, turn to Chapter 31.

THE MONEY DOCTOR SAYS ...

- Know your financial rights as an employee and don't let your employer bully or cajole you into accepting anything less.
- Remember, there are lots of circumstances in which your employer must pay you. And lots of circumstances in which your employer must let you have time off.

7

YOUR RIGHTS AS A FINANCIAL CONSUMER

Do you suspect your bank of over-charging you? Have you felt that an insurance salesperson has sold you a product you don't need? Are you worried about personal financial information being used for marketing purposes?

If you have any concerns about the way you've been treated by a financial institution, this chapter is for you. In it you'll learn how the law protects you, and what you can do if there's something you are unhappy about.

Your basic rights

As the customer of a financial institution you have a wide range of rights. You don't need to suffer poor service, over-charging, mis-selling or fraud. If you're unhappy, there are dedicated, independent organisations that will assist you. Furthermore, if you have lost money, you may be entitled to compensation.

HOW TO COMPLAIN

If you are unhappy and wish to complain, then, in the first instance, you should write to the financial institution concerned and offer them an opportunity to redress the situation. If you are not satisfied with the response you receive, follow the course of action outlined in the relevant section below.

If you're unhappy with your bank, building society, credit union, pension scheme or insurance company

If you're unhappy with your bank, building society or credit union, you can appeal to the Financial Services and Pensions Ombudsman. This body also covers insurance complaints and is authorised to make awards of up to a limit of €250,000.

All banks in Ireland now offer a wide range of financial services, including insurance and pensions, so this body will cover all of these areas should you have a complaint to make.

A finding of the Financial Services and Pensions Ombudsman is legally binding on both parties, subject only to appeal by either party to the High Court. A party has 21 calendar days from the date of the finding in which to appeal.

Financial Services & Pensions Ombudsman's Bureau
Third Floor
Lincoln House
Lincoln Place, Dublin 2
Tel: (01) 5677000
Email: info @FSPO.ie

Financial Services
Ombudsman

If you're unhappy with your financial advisers

In order to make sure that consumers receive reliable and independent advice, the government set up the **Financial Regulator**, now operating within the Central Bank of Ireland. Before you even consider dealing with any professional adviser, you should check that they are regulated by the Central Bank of Ireland and what services they are authorised to provide. They must give you a **Terms of Business** letter, which outlines their terms of business, fees chargeable, appointments with product providers, Central Bank of Ireland authorisation, and notification of the Investors' Compensation Act. You'll find more information about choosing a professional adviser in Chapter 4.

There are three different bodies to which your adviser may belong:
- Brokers Ireland (BI)
- Institute of Banking in Ireland (IoB)
- Life Insurance Association (LIA)

IF YOU HAVE BEEN TURNED DOWN FOR A LOAN OR CREDIT CARD FOR NO APPARENT REASON

If you have been turned down for a loan or credit card, it is probably because of your **credit rating**. Almost all the lenders in Ireland rely on credit bureaux to provide them with information about their potential customers. If the information that any particular credit bureau holds is incorrect, it can result in you being turned down for credit. The three bureaux which operate in Ireland are legally obliged to advise you of the information they hold about you. Their details are:

The Central Credit Register (CCR)
First Floor, Block E, Adelphi Plaza
George's Street Upper
Dún Laoghaire, County Dublin
Tel: (01) 224 5500
Lo-call: 1890 100 050
www.ccr.ie

The Irish Credit Bureau (ICB)
Newstead House, Newstead,
Clonskeagh, Dublin 14
Tel: (01) 260 0388
www.icb.ie

Experian Ireland
Newenham House, Northern Cross
Malahide Road, Dublin 17
Tel: (01) 846 9200
www.experian.ie

You will not pay any fee as an individual for CCR, but will pay a small charge for the other two services. For instance, the ICB charge €6. Do note that they respond only to written or online requests. The service usually takes no more than three days.

If you're worried about Big Brother
Many of us, with a certain amount of justification, worry that large organisations – such as banks and insurance companies – hold incorrect and unnecessary information about us on their files. Under the Data Protection Act you have the right of access to any personal file relating to yourself held by any company or organisation. To discover what data a company or organisation holds about you, you simply have to write to them saying that you're making your request under the Data Protection Act. If you encounter any resistance, then you should contact the Data Protection Commissioner at:
  The Data Protection Commissioner
  21 Fitzwilliam Square South, Dublin 2
  Tel: (076) 1104800 or (057) 8684800
If you discover that an organisation has incorrect information about you, you are entitled to have it corrected.

MONEY DOCTORS WEALTH CHECK

The Deposit Guarantee scheme

With the level of uncertainty about the future of some of our financial institutions, it should be reassuring to know the details of this scheme. This has been in place since 1995 and guarantees individual deposits of up to €100,000 held in any bank, building society or credit union regulated by the Central Bank of Ireland. This consists of a number of Irish and non-Irish deposit-taking institutions operating in the Irish market.

You are covered for up to €1 million for 6 months if you come into a sudden windfall (lotto, inheritance, etc), but after 6 months, it is back to the €100,000 threshold.

THE MONEY DOCTOR SAYS ...

- If you are unhappy with the service you have received from a financial institution you should, in the first instance, offer them the opportunity to put things right. The best way to do this is to put your complaint in writing.
- If you aren't satisfied with the response you receive, take it further. Complain to the relevant ombudsman.
- Legal action is always an option – but remember, it will cost you money, whereas there is no charge involved in asking an ombudsman.

PART 3

BANKING, BORROWING AND GETTING OUT OF DEBT

This section deals with three extremely important topics. Firstly, it offers a comprehensive guide to modern banking services in Ireland, together with tips on getting the most from your bank at the lowest possible cost. Secondly, it explains how you can pay off all your debts – including credit cards, loans, overdrafts and even your mortgage – quickly and easily. Thirdly, it looks at the different ways in which you can borrow money and suggests the most inexpensive ways to do so.

8

BANKING

HOW TO ENJOY THE BEST BANKING IN IRELAND

What do you demand from your bank – first-class service? Free banking? Total security? A range of competitively priced financial products? With a little careful planning, as I will explain in this chapter, you can enjoy the best banking in Ireland.

UNDERSTANDING THE BANKING SYSTEM

The first step to enjoying better banking is to understand how the banks themselves operate.

To begin with, despite the charges they impose, banks don't make their profits from providing day-to-day banking services. This is because it is incredibly expensive to run a branch network, handling millions of transactions, dealing with vast quantities of cash and providing customers with all the other services we (rightly) demand.

So, how *do* banks make their profits? The answer is by selling their customers a wide range of other financial services – everything from mortgages and loans/overdrafts to credit cards, and from insurance to investment products.

Every time you use your bank, whether you are withdrawing cash from a machine, paying a bill, or ordering a statement, you present your bank with another opportunity to sell you something. Much in the same way as supermarkets use 'loss leaders' (popular products sold at below cost price in order to attract customers), banks offer banking services – especially current accounts – as a way of attracting and keeping customers.

In fact, *operated properly*, a current account is one of the greatest financial bargains of all time.

Why have I put the words 'operated properly' in italics? Because in order to recoup some of their expenses, banks stipulate that you must follow the terms and conditions relating to your account. If you don't, they hit you with all sorts of extra charges.

Making the banking system work for you

How, then, can you get the most from your bank? Here are four straightforward and easy-to-follow rules:

- Only buy the services and products you need from your bank. Don't allow them to persuade you to buy something you don't really require.
- Make sure the services and products you buy are competitively priced. Buying a financial product from your bank may be more convenient – but it could cost you a lot of money.
- Don't hesitate to shop around or move your business. Banks rely on customer inertia. In other words, they know that many people can't be bothered to ring around for a better price, let alone move their account elsewhere for a better deal.
- Avoid breaking the terms and conditions attached to any product you purchase from your bank, as the consequences will undoubtedly be expensive.

You may imagine from what I am saying that I am 'anti-bank'. Far from it – I think today's modern banks offer customers fantastic choice, and – if you buy wisely – you can pay little or nothing for your day-to-day banking.

WHAT BANKS DO BEST

At the heart of all banking lies the **current account**. This basic bank account should provide you with the following facilities:

- A safe and secure place to deposit cheques or cash.
- Somewhere convenient to keep your money in the short to medium term, until you need to spend it.
- Access to your cash via branches and cash machines.
- A simple and easy way to pay your bills.

- A comprehensive record of your day-to-day financial transactions.

In order to provide all of this, the typical current account will offer you some or all of the following services:

- A **cheque book**.
- An **automated teller machine** (ATM) **card** or visa debit card, which allows you to get cash 24 hours a day and to arrange direct payments in shops, online and even overseas.
- A **direct debit facility**, so that you can pay your bills automatically.
- A **standing order facility**, allowing you to make regular payments.
- **Regular statements**.
- **Overdraft facilities**.

Your current account should also give you access to a telephone banking facility and – if you use the internet – online banking. Both of these should allow you to access your account and arrange transactions without having to go into a branch.

Although you can obtain most of the services listed above from An Post Money, one 'building society' and some credit unions, only five banks in Ireland offer you *full current account banking facilities*. These are:

 Bank of Ireland

 KBC

 Ulster Bank

 permanent tsb

BASIC BANKING SERVICES EXPLAINED

There are some banking terms that regularly cause customer confusion. I know, because I used to be a banker. Below, I explain them in plain English.

Standing order

A **standing order** is exactly that – a regular ('standing') instruction ('order') to your bank to make the same payment to the same person or organisation on an agreed date. For instance, you might order your bank to pay €200 a month to me because you appreciate this book so much. Or, for that matter, you might instruct them to pay me a much larger amount every other month or every quarter, six months or year. You can instruct them to do this until further notice or until a date you specify.

Direct debit

A **direct debit** is an authorisation to your bank to pay a regular bill on your behalf. For instance, you might sign a direct debit instructing them to pay your Electric Ireland bill when it's presented. With a direct debit you don't specify the amount that is going to be paid, and because of this there are some very strict safeguards in place to protect you. One of these is that only reputable organisations are allowed to use the direct debit system.

Visa debit card

A **Visa debit card** works exactly like a cheque book, but using plastic instead of paper. When you pay someone with a Visa debit card, they apply to your bank for the money, which is then transferred to their account.

You should only make a payment by debit card if you have sufficient funds in your account, or if your overdraft facility is large enough to meet the payment. From 1 January 2016, the current annual €2.50/€5 stamp duty on ATM cards will be replaced with a new 12 cent ATM withdrawal fee capped at €2.50/€5 per annum. All debit cards also double as ATM cards. Thanks to debit cards, you no longer need to bring cash when shopping or wait for a cheque to clear before collecting goods.

Overdraft

An overdraft is a short-term loan offered by your bank as part of your current account facility. There are two types:

- An **authorised overdraft** is one that has been arranged in advance – though you don't, necessarily, have to use it. The bank normally charges for agreeing this facility, usually €25.
- An **unauthorised overdraft** is where the bank decides that despite the fact that you have no agreement to borrow from them, they will still make some payment on your behalf. Unauthorised overdrafts attract penalties and high rates of interest called surcharges. With one bank, it can amount to over double the normal overdraft rate!

What many bank customers do not realise is that banks expect your current account to be in credit for 30 days a year, and will charge you extra if it isn't.

WHAT PRICE BANKING?

So, what can you expect to pay for your current account banking? There isn't an easy answer. All banks have different pricing structures – what one bank offers for free, another will charge for.

In 2004, the Irish Financial Services Regulatory Authority (now known as the Central Bank of Ireland) surveyed bank customers and found that on average they were being charged between €50 and €137 for current account transactions. The level of charges was linked to the customer's choice of bank and level of usage. Today these charges are greater.

A direct comparison of current account charges isn't possible, because all five banks offer different products and make different charges, plus they change endlessly. Check out the National Consumer Agency website (www.consumerhelp.ie) for a snapshot comparison of different accounts. If you want to save money on your current account fees, the best way is to follow the money-saving tips below.

CUTTING THE COST OF YOUR CURRENT ACCOUNT

There are a number of ways to dramatically reduce the cost of your current account banking. These include:

- With competition hotting up, most banks now offer free banking, subject to various conditions. Shop around for the best package to suit your individual circumstances.
- Don't use a bank overdraft facility. Banks will charge you for setting it up. They'll charge you interest on it, and if you exceed the overdraft, there will be a surcharge on top of this interest! Also, they'll use it as an excuse to charge you for other facilities.
- Don't, whatever you do, go overdrawn without formal agreement. An unauthorised overdraft will result in you being charged an extremely high rate of interest plus huge additional fees. Even going overdrawn for a couple of days could result in you paying €20 or more for the privilege.
- Don't allow your cheques or payments to 'bounce', referred to as being 'returned unpaid'. All five banks impose heavy charges if your cheque or direct debit is returned unpaid. This happens, of course, if you haven't sufficient money in your account or you don't have a large enough overdraft limit. 'Refer to drawer' or 'payment stopped' is stamped on the cheque. With the former, your credibility is shot, and there is a question mark on your ability to honour a debt.

- Don't bank a cheque that might not clear. A cheque which is lodged to your account, but not honoured, could cost you as much as €17.14 including unpaid charges and referral fees per transaction.
- Consider using An Post Money (their **BillPay** service or online service at www.mybills.ie are excellent, with over 120 bills payable through any of the approximately 900 post offices throughout Ireland, six days a week and completely free of charge) or a credit union account for limited banking facilities – a far more economical way to do one's banking, see **[p.68]**. They also operate their Smart account (with debit cards and so on) and offer credit cards (0% interest on balance transfers for 12 months) and loans (€5,000 to €75,000 up to 5–7 years for home improvement loans, at competitive rates).
- Consider using a credit card to pay all your bills. If you settle your credit card statement in full every month, this won't cost you anything. See the section on credit cards below for more information about this.
- Using Internet and telephone banking enables you to make payments and transfers between accounts online or over the telephone with a secure password, and eliminates cheque costs and other bank charges.

MONEY DOCTORS WEALTH CHECK

The advantage of a joint account

If I am advising someone who is married or co-habiting, and/or has dependants, I often recommend that they open a joint account and keep a bit of emergency cash in it. Why? When someone dies, it often takes months before his or her affairs can be wound up. During this time, all bank accounts and other assets will be frozen. This frequently leaves the bereaved worrying about money. If you have a joint account, however, no such problem arises. Joint accounts are useful in other circumstances too, as everyone named on the account has the right to operate it, subject to the signing authority given.

Note: Joint accounts do not automatically escape inheritance tax.

OTHER TYPES OF BANK ACCOUNT

In addition to offering current accounts, all five banks offer a range of **deposit** and **saving accounts**. The usual rule with these is that the longer you leave your money, and the more money you deposit, the better the rate of interest you will receive.

In the current climate of low interest rates, many bank deposit accounts offer an extremely poor return.

To give you an idea, if you deposit €1,000 with your average high street bank for one year, you will earn about €1 in interest before tax. Unless you are not liable to income tax, you will have to pay Deposit Interest Retention Tax (DIRT) on this at 33%, meaning you will be left with a rather modest 67 cents for your trouble.

I examine the whole question of what to do with your savings in Part 6. In the meantime, I would suggest that you should not leave your short-term savings in a current account, where it's unlikely to earn any interest at all, and instead you should shop around and put any spare money where it gets the best rate.

Other bank services to consider

As already mentioned, all five banks offer a wide range of other services, from credit cards to personal loans, and from pensions to mortgages. If you have your current account with a particular bank, there is a great temptation to use them for these other services also. I would advise you to resist this temptation. Let me give you two examples of why it's such a bad idea.

At the time of writing I checked the market for the best and worst mortgage rates.

- The best 90% mortgage for a first-time buyer could be a fixed rate of 2.3% (fixed for 2 years). (New Central Bank guidelines limit lending to 90% loan-to-value.)
- The worst 90% mortgage for a first-time buyer on a standard variable rate (no interest-only facility) is 4.2%.

I also checked credit card interest rates:

- The best credit card interest rate (after the 'loss leader' rates) is 13.8%.
- The worst rate is a store card in the range of 22.9%.

As you can see, it definitely pays to shop around.

MONEY DOCTORS WEALTH CHECK

Switching is easy!

All five banks have adopted a code of practice to make it easier to move from one bank to another. Under this code, it should take you less than ten days to get a new account up and running, and all your standing orders and direct debits should be transferred from your old account within one week after that. If you have any trouble changing your bank, you should contact the Financial Services & Pensions Ombudsman's Bureau. You'll find their address on **[p. 54]**.

STATE SAVINGS: ACCOUNTS FROM THE NATIONAL TREASURY MANAGEMENT AGENCY (NTMA)

State savings products from the NTMA are sold in all post offices. Although post offices do not have ATMs, there are about 900 branches and, of course, they're open 6 days per week. You can also use post offices – without cost – to pay about 120 different household bills, and you can buy money drafts at minimal cost.

THE CREDIT UNION OPTION

Credit unions are owned by their members. There are around 400 credit unions in Ireland, each serving a local community. Their original role was to help people to save and also to provide inexpensive loans. In the last few years, though, many have dramatically expanded the range of financial services they offer. For instance, many now offer budget accounts, which are perfectly suitable for paying regular bills, and they are embarking on a new debit card service to compete with banks. The main drawback to using a credit union for your day-to-day banking is that at the moment you can't take advantage of a national branch network or ATMs. Plus, following the Financial Regulator's advice, very few credit unions now offer interest or dividends. However, for some people they do offer an acceptable option.

creditunion.ie

BANKING ON HOLIDAY

If you're going abroad, what should you do about money? Here are a few tips:

- Since Ireland is one of the 18 countries that comprise the eurozone, you can pay with euro when visiting Austria, Belgium, Cyprus, Finland, France, Germany, Greece, Italy, Latvia, Luxembourg, Malta, The Netherlands, Portugal, Slovakia, Slovenia, Estonia and Spain. Like the American dollar, the euro is also accepted in many other countries.

- Wherever you're travelling in the world, whether in the eurozone or not, a credit card is probably the least expensive, most secure and most convenient way of paying. Visa and MasterCard are the most widely accepted credit cards overseas. However, I would not recommend credit cards as a means of obtaining cash when overseas, as credit card companies charge a fee for cash advances plus a high rate of interest from the day of withdrawal. You will also find the exchange rate is not to your advantage!

- If you have a Visa debit card from one of the five Irish banks, you'll find that you can use it extensively all over the world. The advantage of this is that you need not carry a great deal of cash with you, providing you have sufficient funds in your current account. Note, however, that you may not get the best rate of exchange and there could be special charges. Check with your bank before you head off.

- The practical option is to ask for the minimum credit limit on your current credit card and pre-lodge all the funds you expect to spend on your holiday.

THE MONEY DOCTOR SAYS ...

- It is possible to enjoy free or very low-cost banking if you take advantage of the system.
- Unauthorised overdrafts are very expensive and should be avoided if at all possible.
- Bank loyalty doesn't pay. Always shop around for the best deal.
- If you settle up each month in full, a credit card can be a very inexpensive way to manage much of your banking.
- There are alternatives to the banks – An Post and credit unions.

9

GETTING OUT OF DEBT

HOW TO PAY OFF ALL YOUR LOANS – INCLUDING YOUR MORTGAGE – QUICKLY AND EASILY

The greatest threat to your financial well-being is borrowing. I am not talking about reckless borrowing either, but ordinary borrowing in the form of personal loans, overdrafts and credit cards. This is because the cost of borrowing money is a huge drain on your most valuable asset – your income.

What's more, the cost of borrowing can't just be measured in terms of the interest you are paying. You must also factor in the opportunity cost – the money you would otherwise be making if you were investing your income instead of spending it on servicing your debts. Let me give you one simple example:

> €10,000 repaid over seven years at an interest rate of 10% will require monthly repayments of €166. Total interest cost €3,945.

> Invest €166 a month into, say, the stock market for the same period and, assuming the same sort of growth we have seen over the last ten years bar the last few, you'll have a lump sum of almost €20,000 in seven years.

Which is why, in this chapter, I explain the benefits of being debt-free, together with two proven methods to make paying off all your loans fast and painless. For those who are beyond the point of being able to get out of debt, see Chapter 35: MARP, personal insolvency and bankruptcy.

YOU MAY NOT EVEN REALISE YOU HAVE A PROBLEM

Most people borrow money but fail to think of themselves as being in debt. The fact is:
- You don't have to be in any sort of financial difficulty to be in debt.
- When you add up the cost of servicing your debt – including your mortgage – it may come to more than you imagine.
- Debt is the single greatest threat to your financial freedom and security. It is sucking away your most valuable asset: your income.
- The first benefit of being debt-free is that your money becomes your own to spend or invest as you prefer.

- Not having any debt will make you less vulnerable. You won't need so much insurance, for instance.

SIZING UP THE PROBLEM

Over the last 20 to 30 years, consumer debt has increased at a frightening pace. Why should this be? Some borrowing is unavoidable – for instance, loans taken out when ill or unemployed. Some can be attributed to factors such as changing social values, lack of education at school, our consumer society and 'impulse' spending. However, I believe the main reason for the borrowing boom is that debt has become a hugely profitable business. Bluntly, lenders use clever marketing tricks to 'push' debt onto innocent consumers. They do this because the returns are irresistible. Look at how much money they can make:

- If you leave money on deposit at a bank you'll typically earn much less than 0.1% (10 cents for every €100) a year by way of interest.
- That bank, however, can lend your money to someone else at anything up to 24% (€24 for every €100) a year.

Under the circumstances, is it any wonder that financial institutions are falling over themselves to lend money? Or that they devote themselves to coming up with new ways to sell loans to their customers?

DEBT COMES IN MANY DISGUISES

The trouble with the word 'debt' is that it has all sorts of negative connotations. Many people believe that providing they are never behind on their repayments they are not in debt. This isn't true. A debt is when you owe someone money. It could be:

- an unpaid balance on a credit card;
- an overdraft;
- a personal loan;
- a car loan or loan for some other specific purchase;
- a mortgage on your home;
- a secured loan;
- a hire-purchase agreement;
- an unpaid balance on a store charge card;
- a business loan; or
- a loan made by a friend or family member.

It is important to remember that just because you are never in arrears and have an excellent credit rating, it doesn't mean you are debt-free.

MONEY DOCTORS WEALTH WARNING

It is compound interest that makes debt so expensive

When you are earning it, it has the power to make you very rich. When you are paying it, it has the power to make you very poor. Albert Einstein described it as 'the greatest mathematical discovery of all time'. It is the reason why banks, credit unions, credit card companies and other financial institutions make so much profit from lending money. And it is the reason why ordinary investors can make themselves rich simply by doing nothing. It is a fiendishly simple concept called compound interest.

Perhaps the easiest way to understand compound interest is to look at two hypothetical examples:

Imagine that you borrow €1,000 at a rate of 10% a year. At the end of one year – assuming you have made no repayments – you will owe €100 in interest (10% of €1,000) or a total of €1,100. If you wait another year then you will owe an additional €110 in interest (10% of €1,100) or a total of €1,210. In other words, you are paying interest on the interest.

Now imagine that you have €1,000 to invest and you deposit it in a savings account, which pays interest at a rate of 10% per year. At the end of one year you will be entitled to €100 interest. If you withdraw this interest but leave your capital, at the end of the second year you will be entitled to another €100 interest. Supposing, however, that you don't withdraw the interest but leave it to 'compound'. At the end of your first year your €1,000 is worth €1,100. At the end of your second year you will have earned €110 interest, meaning that your original €1,000 is worth €1,210. Put another way, your interest is earning you more interest.

When you borrow money, compound interest is working against you. Supposing, for instance, you borrow €5,000 on a credit card at an interest rate of 15% – which isn't high by today's standards. The credit card company allows you to make a minimum payment of 1.5% each month. After two years you will still owe approximately €4,700, having made repayments of €1,750, of which €1,450 has been swallowed up in interest.

Compound interest can be your greatest enemy or your greatest ally. When you are in debt, it works against you. But when you have money to invest, you can make compound interest really work for you.

'Compounding is man's greatest invention as it allows the reliable systematic accumulation of wealth.' Albert Einstein

BEWARE THE MINIMUM PAYMENT TRAP

You make your lender happy when you:
- borrow as much as possible;
- pay it back over as long a period as possible;
- borrow at the highest possible interest rate; and
- make the minimum monthly payment.

You should be particularly wary of the **minimum payment trap** – where the lender allows you to pay back very little of the debt each month. This is particularly prevalent in the credit card and store card sector. If you opt for the minimum monthly repayment, your repayment will be made up almost completely of interest, so that the debt itself hardly gets reduced. Another thing to watch for is 'revolving credit', where the lender keeps upping your credit limit or offering you new loans. It can take up to 20 years to repay some credit card debt if you make only the minimum payment each month!

DEBT THREATENS YOUR FUTURE FREEDOM

I wouldn't go so far as to say that all debt is bad. There are plenty of instances where borrowing money makes financial sense – in order to buy your own home, for example, or to pay for education. However, **when you borrow money to finance your lifestyle, you are getting into dangerous territory**. Living beyond your means threatens your future financial freedom. Let me give you an example:

Cathal is the manager of a supermarket and earns a good income. However, it isn't enough to cover all the things he and his family like to enjoy, so he borrows frequently. In a typical year, he might borrow to pay for Christmas presents, for a holiday and just to cover other shortfalls in his monthly expenditure, such as clothes or eating out. He views this as 'short-term' debt, but the reality is that every year between the ages of 35 and 55 he borrows an average of €4,000 more than he earns. Because this is short-term, unsecured debt, he pays an average of 12% a year in interest. His monthly debt repayments (excluding his mortgage) are €360.

Cathal's twin brother, Ray, is also a supermarket manager and earns exactly the same income. However, he lives within his means. He doesn't eat out as often, go on holiday as frequently or drive such a nice car. He saves the €360 his brother spends each month on servicing his debts and instead he invests the money. He manages a return of 6% a year on average between the ages of 35 and 55, and so he builds up a tax-free lump sum of €160,000.

The fact is, your most valuable asset is your income, and there is only so much that each of us will ever earn during our lifetimes. By spending a large portion of it on servicing debt you are, essentially, giving it away to your lenders. Surely your need is greater than theirs?

SEVEN EXCELLENT REASONS TO BECOME DEBT-FREE

Here are seven reasons why you should pay off all your debts – including, perhaps, your mortgage.

1. It will make you less vulnerable. If you are in debt and for some reason your income is reduced or stops altogether (suppose, for instance, you fall seriously ill and don't have permanent health insurance), then not being able to repay your loans could have serious consequences.
2. It will make your family less vulnerable. I don't want to depress you, but when you die your debts won't die with you – your estate will have to pay them all.
3. You won't have to worry about inflation. If you owe money and interest rates rise (as recently as 1981 interest rates were as high as 20%), you could easily find yourself struggling to make your monthly payments.
4. You won't have the stress that comes with debt. The fact is, owing money is stressful.
5. You'll enjoy a genuine sense of satisfaction. There is a real peace of mind that comes with not owing money and with owning your home outright.
6. It will open up new choices. Suddenly all the money you are spending on servicing your debts will be available for you to spend or save as you prefer.
7. It will ensure you have a comfortable retirement. In fact, it may allow you to retire early. Why should you have to wait until you are 60 or 65 to give up work?

MONEY DOCTORS WEALTH WARNING

How lenders will try to trick you

With so much profit at stake, lenders put a lot of effort into persuading consumers to borrow. There is a catch to every offer! Let me give you one example:

Josephine goes to buy a new bed in the local store sale. It is marked down from €1,300 to €1,100 and, as she goes to pay, the shop assistant persuades her to take out a store card as it will give her an extra 10% saving. So instead of €1,100 she pays just €990. However, Josephine doesn't pay off her store card at the end of the month, but instead takes 36 months to do so. The result? Because she is being charged 15% interest, the bed ends up costing her €1,548. Not so much of a saving after all!

There are a couple of other things to watch out for. Firstly, **loan consolidation**. When used properly – as I will explain in this chapter – loan consolidation can be an excellent way to speed yourself out of debt. However, unscrupulous lenders often lure borrowers into taking out expensive consolidation loans – even encouraging them to borrow extra for a holiday or other luxury item. Secondly, if **transferring credit card debt** to save money, very often a low-interest or zero-interest period is followed by a much higher rate. Check the conditions carefully and don't be taken in by lenders.

THE FIRST STEP TO GETTING OUT OF DEBT

There is one thing you must do before you set out to eradicate all your debt: stop borrowing. After all, you can't get yourself out of a hole if you keep digging. Take a once-and-for-all decision:

- not just to pay off your debts, but to stay out of debt;
- not to borrow any more money unless it is absolutely unavoidable (or there is a very reasonable chance that you can invest the money you borrow to make more than the loan is going to cost you to repay);
- not to live beyond your means; and
- to avoid 'bargains'. In my book, a genuine bargain is something you need to buy and you manage to get at a lower price than you expected to pay for it. Something that you don't need but you buy because it seems to be cheap is definitely not a bargain.

There are various actions you can take to make this easier on yourself. You can:
- Cut up all your credit cards and store cards.
- Cancel your overdraft limit. But remember, most banks will allow a 'shadow' overdraft on your account. This means that, informally, they may allow your account to overdraw by, say, €500 before you are contacted. This is costly and may eventually have to be formalised, so you are back in the overdraft trap again. Keep track of all transactions on your account.
- Use a charge card where the balance has to be paid in full at the end of each month, or take the prepaid card option.
- Avoid buying any unnecessary items.
- Avoid taking out any new loans, including hire-purchase agreements and overdrafts.
- Avoid increasing the size of any existing loans.
- Pay with cash whenever possible – nothing reduces one's tendency to spend money as much as paying with cash.

American money expert Alvin Hall (you may have seen him on television) suggests that anyone who has trouble curbing his or her expenditure should keep what he calls a **money diary**. The idea is that you carry a small notebook with you wherever you go and write down details of every single penny you spend. You should include everything – from your daily newspaper to your mortgage repayments. After a couple of weeks, you'll have a precise picture of where your money is going and this, in turn, will help you avoid spending money on things you don't really want or need. If you are prone to impulse spending, or if you always spend more than your income, I can see the good sense in this approach. Download the **free Money Doctors app** that will track your spending. Simply type 'Money Doctor' into iTunes or Google Play to download.

TAKING STOCK OF YOUR SITUATION

Once you have stopped making the situation any worse, you need to take stock of your situation. In particular, you should gather together full details of your debts. The information you require about each of your debts is:
- to whom you owe the money;
- how big the debt is;
- how long you have to pay it back (the term), if relevant;
- what the rate of interest is and whether it is fixed or variable;
- whether you will be penalised for paying back the debt early (and if so what the penalties are);

- what the minimum monthly payment is (if this is relevant); and
- whether the interest is calculated daily, monthly or annually.

It is important not to overlook any debts, so here is a quick checklist to remind you. Don't forget to include any money that your spouse or partner may owe, too!

- mortgages
- secured loans
- credit cards
- store cards
- overdrafts
- personal loans
- car loans
- hire- or lease-purchase
- catalogue company loans
- family or friends who may have lent you money
- student loans

Most of the information you need should be supplied to you each month by your lenders. If it isn't, you should telephone or write to them asking for full details.

MONEY DOCTORS WEALTH CHECK

The 'savings' conundrum

The Money Doctor often encounters 'patients' who have debts but are saving money at the same time. If the return on your savings is merely the deposit interest rate from a bank, it may make very good sense to reduce your debt instead. The interest you are charged on your debt is very likely far higher than the interest you earn on your savings.

In most cases, it makes sense to stop saving money, and to use existing savings to pay off some or all of your debts. Why? Because usually what you earn from your savings will be substantially less than what you are paying out to borrow.

- €100 in a savings account may earn you as little as 1c in interest after tax per year.
- €100 owed on, say, a credit card may cost you as much as €24 or even more per year.

So if you have savings of €1,000, and use it to pay off €1,000 of credit card debt, you could save yourself as much as €240 a year – more if you have borrowed on a store card.

Note, however, that it does not make sense to cash in your savings if, for example, you have an endowment policy that you may need to leave to mature. You would be well advised to take professional advice on this, since some are worth more than others.

Overall, however, it does not make financial sense to be investing a small amount of money each month if, at the same time, you are spending a small fortune on servicing a debt.

THE ART OF DEBT ELIMINATION

You've taken the decision not to incur any extra debt. You've got a real grip on the size and nature of your problem. What next? You have two options:

- the **consolidation** approach.
- the **sniper** approach.

Option 1: The consolidation approach

The idea behind 'consolidation' is to reduce the cost of your debt dramatically. Instead of having lots of different loans, all at different rates, you have a single loan at one, much lower rate. This works particularly well if you own your own home. What you do is:

1. Add up all the money you currently spend on making debt repayments.
2. Consolidate all your debts into a single, much cheaper loan.
3. Keep on making the same monthly payments.

This is best explained with an example. Below, I have listed all the debts that Brian and Sheila have, along with the interest rate they are paying on each one:

Type of debt	Monthly cost	Interest rate (%)
Mortgage	€900	5.5
Home improvement loan	€16	10
Credit card 1	€45	16
Credit card 2	€30	16
Store card	€71	17
Car loan	€225	10

The total amount Brian and Sheila spend on their debts is €1,287 a month. Since they own their own home, they may be able to consolidate all their debts in with their mortgage. At the moment their mortgage is for €128,000 and has 19 years to run. Although consolidating their loans increases their mortgage to €152,000, by continuing to pay €1,300 a month they can shorten the length of their mortgage to just 14 years. At the same time they will save themselves €27,000 in interest!

Debt consolidation like this is a once-in-a-lifetime course of action. Please remember, it only works to your advantage if you carry on making the same monthly payments – otherwise you are merely spreading the cost of your short-term debt over the longer term. I believe one should never borrow money for a longer period than the life of the asset you are buying.

Currently it is virtually impossible to obtain such a consolidation loan with any of the lenders in Ireland. I would strongly advise using professional help.

Option 2: The sniper approach

If you don't own your own home – or if you don't have sufficient capital tied up in your property to consolidate your debts in with your mortgage – you can take what I call the 'sniper' approach. This involves 'picking off' your debts one at a time, starting with the most expensive. What you do is:

- Find some extra money. Just because you don't have a mortgage doesn't mean that you can't consolidate your debt. Move your borrowing to where it is costing you the least.
- Use the money you are saving each month to pay off your most expensive debt – in other words, the one with the highest rate of interest.

Do you sometimes pay more than the minimum amount required each month? If you do, make sure you pay it to whichever of your debts is costing you the most. Incidentally, you may find that one or more of your existing lenders will be open to negotiation.

For example, imagine that Neil has the following debts:

Type of debt	Monthly/minimum cost	Interest rate (%)
Credit card €4,000	€60	16
Store card €5,000	€75	17
Car loan €8,000	€258	10

Every month he usually pays about €100 more off one or other of the debts – on a purely random basis. Also, he is able to find €100 from other sources (see below) to help speed himself out of debt. In other words, Neil has €200 extra to apply to getting himself out of debt. What he needs to do is pay off his most expensive debt first – his store card. By paying an extra €200 a month he can do this within 20 months. This frees up the store card minimum payment of €75 to help pay off his next most expensive debt – which is his credit card.

MONEY DOCTORS WEALTH CHECK

Putting your money to the best possible use

The secret to getting rid of your debts is in putting your money to the best possible use. Your objective is to get your loans onto the lowest possible rate of interest, and then to use this saving to speed up the process of paying off your debt.

Of course, if you can find some extra money each month, then you can get out of debt even faster. One way to find extra money is to look at how you spend your income and see if you can make some basic savings without necessarily cutting back. For example:

• Many people pay more than they have to for their banking. Review your arrangements. Could you be earning extra interest? Saving interest? Avoiding unnecessary costs?

• Don't pay for anything you neither need nor use. For instance, membership fees, internet charges and magazines.

• Double-check you aren't overpaying your tax. Are your tax credits correct?

• Review all of your insurance costs. This is a fiercely competitive market, and you may be able to save a substantial amount.

In general, it isn't what you earn but how you spend it that will make the difference to your finances. You could be on an enormous salary, but if you are up to your neck in debt (as many high-income earners are) it is useless to you.

THE MONEY DOCTOR SAYS ...

- If you only take action on one aspect of your finances, make it your priority to get yourself out of debt.
- The first step is to stop borrowing and to get a realistic assessment of what you owe and how much it is costing you.
- Consider consolidating your debt in with your mortgage, if you can.
- Remember, if you save money or have any spare cash, you should put it towards paying off your debts, providing you still maintain a Rainy Day Fund or Emergency Fund.
- Pay your most expensive debts off first.

10
BORROWING

HOW TO BORROW SENSIBLY AND INEXPENSIVELY

There are times when it makes sense to borrow. And there are times when borrowing is unavoidable. Either way, you want to make sure that you don't pay a cent more than you have to. If there is one area of personal finance where consumers get ripped off regularly, it is when they borrow.

Look at the difference!
Nothing better illustrates how consumers can overpay for a loan than a quick comparison of rates:

Secured loan from one of the specialist lenders	4%+
Personal loan (unsecured) from any high street bank	10%+
Credit card from any of the main providers	17%+
Store card from any of the major retail outlets	20%+

As a consumer, it is not impossible that you might simultaneously be paying 4% and 20% to borrow money – which is ridiculous.

MONEY DOCTORS WEALTH CHECK

How to compare loan rates
So that consumers can compare interest rates, the government insists that the cost of loans is expressed in terms of an **annual percentage rate** (APR).

Confusingly, there is more than one way to calculate the APR – but broadly speaking, it is an accurate way to assess how much a loan is going to cost you, including all the hidden costs such as up-front fees.

Clearly, the lower the APR, the cheaper the loan, the better it is for you.

Remember, financial institutions make enormous profits from lending money. You should never, ever be shy about shopping around or asking for a lower rate.

So, what is 'sensible borrowing'?

There are times when it makes excellent sense to borrow. For instance, if you want to:
- buy, build or improve your home;
- finance a property investment;
- pay for education;
- pay for a car or other necessary item; or
- start a business.

There are also times when it is impossible not to borrow money – if you are temporarily unable to earn an income, for instance, for some reason beyond your control.

There is no intrinsic harm, either, in genuine short-term borrowing for some luxury item. What is really dangerous, however, is short-term borrowing that becomes long-term borrowing without you meaning it to do so. This is not only very expensive, but makes you more vulnerable to financial problems. I can't emphasise enough how bad it is for your financial well-being to borrow money to pay for living expenses. In particular, you should definitely avoid long-term credit card and store card debt.

If you have succumbed to the temptation of credit card or store card debt, and you want to pay it off, read Chapter 9 on getting out of debt.

Never borrow for longer than you have to

Making sure that you pay the lowest rate of interest is one way to keep the cost of borrowing down. Paying your debts back quickly is another. Compound interest (see Chapter 9) really works against you when borrowing money. The difference between paying back €1,000 at 15% APR over one year and, say, three years is a staggering €300 in interest!

Build up a good financial/credit rating history

It is vital to be aware that defaulting on loans or credit cards is registered with the Irish Credit Bureau (ICB) and the Central Credit Register (CCR), and will greatly affect your ability to borrow at attractive interest rates in the future. Never let unauthorised arrears build up on any loan. If your circumstances change during the term of a loan, inform the lender and come to an agreed and realistic repayment schedule. (See Chapter 14, 'If I have trouble making my mortgage repayments, what should I do?') Even negotiating an extension to an interest-only repayment will be recorded on these registers.

WHY RATES DIFFER SO WIDELY

Financial institutions set their charges according to the level of risk involved and prevailing market conditions.

As far as they are concerned, loans fall into two categories:

Secured loans, where, if a borrower fails to make the repayments, there is a physical asset – such as a house or even an insurance policy – that can be 'seized' and sold to meet the outstanding debt. Because of this, secured loans should cost considerably less.

Unsecured loans, where, if a borrower fails to make the repayments, the lender has no security and thus risks never getting paid (though this is rare). Such loans cost considerably more.

THE FIRST RULE OF CHEAPER BORROWING

The first rule is, therefore, to take out a secured rather than an unsecured loan. This isn't always practicable – but where it is, you'll save a substantial amount of money.

Secured loans
Secured loans include:
- a mortgage on your property;
- a secured loan (which is like a second or extra mortgage) on your property; and
- asset-backed finance (used, for instance, for major purchases such as cars).

Unsecured loans
Unsecured loans include:
- bank overdrafts;
- credit union loans;
- personal or term loans, including car loans;
- credit cards;
- store cards;
- hire-purchase; and
- loans from money lenders.

Interest rates have not always been so low

We have enjoyed relatively low and stable interest rates in recent years. Things were very different in the not-so-distant past. Indeed, in the early 1990s, mortgage rates went up to 15% at one point, and some people were paying over 30% a year on their credit card debt.

We saw in 2008 that interest rates rose by nearly 2%. Therefore, don't borrow so much that a change in interest rates (or a change in your personal circumstances) would leave you in crisis.

Rates plummeted to 1% ECB rate during 2009 and remained there for 18 months, and while they increased up to 1.5% in 2011, they have continued to fall since early 2013, falling to 0% ECB rate from March 2016 to date.

CHOOSING THE BEST LOAN FOR YOUR NEEDS

With the possible exception of borrowing to fund a major holiday or a special event such as a wedding, you should try to make sure that the useful life of whatever you're using your loan for will be longer than the time it takes you to repay it. Remember, the rate of interest being charged is only part of the equation. The other part is the length of time it will take you to repay the loan. For instance, you might think it was sensible to take out some extra money on your mortgage to buy a car, since mortgages are, undoubtedly, the least expensive way to borrow. If, however, your mortgage still has 15 years to run then you'll be paying for your car over all that time. Under these circumstances, you should opt for an alternative method, or else ensure that you overpay your mortgage in order to clear that part of the debt sooner.

THE MONEY DOCTORS BEST LOAN GUIDE

Here are the ten most common ways of borrowing money, listed in order of value – with the least expensive first and the most expensive last.

1. **Loans from family, friends and employers:** Often family members, friends and employers will make interest-free or low-interest loans. My advice is always to regularise such loans with a written agreement, so that there is no room for misunderstanding or bad feeling at a later date. Also, such loans may give rise to tax liability.

2. **Mortgages and secured loans:** Since the demise of tracker mortgages, interest rates have increased, but they are still low in relative terms. However, because of funding difficulties, most lenders will no longer consider equity releases or top-up mortgages to finance other non-property purchases. If you are fortunate enough to have a sympathetic lender and have sufficient equity in your property, this can still be an inexpensive way to finance a major purchase. However, if you buy, say, a car and add it to your mortgage, you should increase your monthly repayments so that that part of your debt is paid off sooner. Otherwise, you could be paying for your car over the whole term of your mortgage. Ensure that any extra payments made are reducing the capital (loan), rather than merely crediting your repayment account.

3. **Asset finance and leasing:** I am a big believer in asset finance and leasing when available. Although not as cheap as a mortgage, this can be an economical way to fund major purchases, and it has the benefit of being very tax-efficient if you are self-employed or running a business. You should ask an authorised financial adviser with access to all providers to find you the best possible rate. Leasing is also very quick – you can receive your cheque within 48 hours of an application.

4. **Overdrafts:** If you have a bank current account, you can ask your manager for an overdraft facility. Once approved, you will be able to spend money up to this amount. There won't be a set repayment period, but there may well be an annual charge. Authorised overdrafts are usually fairly competitive (though you shouldn't be afraid to negotiate). Exceeding your overdraft limit, however, can lead to heavy charges and the embarrassment of bounced cheques – unauthorised overdrafts should be strictly avoided. Bear in mind, too, that most banks expect your current account to be in credit for 30 days a year and will charge you extra if it isn't.

5. **Credit union loans:** We are fortunate in Ireland to have a network of local credit unions, willing to lend money to its members at competitive rates of interest. To qualify for a loan you must first be a member of the credit union – usually for a minimum of one month – and then normally save a regular amount with them for a set period of time, though some CUs just require a percentage of the loan you are looking for to be on deposit. While once it was 25%, some CUs are now only looking for 2.5%. Because credit unions are non-profit making, they tend to offer much better value for money. Not all credit union rates are the same and, while it is

worth shopping around, you can only open a credit union account in the nearest office to where you live or where you work.

6. **Personal or term loans:** The cost of personal or term loans can vary enormously. Essentially, when you borrow the money, you agree to a set repayment period or 'term'. The rate of interest charged is normally variable and you should always pay close attention to your statements to check that it hasn't risen out of line with market rates. Where a rate is fixed in advance – giving you the security of knowing what your repayments will be – it is likely to be higher.

   Where a loan is provided by a dealer or retailer, check the conditions closely. Sometimes you may be offered a low or zero rate for an agreed period, which will then rise dramatically in cost after the set term. Also, the cost of providing this credit will be built into the price of whatever you are buying.

7. **Credit cards:** Used properly, a credit card will give you as much as 45 days of interest-free credit. On a certain day every month, your bill will be calculated for the previous 30 days and sent to you for payment by the end of the following month. If your cut-off date is, say, the 17th of the month, all charges from 17 December to 17 January would have to be paid for by the end of February. If you can't pay the full amount, you are given the option of paying a reduced amount. This could be less than 3% of the total outstanding. The catch is that you will be charged an extremely high rate of interest – possibly 20% a year – on the balance. Credit cards are an extremely expensive way to borrow, and credit card companies are very aggressive in their marketing methods. If you are going to use a credit card then don't fall into the trap of making the minimum payment each month. A relatively small balance could take you years to clear.

   Note: if your income is high enough, your bank may offer you a 'gold' credit card with a built-in overdraft facility at a preferential rate. Your credit card balance will be settled each month using the overdraft. This can be a cost-effective way to borrow, and is worth investigating.

8. **Store cards:** I am afraid I am not at all enthusiastic about store cards. They work in the same way as credit cards except, of course, you can only use them in the store (or chain of stores) that issues the card. Their single advantage is that having the card may entitle you to an extra discount on first purchase and again during any sales. Their huge disadvantage is that the rate of interest charged

on outstanding balances almost always makes normal credit cards look cheap by comparison. My strong advice – unless you are extremely disciplined with money – is not to use store cards.

9. **Hire-purchase:** Hire-purchase allows you to buy specific goods over an agreed period of time. In other words, it is a bit like a personal or term loan. The difference is that the rates charged for hire-purchase are normally somewhat higher, and you might be better off looking at alternatives such as a personal loan or a lease. Remember, too, that with hire-purchase you don't own whatever you are buying until you have made your last payment. This is not the case with, for example, a personal loan. However, if you have paid over half the term in the HP agreement, you can then return the goods (e.g. a car) and the loan is scrapped at that point.

10. **Money lenders:** Whether licensed or unlicensed, money lenders are just about always the most expensive possible way to borrow. The rates they charge are outrageous. If they are trading illegally, there is the added risk of violence or intimidation if you don't pay what they say you owe them. You should avoid them like the plague! Incidentally, the definition of a money lender – and licensed at that – is an entity or person that charges you a minimum of 23% interest a year – but most charge up to 200%! A list of licensed money lenders is available from the Central Bank web site.

(See Chapter 14: 'If I have trouble making my mortgage repayments, what should I do?' for details of who to contact to avoid money lenders if you are in dire circumstances.)

THE MONEY DOCTOR SAYS ...

- Think carefully before you borrow money. Is it sensible to take out a loan for whatever you are planning to buy? Don't borrow money to pay for 'lifestyle' items. No loan should ever last for longer than the thing you are spending the money on!
- Shop around for the most competitive rate. There is a huge difference, and you can save yourself literally thousands of euros by making sure you get the cheapest possible loan.
- Read any credit agreement very carefully and seek clarification of any sections you don't fully understand.
- Don't allow short-term borrowing to become long-term by mistake.
- Don't be blindly loyal to any particular lender. Go where the best rate is.
- If in doubt, seek expert help – www.moneydoctors.ie.

PART 4

A COMPLETE GUIDE TO INSURANCE

Life insurance … home insurance … pet insurance … medical insurance … product warranty insurance … travel insurance … income protection insurance … there is no shortage of insurance policies to choose from. In principle, so much choice is a wonderful thing. It allows you to protect yourself, your family and your possessions from a whole range of risks – at one end catastrophic, at the other mildly irritating.

In practice, of course, so much choice can be confusing and can easily lead to you:

- *not taking out cover you should really have;*
- *taking out cover that you don't actually need;*
- *taking out the wrong amount of cover (too much or, more worryingly, too little); and/or*
- *paying more than you have to.*

The problem is often compounded by the fact that many people receive poor or heavily biased advice.

This section of the book has a single purpose: to make sure that you have the appropriate cover for your needs and that you aren't paying more for it than is necessary. It is divided into two chapters. In the first, we will consider cover for people; and in the second, cover for things.

11

PROTECTING YOURSELF AND YOUR FAMILY

HOW TO BUY THE MEDICAL, INCOME AND LIFE INSURANCE YOU ACTUALLY NEED – AT THE LOWEST POSSIBLE PRICE

First-class medical protection, critical illness cover and life insurance are available at relatively low prices, providing you know how to buy it.

In this chapter you'll discover how to:

- make sure you aren't sold cover you don't need;
- decide what cover it is sensible for you to take out;
- find out who you can trust to advise you; and
- make sure you get your cover at the lowest possible price.

American filmmaker Woody Allen quipped that his 'idea of hell is to be stuck in a lift with a life insurance salesman'. Mr Allen is by no means alone in his distrust both of life insurance and of the people who sell it. Why should this be? It is partly because no one likes to think about anything bad happening to them, and partly because – in order to draw attention to a very real need – life insurance salespeople are forced to bring up uncomfortable subjects with their prospective clients.

However, although it is not something you may rush to tackle, making certain that you have adequate life – and health – insurance will bring you *genuine* peace of mind.

You know you should ...

It isn't pleasant to dwell on being ill, having an accident or – worst of all – dying. Nevertheless, you owe it to yourself, and those you care for, to spend a little time making sure you are protected should the worst happen. This means being:

- *protected* by permanent health insurance (PHI) if you are too unwell to earn an income;
- *protected* by private medical insurance if you should need medical attention; and

- *protected* by life cover if you, or your partner, should die.

For a relatively small amount of money you can take out a range of insurance policies designed to:

- provide for you, or your dependants, if you, or your partner, should die;
- give you a lump sum or a regular income if you find you have a serious illness, are incapacitated or cannot work; and
- meet all your private medical bills in the event of an accident or illness.

There are, of course, plenty of facts and figures available proving just how likely it is for someone of any age to fall ill or die. Sadly, such statistics are borne out by everyone's personal experience. We all know of instances where families have had to face poor medical care and/or financial hardship as the result of a tragedy. We all know, too, that spending the small sum required to purchase appropriate cover probably makes sound sense.

Spend time, not money

In reality, none of the insurance dealt with in this chapter is expensive when you consider the protection it offers. The secret is to identify exactly what cover you *really* need and not to get sold an inappropriate or overpriced policy. It is also important to review your needs on a regular basis. What you require today and what you'll require in even two or three years' time could differ dramatically.

The best way to start is by considering what risks you face and deciding what action you should take. Here are three questions that everyone should ask themselves, regardless of their age, gender, health or financial circumstances.

Question 1: What would your financial position be if you were unable to work – due to an accident or illness – for more than a short period of time?

Obviously, your employer and the state will both be obliged to help you out. However, if you have a mortgage, other debts and/or a family to support, your legal entitlements are unlikely to meet anything like your normal monthly outgoings. If you do have a family then your spouse will have to balance work, caring for you and, possibly, caring for children. Is this feasible or – more to the point – desirable? How long will your savings last you under these circumstances? Do you have other assets you could sell?

Unless you have substantial savings and/or low outgoings, **income protection cover** (sometimes known as permanent health insurance) and/or **critical illness insurance** could both make sound sense.

Question 2: Do you have anyone dependent on you for either financial support or care? Are you dependent on someone else financially? Do you have children, or other family members, who would have to be cared for if you were to die?

If you are single and don't have any dependants, then the purpose of **life insurance** could be to settle your debts and/or leave a bequest. If, on the other hand, there is someone depending on you – either for money or for care – then life cover has to be a priority.

If you are supporting anyone (or if your financial contribution is necessary to the running of your household), you need to take out cover so that you don't leave those you love facing a financial crisis.

If you are caring for anyone – children, perhaps, or an ageing relative – then you should take out cover so that there is plenty of money for someone else to take over this role.

Question 3: Does it matter to you how quickly you receive non-urgent medical treatment? If you needed medical care would you rather choose who looks after you, where you are treated and under what circumstances? How important is a private room in hospital to you?

We are fortunate enough to enjoy free basic health care in Ireland. However, if you are self-employed or if you have responsibilities that make it important for you to be able to choose the time and place of any medical treatment, then you should consider **private medical insurance**.

INCOME PROTECTION COVER

If you are of working age, the chances of you being off work for a prolonged period of time due to illness or an accident are substantially greater than the chances of you dying.

For this reason, **income protection cover** is valuable. As its name suggests, it is designed to replace your income if a disability or serious illness prevents you from working. If you are in a company pension scheme – or if you have arranged your own pension – you should check to see what cover you have already, since it is sometimes included.

Incidentally, most policies only pay out after the policyholder has been off work for a minimum of 13 weeks, although there is one scheme that operates from day one – email the Money Doctor for details (info@ moneydoctors.ie). If you want to reduce costs, you can alternatively opt for a policy that doesn't pay out until you have been off work for 26 weeks. Income protection is the only type of insurance, outside of pension-related life cover, that allows for tax relief on the premium paid at your marginal rate.

THE MONEY DOCTOR SAYS ...

As with anything, you should shop around for all your insurance cover. Costs vary dramatically. Remember, too, that an authorised adviser, regulated by the Central Bank of Ireland, can explain all the policies to you and can steer you to the best for your needs.

MONEY DOCTORS WEALTH WARNING

Don't be sold something you don't need

I don't believe it is advisable to buy insurance from anyone who isn't qualified to inform you about every single option available to you. A salesperson who is tied to one company – or even a small selection of companies – is clearly not going to offer you the same quality of advice as someone who has a detailed knowledge of the entire market. For further advice on this crucial area see Chapter 4.

CRITICAL OR SERIOUS ILLNESS INSURANCE

Horrible as it is to think about, imagine being diagnosed with a serious illness. I am talking about something like cancer, heart disease or multiple sclerosis. Naturally, under these circumstances, you might need special care and/or want to make life changes. This is where **critical** or **serious illness insurance** comes in. (The name of this insurance cover is changing to **specified illness cover**.) Providing you survive for two weeks after your diagnosis, you will receive a lump sum of tax-free money to spend however you wish. Clearly, such a sum would help you to seek specialist treatment, pay off your debts or in other ways ensure that you didn't have any financial problems.

This cover provides you with a lump sum – not an income.

LIFE COVER

There are several different types of life cover – but they are all designed to do one thing. For a relatively low monthly payment, they provide a lump sum if the insured person dies. The lump sum is tax-free and may go into the insured's estate or may be directly payable to a nominated person (such as his or her spouse). Some of the uses to which this lump sum might be put include:

- paying off a mortgage;
- paying off other debts;
- investments to provide a replacement income; or
- investments to provide money for childcare or the care of someone else, such as an ageing relative.

In the case of more expensive life cover, the policy can have a cash-in value after a period of time has elapsed. The cost of life cover will be determined by your age, gender and lifestyle. If you are a non-smoker and don't drink heavily, you will save quite a bit of money.

There are two main types of life cover: term insurance and whole of life assurance.

Term insurance

As its name implies, term insurance is available for a pre-agreed period of time – usually a minimum of ten years. It is mandatory when you take out interest-only home loans.

It is particularly useful for people with a temporary need. For instance, if you have young children, you and your spouse might take out a 20-year plan giving you protection until your family has grown up and left home. By the same token, you might take out a policy that would pay off the exact amount of your mortgage.

Term insurance is the least expensive form of life cover. You can opt for:

Level term: The amount of cover remains the same (level) for the agreed period. For instance, you might take out €50,000 of cover for ten years. The cost remains fixed for the same period, too.

Decreasing term: The amount of cover drops (decreases) every year. For instance, you might take out €50,000 of cover that drops to €48,000 in the second year, €45,000 in the third year and so forth. Such policies are almost always taken out in conjunction with mortgages in order to pay off the outstanding debt should the insured die. Note this sort of cover can't be extended or increased in value once you have taken it out.

Convertible term: Although the cover is for a set period of time, a convertible policy will allow you to extend your insurance for a further period regardless of your health. This is a very useful feature because it means that if you suffer some health problem you won't be denied life cover because of it. In fact, if you extend the policy, the insurance company will charge you the same premium as if you were perfectly healthy. Convertible term cover is normally not much more expensive than level term cover, and is therefore usually the better option.

Whole of life assurance

There are two benefits to taking out a whole of life assurance plan. Firstly, providing you carry on making your monthly payments, the plan is guaranteed to pay out. In other words, you are covered for the whole of your life. Secondly, there can be an investment element to the cover. So if you decide to cancel the plan you'll receive back a lump sum.

There are various features you can opt for with whole of life cover. You can vary the balance between actual life cover and the investment element, for instance. Also you can decide to end the cover at a particular point – when you retire, for instance. Some whole of life policies are designed to meet inheritance tax liabilities (Section 72 – the proceeds of the policy are tax free when used to pay capital acquisitions tax (CAT) liability on inheritances).

However, whole of life cover is more expensive than term cover and, in most cases, the premiums are reviewed upwards at regular intervals.

PRIVATE MEDICAL INSURANCE

This type of insurance is designed to meet some or all of your medical bills if you opt to go for private treatment.

Only three companies provide this cover in Ireland: Voluntary Health Insurance (VHI), Laya Healthcare and Irish Life Health. Between them they offer a wide range of plans with an array of options, conditions and limits.

The basic decisions you have to make are:
- Do you want a choice of consultant?
- Do you want a choice of hospital?
- Do you want private or just semi-private hospital accommodation?
- Do you want outpatient cover?

Discounts can be available if you join through a group – your employer, for instance, or a credit union.

As with all insurance, it is well worth getting expert help in deciding which option is best for your needs.

WHICH TYPES OF COVER SHOULD YOU CHOOSE?

Is it better to take out income protection or critical illness insurance? Should you opt for term life or whole of life cover? If term cover – which sort? If whole of life – what investment element should you include? Do you need private medical insurance, or is it a luxury you can do without?

Although these are personal decisions that only you can make, a professional authorised adviser will be able to guide you. You could also go to the Health Insurance Authority website, www.hia.ie, which has comparisons of the three insurers.

Keep the following points in mind when making your decision:

- If you have a limited budget, I would opt, first and foremost, for either income protection or specified illness cover. Depending on your circumstances, you might take out both.
- If you are on a tight budget, then take out decreasing term insurance to cover your mortgage.
- If you have joint financial responsibilities – for instance, if you are married – and you have limited resources, it is more important to cover the main income earner.
- Covering a husband and wife together on the same policy often doesn't cost that much more than covering just one person.
- If you are self-employed, private medical cover is not really a luxury but more of a necessity, and the premiums are tax deductible for everyone.

MONEY DOCTORS WEALTH WARNING

Six things every life assurance company must tell you

The sale of life assurance is strictly regulated and your life assurance company must provide you with six important pieces of information before you sign on the dotted line. These are:

- The **cost:** Not just the monthly premium, but also whether the cost will ever be subject to review. If the cost is fixed, this is referred to as level premiums. There are reasons why the cost could be increased. For instance, it could be because the benefit will be going up at some point in the future.
- A description of the main **purpose** of the product: For instance, whether it's a savings or protection policy.

- Full details of all the **charges** and any **commission** that is going to be made to a broker or salesperson.
- If there is an investment element to the policy, you should be given examples of the **expected return**, together with details of any future **tax liability**. Any guarantees should also be explained.
- You should be told what will happen **if you cancel** (or 'surrender') the policy early. What will this do to the projected value?
- **Background information** about the insurer and anyone else involved, such as the broker or intermediary.

Note: by law, you must also be given a 'cooling-off' period. This is time in which you can change your mind about the policy you have purchased and cancel it, without cost or penalty.

MONEY DOCTORS WEALTH WARNING

You <u>must</u> be truthful

When you complete an application for life cover – in fact, for any sort of insurance – the onus is upon you to advise the insurer of any facts that may affect the risk they are taking on. You'll be asked to sign a declaration to the effect that you haven't withheld any relevant information. If you lie, or if you fail to reveal something that may be important, your policy may end up being invalid. Clearly, it would be a complete waste of your money if, when you came to claim, the insurer were not legally bound to pay up. In the case of life cover, you must provide information about your medical history and also about any risks (such as dangerous sports) that might have some bearing on your life expectancy.

HOW MUCH LIFE COVER DO YOU NEED?

One of the most difficult questions regarding life cover is deciding just how much you need. If you want to replace your income, you will require roughly between 10 and 15 times your annual after-tax earnings.

So, if you take home €1,000 a month, you should aim to have a minimum of €120,000 cover, which is €1,000 (your salary) x 12 (number of months in the year) x 10 (minimum advisable level of cover).

Remember, it is possible to keep the cost of life cover down by going for a 'term' policy. Bear in mind too that it's better to have some cover than no cover at all, especially when you have dependants.

LIFE COVER TAX TIP

If you're worried that you may have to pay inheritance tax (see Chapter 27 for further information about this), one solution is to set up your life assurance policy (Section 72) so that it is not counted as part of your estate when you die. This is done by 'writing the policy under trust' – which is as simple as completing a form that your insurer or agent will provide. If you do this, not only will the proceeds from your life cover escape inheritance tax, but the money will also be paid to your chosen beneficiaries relatively quickly – usually in a matter of weeks. It doesn't cost anything to put your life assurance under trust, and you can change the beneficiary (or beneficiaries) at any time.

KEEPING THE COST DOWN

There are two ways to keep the cost of your insurance down to an absolute minimum:

1. Always get independent professional assistance from someone who is authorised to look at *every option* for you. This is one purchase where shopping around and expert knowledge can save you serious money.
2. Refine your needs. By taking out the right sort of cover, and the right level of cover, you won't be wasting money. Quitting smoking can be beneficial both in terms of your health and your finances. If you are free of the habit for over 12 months, it could mean up to a 50% reduction in your monthly life cover premiums. Email the Money Doctor for details (info@moneydoctors.ie).

THE MONEY DOCTOR SAYS ...

- Don't stick your head in the sand, believing that 'it won't happen to me'. Protecting yourself and your family should be one of your key financial priorities.
- Choose an independent, professional authorised adviser who you feel comfortable with to advise you.
- Don't get sold cover you don't need.
- Review your needs regularly – every two or three years – to make sure you have adequate protection.
- This is a fiercely competitive market. Having an expert shop around for you could mean big savings – email consultation@moneydoctor.ie.

12

PROTECTING YOUR POSSESSIONS

INSIDER TIPS ON HOW TO KEEP THE COST OF YOUR GENERAL INSURANCE TO A BARE MINIMUM

With the cost of general insurance only going one way, it is important to make sure you are getting value for your money. In this chapter you'll discover:

- details of all the different types of cover you should consider;
- how to ensure that you aren't paying more than you have to; and
- other buying tips.

THE IMPORTANCE OF PROPER COVER

The temptation, when insurance premiums rise, is to reduce the amount of cover you have or – where cover isn't obligatory – to cancel the policy completely.

There are two reasons why it is important to make sure that you have adequate 'general' insurance.

Firstly, if you have borrowed money in order to pay for something, you should always ensure that there is sufficient insurance to repay the debt in case disaster strikes. To quote just one real case history:

> Frank borrowed €15,000 to buy a car, and only took out the cheapest motor insurance he could buy – third party, fire and theft. The car was involved in an accident and completely destroyed. Because Frank didn't have comprehensive insurance, he is now saddled with paying off the original car loan plus paying for a replacement car.

Secondly, if you under-insure, you risk receiving less of a pay-out when you come to claim. This is particularly true when it comes to home insurance. Again, let me quote a real case history:

> John and Moira didn't have a mortgage on their house. Although they had buildings and contents protection, they hadn't bothered to check the amount of cover for many years. Unfortunately, an electrical fault resulted in the house being burned down (thankfully, no one was hurt). When they came to claim, because they were under-insured, the insurance company would only pay three-quarters of the cost of rebuilding.

Shopping around for insurance is no one's idea of fun. But the cost of not taking out adequate insurance can be huge. If you invest just a small amount of time reading this chapter and acting on it, you will keep the cost to a bare minimum.

THE DIFFERENT TYPES OF 'GENERAL' INSURANCE

So, what is 'general' insurance anyway? This catch-all expression encompasses the following areas:
- Home and other forms of property insurance
- Motor insurance
- Public liability
- Insurance for other possessions, such as boats, caravans and mobile telephones
- Pet insurance
- Travel insurance
- Credit insurance
- Professional indemnity insurance
- Other risk insurance (e.g. Golfsure – for that round of drinks after a hole in one!)

DON'T JUST RELY ON BROKERS

General insurance is the one area where I would suggest that you shouldn't turn to brokers to get you the best deal. In many areas there are now 'direct' operations that can undercut brokers substantially. To find details of these direct operations look in your *Golden Pages* and keep an eye out for companies advertising in the national press. Remember too that insurance companies tend to rely on customer inertia when it comes to renewal. Having won your custom, they may push the cost of cover up in the second year, hoping you won't be bothered to check elsewhere. Telephoning around and filling in extra paperwork is a nuisance, but think of it this way: if it takes you, say, three hours' work to save €200 then you are effectively paying yourself nearly €70 an hour after tax.

HOME INSURANCE

Home insurance is divided into **buildings cover** and **contents cover.**

Buildings cover

Buildings cover is obligatory if you have a mortgage, and you may find that your lender automatically provides this protection (or at the very least a quotation) for you. The insurance is to protect the structure of your home (the building itself, outbuildings, fixtures and fittings and so forth) against fire, storm damage, flood, subsidence and other similar occurances. Most policies also include **public liability** cover, so that if something happens to someone on your property (for instance, if they have an accident), you are protected.

It is vital to have sufficient buildings cover protection for your home. The cost is linked entirely to the rebuilding cost. Where your home is located, how old it is, its size and the materials from which it is constructed will all influence the premium. If you would like help deciding how much cover to take out, the Society of Chartered Surveyors Ireland (www.scsi.ie) produces an annual guide. Not all buildings policies cover you for the same things, so you should check the small print. One way of keeping the cost down is to make sure you have smoke alarms fitted; another is to join your local neighbourhood watch scheme.

Contents cover

Contents cover is even less standard than buildings cover. The sort of protection you'll receive can vary enormously, so bear this in mind when comparing prices. For instance, are you being offered **new for old** cover, which means that if you claim you'll receive the cost of replacement with no reduction on account of the age of your possessions? Also, how much of any loss will you be expected to pay for yourself (known as an **excess**)? And to what extent are valuables – such as jewellery or cash – actually covered? You'll find that there are all sorts of 'extras' that may or may not be included – from employer's liability to theft of bicycles and from liability to third parties to personal liability. Tedious as it is, the only way to know what you are actually getting is to read the small print. Happily, there are a number of ways to keep the cost of your contents cover down:

- Fit an approved alarm system.
- Fit approved locks to doors and windows.
- Join your local neighbourhood watch scheme.

Note that discounts are sometimes offered to people who are at home most of the day – for instance, if you are retired.

MOTOR INSURANCE

With such high insurance premiums, you may be tempted to try to reduce the cost by any means possible. For instance, city-based car owners usually pay higher premiums than their rural counterparts, and some are tempted to pretend that their car actually 'lives' in the country. Remember, if you ever come to claim, many insurance companies now send out an investigator to make independent inquiries – a false statement could result in you being taken to court for fraud.

Motor insurance is more expensive if you:
- don't have a full licence;
- have a history of motor offences;
- are under 25 years old;
- have made claims in the past; or
- have a criminal record.

You can't make yourself any older than you actually are, but if you don't have a full licence it is well worth putting in the effort to pass the test. Remember, don't rush to put in a minor claim, as it may result in higher premiums. Also, remember that fines may not be the only cost of speeding. Insurance companies check your driving penalty points. In Ireland, it's 12 and you are off the road.

INSIDER TIPS ON BUYING OTHER GENERAL INSURANCE

In my opinion, many types of general insurance do not offer value for money. I am particularly suspicious of:

Extended warranties: These cover you against faults developing in electrical and mechanical goods. Often the retailer makes more money from these insurance policies (by way of commission) than on the sale of the actual product. As legislation offers you 12 months' protection anyway (and as, in general, such goods are much better made nowadays), I am suspicious of such policies.

Mobile telephone insurance: This protects you against loss of or damage to your phone. This is often expensive in relation to the actual cost of replacing your telephone. Furthermore, many people end up buying this cover without meaning to because they don't pay proper attention when completing the contract.

Credit card insurance: There are two types of cover offered by credit card companies. The first protects you against fraud, and the second against you being unable to make your repayments due to an accident, illness or redundancy. Both types of cover are expensive and in most cases I would advise against them.

Pet insurance: This protects you against having to pay vet bills if your pet is ill or involved in an accident. Again, I would strongly suggest examining the value for money offered by such policies.

Travel insurance is often sold by travel agents at highly inflated prices since they earn good rates of commission on every policy sold. Travel insurance is important – but there are many different sources of cover. If you are a regular traveller, you may like to consider an annual policy. Also, if you have certain credit cards, an amount of cover may already be included in your annual fee.

THE MONEY DOCTOR SAYS ...

- Check the small print! All insurance policies are not equal.
- It may not be much fun shopping around, but it helps to think of the saving in terms of effort and reward. Three hours spent saving €200 is worth virtually €70 an hour after tax to you.
- Don't get sucked into buying cover you don't really need.
- Don't be tempted to under-insure – it could leave you exposed.

PART 5

A COMPLETE GUIDE TO PROPERTY PURCHASE

I don't think it would be an overstatement to say that property – and, in particular, owning it – has been something of a national obsession. It is easy to understand why: home ownership offers security and the potential to make a capital gain. In the ten years up to 2006, residential property prices grew at an average rate of 12% per annum. Sadly the downturn took hold, but there are still opportunities in the property market, especially for those with money, as property prices have been rebounding since 2012.

Only the fortunate few can now afford to buy a home outright. For the rest of us, saving up until we had the full cost of the apartment or house we wanted to buy would be impractical. The fact is that it would probably take decades, and we would need to live somewhere else in the meantime. The solution is to take out a mortgage or home loan. Such loans are 'secured' against the value of the property being purchased and – because this means the lender faces much less risk – they are normally the least expensive type of borrowing you can undertake.

From a financial perspective, mortgages are the most important consideration when buying a property, which is why the longest chapter in this section is devoted to them. They are not, however, the only thing you need to think about if you own – or are thinking of owning – a property. There is also the question of whether it is better to rent or buy, and issues regarding investing in property, property-related costs, tax and a host of other related topics, all covered extensively in what follows.

13

MORTGAGES

The number of active lenders in the mortgage market has decreased sharply in the last ten years, and so has the range of products and options. This chapter explains:

- how to make sure you've got the mortgage that suits you best;
- how to make sure you are paying the lowest possible price; and
- who to trust for mortgage advice.

We will also look at how mortgages work, re-mortgaging, tax relief and just about every other property-related question you can think of.

TAKING ADVANTAGE OF THE MORTGAGE REVOLUTION

Please put any preconceptions you have about buying a home or arranging a mortgage to one side. The truth is:

- Your home is *not* necessarily your most important investment.
- Your home is definitely *not* your most expensive purchase.
- You *don't* have to take 25 to 35 years to pay back your mortgage.

Also, and this is crucial to keeping the cost of buying your home or investment property to a bare minimum:

- The interest rate your mortgage lender charges you makes a huge difference to the cost of buying your home.
- The type of mortgage you have also makes a huge difference to the cost of buying your home.

Changes in the mortgage market have meant that for the foreseeable future you may be tied to the lender from whom you originally got your mortgage. For this reason, it is essential that you do careful research before selecting a particular lender or product. Independent advice from an authorised adviser will stand you in good stead over the whole term of your mortgage.

Not necessarily your most important investment. Definitely not your most expensive purchase.

Received wisdom has it that the most important investment most of us will probably ever make is in our home. There is no doubt that owning your home is a significant part of being financially secure:

- The cost is not dissimilar to renting a home – making it a good financial decision.
- You aren't at the mercy of unscrupulous, unpleasant, greedy or inefficient landlords.
- With luck, you'll see the value of your property rise in the longer term – giving you a tax-free gain.

Nevertheless, although it makes sense to buy your own home, you shouldn't be fooled into thinking that it is the 'be all and end all' of investments. It is arguable, in fact, that building up your other investments – especially a pension plan – is more important. Furthermore, the stock market has, traditionally, always produced a better return than property. I'm not trying to put you off buying your own home – far from it – but don't forget it is only one part of establishing your personal wealth.

It is also worth remembering that your home won't automatically be your most expensive purchase. Depending on interest rates, that honour could easily go to your mortgage. If you buy a house for €300,000, taking out a traditional, repayment mortgage for €240,000 (80% of the purchase price) and paying it back over 25 years at an average rate of 3%, the total cost of your mortgage (including interest) will be €341,342.15. That's €41,342.15 more than the actual cost of your home, a total of €101,342.15 in interest over the period. This is why it is crucial that you choose the least expensive mortgage option available to you. Every cent counts.

INTEREST: ALL THE DIFFERENCE IN THE WORLD

The rate of interest you are charged on your mortgage makes a huge difference to the total cost of your home, as the following table indicates:

Cost of €100,000 25-year repayment mortgage: interest payable

Annual interest rate (%)	Cost per month	Total interest over term (€)
3	474.21	42,263
3.25	487.32	46,195
3.5	500.62	50,187
3.75	514.13	54,239
4	527.84	58,350
4.25	541.74	65,251
4.5	555.83	66,750
4.75	570.12	71,034

The difference between paying, say, 3% and 4.75% (which doesn't sound like much) is an increase in repayments by €95.91 per month, and actually equates to €28,771 of interest over the 25-year term. Think how much extra you would have to earn after tax to end up with €28,771 in your pocket. Paying more mortgage interest than you have to can seriously damage your wealth. Shopping around makes excellent sense.

TWO MORTGAGE OPTIONS: REPAYMENT VERSUS INTEREST-ONLY

Although there is a whole range of mortgages to choose from, they all fall into two categories:
- repayment (annuity) mortgages; and
- interest-only mortgages.

Repayment (or annuity) mortgages
In this type of mortgage, your monthly repayments are divided into two parts. The first is the interest you owe on the total amount borrowed. The second is repayment of part of the capital you have borrowed. The big advantage of this mortgage is that you are guaranteed to have paid off your whole loan at the end of the term. However, in the early years almost all of your monthly repayments will be in interest. Let me give you an example:

> Sheila takes out a €300,000 mortgage over 25 years at an interest rate of 3.7%. Her monthly payments are €1,542.39. At the end of the first year, she will have paid a total of €18,508 but will still owe over €296,200 to her lender. In year ten she will have paid €185,086 but will still owe €212,000. Put another way, in the first ten years, roughly 60% of what she pays to her lender will be interest, and only 40% will be capital.

MONEY DOCTORS WEALTH CHECK

Save extra interest
When choosing a repayment mortgage, make sure the interest is calculated daily or at least monthly ('monthly rest'). Why? Because over the term of your mortgage this will save you a tidy sum of money. The main thing to avoid is something called the 'annual rest system', which will cost you the most. Some lenders may still have customers on their books who are on this system, and it can add about 0.35% to your interest rate. If you are in this position, go back to your lender and ask them to change you to a monthly calculation.

Interest-only mortgages

The other sort of mortgage is an interest-only mortgage, in which you pay only the interest for an agreed period. With an **investment mortgage**, you pay interest only on the amount borrowed *and* at the same time you set up a savings plan, which – it is hoped – will pay off the capital at the end of the term. Your monthly repayments will, therefore, consist of interest on the loan and a contribution to a savings plan. This is ideal for certain types of loans, e.g. commercial loans where the interest remains constant and the tax relief can be maximised (because the capital is not being repaid, you are receiving the maximum possible tax relief on the interest over the entire term).

In the case of both a home and an investment property there are certain circumstances where you might not bother with the savings element, as I'll explain in a moment.

Around 30 years ago, interest-only home loans got a bad name because many borrowers were advised to take out **endowment policies** (see below for an explanation) to repay the capital at the end of the term. Unfortunately, some of these policies failed to produce a sufficient return to do so. In other words, borrowers found that after 25 years, they still owed money to their lenders.

Despite past problems with endowment mortgages, interest-only home loans can make sound financial sense. For instance, if you are self-employed, the tax benefits of a pension-linked, interest-only mortgage can be very substantial, in particular when taken out for commercial property.

Here is a quick summary of the three main types of interest-only mortgage options available:

Endowment mortgages: These are investments offered by life insurance companies, and there are various types available. The money you pay to the life insurance company is partly used to provide you with **life cover** (so that if you die the mortgage itself can be repaid) and partly invested in the **stock market**. If the money is invested well, then obviously your original loan will be repaid and you might even be left with a tax-free sum. However, if the performance of the endowment policy is not good, then you could be left with insufficient cash to repay your original loan. There is no tax relief on endowment policy premiums. In fact, this type of mortgage has not been available for many years.

Pension-linked mortgages: In this arrangement, the life insurance company (after taking out money to pay for life cover) invests your cash into a **pension fund**. This has very definite tax benefits for anyone who is self-employed or on an extremely high income. Ordinarily, the pension fund is designed to mature on your retirement age at double the original amount being borrowed. Twenty-five per cent of this pension fund is available at maturity for encashment, tax-free, and even though you will have to pay tax on the rest of the fund, you should have sufficient money to pay off the rest of the mortgage.

New rules on self-direct trusts or **SSAPs** (small self-administered pension schemes) now allow pension funds to borrow on properties. Indeed, there are all sorts of other tax benefits available to those who buy property as part of their pension fund. Some of this is covered elsewhere in the chapters on retirement planning and tax. However, as it is such a complicated area you will need to take specialist advice (consultation@moneydoctors.ie) if you wish to take advantage of the rules.

Interest-only mortgages: Some time ago, it was possible to borrow money to purchase property at very competitive rates of interest without any obligation to repay the capital before the end of the term. For instance, if you took out a 20-year interest-only mortgage, all you have to pay each month is the agreed rate of interest. The capital sum isn't due until the 20 years have passed. This could suit you for all sorts of reasons: Perhaps you are expecting to receive a lump sum – such as an inheritance – before the 20 years are up. Maybe you intend to resell the property during this period. Possibly you have other investments that could be cashed in to repay the loan. Possibly you will win the Lotto! Do note that you will have to have level-term life cover covering the entire amount borrowed for the full term of an interest-only mortgage, so that the loan can be repaid in the event of your death. Interest-only mortgages are now a thing of the past.

FIXED OR VARIABLE RATE?

As if you didn't have enough choice already, another decision you must make when mortgage shopping is whether to opt for a fixed or variable rate. A **fixed rate** means that the amount of interest you pay is pre-set for an agreed period of time. This offers you the benefit of certainty. Even if interest rates rise, your repayments stay the same. On the other hand, if interest rates fall you won't benefit. You incur a penalty should you wish to pay off or partly pay off your mortgage while on a fixed rate of interest.

Generally, this sum is set at between three to six months' interest on the amount being repaid.

A **variable rate**, on the other hand, moves with the market. This is fine while interest rates are low, but if they begin to rise, you could be adversely affected. There is generally no penalty if you wish to pay off all or part of the loan before the end of a variable-rate mortgage term.

Tracker mortgages *were* the real deal, and today are costing Ireland's lenders a fortune to maintain. The interest rate tracks the ECB rate (currently 0.00%), and the lender agreed a margin (or profit) that had to be maintained for the entire term of the mortgage; only if the ECB rate moves does your tracker rate move. Today, some lucky mortgagers are paying 0.5% over the ECB rate (total 0.5%), as they negotiated their loan based on only having to borrow less than 50% of the value of their home.

THE MONEY DOCTOR SAYS ...

Unless you are self-employed, on a high-income or have some other source of funds coming to you in the future, the Money Doctor normally recommends that you take out a repayment or annuity mortgage when buying your main home. This said, there are some interesting variations now available, allowing you to combine an interest-only mortgage with a repayment mortgage, in particular pension-based mortgages.

WHY YOU SHOULD TRY TO MAKE MORTGAGE OVERPAYMENTS

Something I have become very keen on in recent years is the idea of overpaying your mortgage each month. This can't be done with all mortgages (for instance, you can't do it if you are on a fixed rate), but where it is possible and your income allows, it brings real benefits. With interest rates low at the moment and likely to stay low for the next few years, it may also be important to remember that if your return/yield is far greater than the cost of the money (the mortgage rate), then investing your surplus monies elsewhere may be more beneficial. Consider these two examples, though, where overpayment can be beneficial:

Mary takes out a repayment mortgage for €250,000 with a term of 25 years at 4.5%. Her minimum monthly repayment is €1389.58. However, she decides that she can afford to pay an extra €250 a month. As a result, her mortgage will be paid off six years earlier and she will save €44,511 in interest.

John also takes out a repayment mortgage for €320,000 with a term of 30 years at 3.5%. His minimum monthly repayment is €1436.94. He 'overpays' by €400 a month and as a result his mortgage will be paid off 10 years earlier and he will save €71,890 in interest!

THE MONEY DOCTOR SAYS ...

With the range of mortgage choices available, many borrowers worry about whether they are making the right decision for their needs. This is where a really good independent financial adviser offering a full choice of lenders can help. He or she will be able to guide you to the least expensive, most appropriate mortgage for your needs. Email consultation@moneydoctor.ie.

HOW THE RIGHT PROFESSIONAL ADVISER WILL SAVE YOU MONEY

It goes without saying that you should shop around for the best possible mortgage deal, as so much of your hard-earned cash is at stake. Two things to watch out for:

- You may not always be comparing like with like. There is a great deal of difference between a ten-year fixed-rate mortgage and a current account repayment mortgage. Each will cost a different amount, and each is designed to meet a different need.
- You may not be offered a full range of options. A bank or building society, for instance, might only have three or four types of mortgage to offer you. Many mortgage advisers deal with less than five lenders.

There are 9 mortgage lenders in Ireland at this point in time. To get the best possible deal you should always deal with an adviser who is authorised by the Central Bank of Ireland to act on behalf of the majority of these lenders.

Please remember, too, that even if you are a customer with a particular financial institution, your authorised financial adviser may still be able to negotiate a better deal on your behalf with that institution. This is because a professional will know what the best deal available actually is, while the lender will know that the adviser has other options should the lender fall short of the client's requirement.

MONEY DOCTORS WEALTH CHECK

The latest information ...

If you want the latest financial information – everything from interest rates to tax-saving tips – log on to the Money Doctors website at www.moneydoctors.ie.

THE MONEY DOCTOR SAYS ...

- Don't be complacent. Even a small difference in the rate you pay can make a huge difference to the cost of your mortgage. No lender deserves your loyalty. Go to where the best deal is.
- Don't trust any adviser who isn't authorised to act for all the financial institutions offering home loans in Ireland, or at the very least use an adviser who can tell you where the best deals can be obtained, irrespective of the agencies held. There are nine lenders, and anyone who can't tell you about all of them isn't going to get you the best deal.
- Do not panic if your home is worth less than your mortgage. As long as your income can meet the monthly mortgage repayment, the loss will only crystallise upon sale of the home. Always obtain professional advice for strategies.
- Remember, authorised financial advisers should be independent. In most cases, you will pay a fee for their services, but their job is to find you the best package for your needs.

14

PROPERTY QUESTIONS

THIS CHAPTER CONTAINS ANSWERS TO ALL OF THE MOST COMMON PROPERTY AND MORTGAGE QUESTIONS, INCLUDING:

- Should I buy or rent my home?
- How much can I borrow on my income?
- What is APR?
- Is it worth switching my mortgage to get a lower rate?
- Help! I'm self-employed. How do I get a mortgage?
- What will it cost for me to buy my home?
- Does it make sense to buy a second property as an investment?
- What are the benefits of owning a home in a designated area?
- What's the story with local authority loans?
- What other state housing grants might be available to me?
- Is it worth repaying my mortgage early?
- What types of home insurance will I need?
- If I have trouble making my mortgage repayments what should I do?

SHOULD I BUY OR RENT?

Ireland is one of the few countries in Europe where buying one's home is the norm. Broadly speaking, at present the cost of buying a home is the same as – or in many cases less than – renting the same property. This is linked to supply and demand, of course, and varies from region to region as well as from property to property. We were in a low-interest environment until 2006, and this favoured house purchase, as did the availability of mortgage interest tax relief. Interest rates rose between 2006 and 2008, and while they are now back to historically low levels, consumers are now more reluctant to borrow. The relatively meagre tax relief for first-time buyers has not been available since December 2012, and the existing relief will finish in January 2024.

If a future government were to introduce greater tenants' rights the situation might change, but at the moment, if you can raise the necessary deposit, buying makes better long-term sense than renting. After all, when you give up a rental property, you receive nothing back. Whereas when you have paid off your mortgage you will own your home and may have seen a nice, tax-free capital gain as well.

House prices in Ireland rose at an unprecedented rate in the ten years to 2007, and most informed opinion at that time was that as long as we continued in a low-interest environment and our economy remained healthy, a sharp fall in house prices seemed unlikely. However, things changed dramatically in 2008, culminating in the 'bottom of the market' in 2012 – those buying in that year made a good investment. Prices since then have nearly come back to those 2007 days, with 2019 being a little stagnant after years of growth.

How much can I borrow?

You should always put down as much of a deposit as possible when buying your home if you are a first-time buyer. You will need a minimum of 10% of the purchase price (that is to say €30,000 if you are buying a €300,000 property), but it is preferable to have more. Why? Because it makes you less vulnerable to moves in interest rates and property values.

Your ability to repay a mortgage will be based on your net disposable income (NDI) (gross income less tax, USC, PRSI and any existing loan repayments), and will be stress-tested to allow for future rises in interest rates. The maximum percentage of your NDI that can be set aside for financial commitments, including a home loan, depends on your income and can be as much as 35%.

You will also have to demonstrate that on your existing expenditure pattern you have the ability to meet the stress-tested repayments (usually an extra 2% over the existing rate) on the proposed new mortgage. This proof can come from a combination of existing mortgage repayments or rent, a regular savings plan and repayments of other existing loans, which will be fully paid before the mortgage is drawn down.

What is APR?

The cost of your loan is expressed as an **annual percentage rate** (APR). This is different from a straight interest rate in that it takes into account not just the interest rate but also the timing of any interest payments, capital repayments and other charges, arrangement fees and so forth. The APR must, by law, reflect the actual rate of interest charged over the full period of the loan.

IS IT WORTH SWITCHING MY MORTGAGE TO GET A LOWER RATE?

The short answer is: it depends if you can find a new lender willing to allow you to switch. If the loan to value of your mortgage is less than 60% there are two things to consider, apart from proof of ability to repay:

- How much can you save by switching lender?
- What is switching lender going to cost you?

The first question is relatively easy to answer. The second question will depend on a variety of factors, including:

- whether you are on a fixed interest rate – in which case there may be a penalty for switching
- how much it is going to cost you by way of legal and other costs.

If you can save 0.25% a year interest or more, it could well be worth the switch. If in doubt, consult an authorised mortgage intermediary or accountant and ask them to do the figures for you.

HELP! I'M SELF-EMPLOYED

Most financial institutions are pleased to lend to someone who is self-employed – though if you have less than three years' sets of accounts it may be harder. This is another instance where a professional authorised mortgage intermediary will help. He or she will know which lenders are keen for your business and willing to offer you the lowest rates. Remember that it is the net profit (after expenses but before tax) that lenders use for borrowing eligibility.

Note: It is no longer possible to get a mortgage in Ireland without a statement from your accountant to the effect that your tax affairs are completely up to date.

WHAT WILL IT COST FOR ME TO BUY MY HOME?

There are various expenses involved in buying a home:

Valuation fees: No lender will let you have a mortgage without a proper valuation. The price of this will vary but is likely to be in the region of €130. You may like to ask an architect or some other type of professional property adviser to survey the building for you to check its condition and the likely cost of any repairs needed. The fee for this will be linked to the amount of work required and could run to several hundred euros or more for a large house.

Legal fees: This is primarily the cost of employing a solicitor to look after the whole transaction for you. The normal cost is around 1%

of the total price plus VAT at 23% and outlay. So for a €200,000 house you will have to find in the region of €2,400. Your lender may also charge you the costs of their legal fees if it is a commercial transaction. Negotiation over legal fees is always possible, and you should ask for a reduction, especially if you are a first-time buyer.

Land registry fees: On a €200,000 property this would be up to €750. The fee is to cover registering the property in your name.

Stamp duty: This is based on the purchase price of the property. The following rates of stamp duty apply to all residential properties, since 8 December 2010:

Property value	Rate
Up to €1,000,000	1%
Balance	2%

Stamp duty on commercial and non-residential property is charged at 6%.

Search fees: This is to check that the property has planning permission, isn't located on the site of a proposed development and so forth. Usually around €150.

Arrangement fees: Some lenders charge application and arrangement fees, but generally only on non-home loans. These are in the region of €100 to €300.

To give you a typical example, for a first-time buyer purchasing a house for €300,000 with a 90% mortgage (€270,000) the total fees will be around €6,000.

THE FINANCE ACT 2012

The Finance Act 2012 included the following changes to the rules on mortgage interest relief:

- First-time buyers in 2012 received mortgage interest relief at a rate of 25% for the first 2 tax years, reducing after that, with certain first-time buyer ceilings.
- Non-first-time buyers in 2012 received mortgage interest relief at a rate of 15% from 2012 until 2017, 22.5% for the next 3 years and 20% for a further 2 years.
- A special rate of 30% for the tax years 2012 to 2017 was introduced for first-time buyers who bought their sole residence for the first time in the years 2004 to 2008 or paid their first mortgage interest payment during this period.
- The maximum relief is €10,000 per person per annum.

With effect from 1 May 2009, mortgage interest relief may be claimed for a maximum of seven years, both for first-time and non-first-time buyers.

- Mortgages taken out on or after 1 January 2013 do not qualify for mortgage interest relief.
- Budget 2018 extended the relief on a tapering basis for 3 years to December 2020.

DOES IT MAKE SENSE TO BUY A SECOND PROPERTY AS AN INVESTMENT?

Buying property and renting it out became an increasingly popular investment in the 2000s. There were various reasons for this, including:

- tax incentives – you can claim 80% of any loan interest you pay on borrowings to acquire and/or improve the property, against any rental income you receive. Plus, if you buy certain types of property or property in particular areas you will receive additional tax breaks.
- potential increases in property values.
- possible high yields compared to other investments.
- the low cost of borrowing money.

In general, the only investors who don't make money from renting out property are those who have over-estimated the return they'll receive, haven't allowed for all the likely costs and lack the patience to wait out any market downturns. The secrets to success are undoubtedly:

- Allow for periods without tenants (known as 'voids').
- Make sure you have calculated all the costs including loan repayments, redecoration, maintenance and repair.
- Don't view it as a short-term investment.

WHAT OTHER STATE HOUSING GRANTS MIGHT BE AVAILABLE TO ME?

There are various other grants available from the state, including:

Improvement grants: A range of loans could be available from your local authority towards improving or extending your home, subject to a number of conditions.

Disabled persons grant: This is given to cover the cost of adapting a private home for the needs of someone who is disabled.

Thatching grant: This is available towards the cost of renewing or repairing thatched roofs on houses. Thatchers are a dying breed, but it is important to reward and help those who are maintaining our heritage.

Home energy savings grants: A range of grants is available to improve home insulation, install renewable energy systems and upgrade existing heating systems to become more energy-efficient. Details can be found at www.seai.ie.

Is IT WORTH REPAYING MY MORTGAGE EARLY?

Should you overpay your mortgage each month? Should you use all your available cash to reduce your mortgage? Should you use a lump sum of cash to reduce or pay off your mortgage? The answer is probably yes if the following apply to you:

- You don't have other, more expensive, debts. If you do, these should be paid off first.
- It won't leave you without some savings tucked away against a rainy day.
- There aren't other investment opportunities that might be worth more to you in cash terms.

If you were thinking of paying off some or all of your mortgage, I would strongly advise consulting an authorised adviser or mortgage intermediary first. He or she will be able to work out the figures for you.

What home insurance will I need?

This is covered in greater detail in Chapter 12 on insurance. In summary, homeowners should take out the following cover:

Buildings insurance: This is compulsory if you have a mortgage. Basically, it means that if damage is done to the fabric of your home (by a fire or a flood, for instance), money is available to repair or rebuild as necessary.

Contents insurance: This protects you against loss of or damage to your home contents.

Mortgage repayment insurance (payment protection insurance): This cover is optional, but means that if you are ill or made redundant, your mortgage repayments will be paid for you. Payments usually last for up to a year. Refunds are underway from some providers who mis-sold this product. Email the Money Doctors for details (info@ moneydoctors.ie).

If I have trouble making my mortgage repayments, what should I do?

Contact your lender immediately. The worst thing you can do is to keep them in the dark about any financial problems you may be encountering.

If you need help with your finances you could contact a qualified, experienced financial adviser. You could contact the following:

- Your local St Vincent de Paul Society – they run a special advice scheme.
- The Department of Social Protection also runs a free advice scheme called the Money and Budgeting Advice Service (MABS). You can obtain details from your local social welfare office or public library.
- The Insolvency Service of Ireland (www.isi.gov.ie), set up in 2012, have different structures to deal with unsecured and secured debts.

There is a solution, no matter how bleak the situation may seem.

THE MONEY DOCTOR SAYS ...

If you have any questions about property or mortgages not answered in this book then please do email the Money Doctor (www. moneydoctors.ie) or book a one-to-one consultation (consultation@ moneydoctors.ie).

PART 6

SAVINGS AND INVESTMENT SUCCESS

My favourite quote about wealth is from Ernest Hemingway. In response to F. Scott Fitzgerald's comment that the rich are different, he replied: 'Yes, they have more money.'

And getting yourself into a position where you have 'more money' is what this section of the book is all about, for, as the entertainer Sophie Tucker observed, 'I've been rich, and I've been poor; rich is better.' Now, I hasten to add, I am not suggesting you get rich for the sake of it. My interest is in making sure you have sufficient money to be free – free from the worry of not having enough, and free to choose how you spend your time.

There are some widely held misconceptions about how to get rich. Some people think the only way they will manage it is by owning their own business; others feel the Lotto offers them their best chance; a third group seem to imagine it will happen all by itself.

In my experience, the only way to get rich is to take it slowly and steadily. Set aside part of your income every month and invest it wisely and you will be amazed at how, over the years, it grows.

Many people feel that there is not much difference between savings and investment, but to my mind there is a clear distinction:

- *Saving is all about short-term goals. This is the money you tuck away on a regular basis to pay for your holidays, or in case of emergency. Because this is money that needs to be available to you, it can't be tied up where you can't get your hands on it.*
- *Investment, on the other hand, is all about medium- to long-term goals. You invest to ensure yourself a more prosperous and secure future. You may invest a lump sum, or a little on a regular basis, but the important thing is (barring an unforeseen crisis) you should be able to leave your money to work for you undisturbed for a reasonable period of time.*

This section is divided into two chapters. In the first, you'll discover the best possible way to save your money with a view to building your own emergency fund. In the second, you'll learn how to invest your money in such a way as to build your wealth. Between the two you'll have all the tools you need to make your money grow, and grow, and grow ...

15

SAVING FOR A RAINY DAY

THE QUICKEST, MOST EFFICIENT WAY TO BUILD UP AN EMERGENCY FUND

One of your key financial objectives should be to have some easily accessible cash savings to pay for larger expenses or simply in case of a 'rainy day'. In this chapter you will discover:
- why it is so important to have cash savings;
- how much savings you should build up; and
- the best way to make your savings grow.

GOOD, OLD-FASHIONED SAVINGS

We are lucky enough to live in a country where the state provides a safety net for widow(er)s, for the seriously ill or disabled, for pensioners and for anyone in dire financial straits. However, the amount on offer is relatively meagre – it won't cover many of the regular minor financial crises ordinary people face. For instance, the state isn't going to help you with an unexpected bill for repairs to your home or car. Nor will they pay all your regular bills if you find yourself without an income for any reason. The fact is you should have a bit of cash tucked away – good, old-fashioned savings – just in case you ever need it. You should probably also have some extra cash to hand so that you can take advantage of an unexpected investment opportunity, for capital expenditure or just in case you see something you want to buy.

Saving up money to create a safety net requires a degree of commitment. It is in our nature, after all, to spend rather than to save. But if you can motivate yourself to tuck a little bit away each month I promise you'll never regret it!

SAVING MADE SIMPLE

It is one thing to think 'I must build up my savings', but often quite another thing to actually do so. Saving can only be achieved by conscious effort. Ideally, you should open your savings account somewhere convenient and arrange to make regular payments into it. For instance, you might set up a standing order to transfer a regular amount each month from your bank current account to a deposit account. Some employers offer 'payroll deduction' schemes, where the money goes straight from your salary to a savings account. Alternatively, if you are entitled to receive a child allowance from the state, you could consider saving all of this on an automatic basis. The important thing is that a savings plan should be regular, and sacrosanct.

HOW MUCH IS ENOUGH?

Just how much savings you should aim to accumulate will be determined by your personal circumstances.
- A single person in his or her twenties without any responsibilities and with low overheads probably only needs to have enough cash to cover, say, three months' worth of expenditure.
- A couple with children, a mortgage and a car to run should probably aim to build up as much as six months' expenditure.

If you aren't already lucky enough to have a lump sum available to form your safety net, the best way to build it up is to establish a pattern of regular saving each week or each month. Remember, something is better than nothing – even if it is a relatively small amount, it will soon add up.

YOUR SAVINGS STRATEGY

If you have, say, six months' worth of expenditure saved up and you don't need instant access to all of it, my advice is to keep about a third where it is readily available and the rest where you can access it by giving notice. This strategy will allow you to earn extra interest.

Incidentally, if you are in a permanent relationship, then ideally you should both have access to the emergency fund. In the event of some problem affecting one of you, the other may need to use this money.

EMERGENCY FUND: THREE BASIC REQUIREMENTS

An emergency fund should meet three basic requirements:
- It should provide you with total security. Your savings must not be at risk.
- It must earn as much interest as possible under the circumstances.
- It must provide you with the level of access you need.

The options available that meet these requirements are limited pretty much to those listed below.

Deposit accounts

If you leave money on deposit with a bank, building society or credit union they will pay you interest. How much interest you earn will vary according to:

- how much money you have on deposit;
- the length of notice you have to give before you can make a withdrawal (notice accounts/fixed-rate accounts); and
- your commitment to saving regularly (check out regular-saver accounts).

Rates can vary substantially, and they change all the time. Shop around and don't be afraid to move your money to where it can earn more for you. Remember, currently the Deposit Guarantee Scheme guarantees €100,000 of your savings.

State savings from NTMA

Available from An Post, these offer a good range of savings products, all of which give competitive returns and some of which are tax-free. If you want to build up an emergency fund the two most appropriate accounts to consider are the instalment savings scheme or the deposit account. An Post's instalment savings scheme requires you to make regular monthly payments for at least one year of between €25 and €1,000. In exchange, you will enjoy tax-free growth. An Post's deposit account is very similar to a bank or building society deposit account. The interest rate isn't high, but it is competitive, and you have instant access. Once you've built up your emergency fund, you may like to consider transferring your money into either a state **savings bond** or **savings certificates**. Both are designed for medium- to long-term growth (at least three years), but you can get your money quickly if you need to. Keep in mind that the interest earned on savings bonds and certificates is tax-free. The National Solidarity Bond (either a four- or ten-year investment) enjoys an element of tax-free returns, with the ten-year bond returning a gross 16% per annum after 10 years (AER 1.5%), tax free. All state savings investments are available in post offices or online (www.statesavings.ie).

SAVINGS AND TAX

On deposit accounts, deposit interest retention tax (DIRT) is levied from January 2020 at source on your interest earned at a standard rate of 33%. However, if you are not liable for income tax and you or your spouse are over 65 years of age or you are permanently incapacitated, then you are entitled to claim back any DIRT deducted from your interest. You can make a back claim for DIRT tax for up to four years. To claim a refund of DIRT already paid, you should submit Form 54 to your local Revenue office. You can then complete Form DE1 and give it to your deposit taker to ensure that your interest will be paid without deduction of tax in the future.

MONEY DOCTORS WEALTH CHECK

How to reclaim DIRT

Nothing could be easier than reclaiming DIRT. All you do is complete a short form available from any larger post office, bank, building society or tax office. You'll need to attach evidence of the DIRT that you have paid. This is done by asking the financial institution (or institutions) concerned to provide you with a special certificate. The DE1 leaflet is available at www.revenue.ie/leaflet/dde1.pdf for those who wish to claim exemption from paying DIRT.

THE MONEY DOCTOR SAYS ...

- Saving on a regular basis may not always be easy, but it will bring you real peace of mind.
- You should have an emergency fund in place sufficient to cover all your bills for between three and six months.
- As with everything: shop around. You could earn a considerably greater return by moving your money to where the best rates are.
- Watch out for regular-saver accounts – you save from €100 to €1000 per month up to 12 months at very attractive rates. E-mail me for details of these deposit takers and their interest rates and terms.

16

INVESTMENT STRATEGIES YOU CAN COUNT ON

HOW TO MAKE YOUR MONEY GROW AND GROW AND GROW

Every investor faces the same conflict: how to balance risk and reward. Should you accept a lower return in exchange for peace of mind? Or should you attempt to make your money grow more quickly and face the possibility of losses? In fact, the best solution to the dilemma is: neither. As this chapter will demonstrate, the optimum way to build up your wealth is to:

- Set clear objectives. Know where you are going and what you want to achieve.
- Diversify. Invest your money in more than one area to combine growth and security.
- Be consistent. Don't chop and change; stick to your strategy.
- Stay on top of it. Keep an eye on performance all the time.
- Avoid unnecessary expenses and charges.

In addition to outlining a proven method of making your money grow, the chapter summarises all the major investment vehicles you should consider, providing you with 'insider' tips in relation to:

- pooled investments;
- stocks and shares;
- property; and
- tax-efficient investment.

BASIC INVESTMENT PLANNING

As discussed in earlier chapters, your primary investment priorities should be to:

- build up an emergency fund;
- start a pension plan; and
- buy your own home.

What you should do next will depend on your circumstances. Whether you have a lump sum to invest or simply plan to save on a regular basis, your options will basically revolve around the following questions:

- How much money is involved?
- How long can you tie your money up for?
- What type of return are you looking for?
- What risks are you willing to accept?
- To what extent is tax an issue?

Let's look at each of these in turn.

How much money is involved?

If you are saving regularly, you have a choice between investing in a specially designed longer-term plan or building up 'blocks' of capital and investing each one somewhere different.

If you have a lump sum – or as you build up 'blocks' of capital – then the choice of investments available to you opens up. For instance, with some capital available, property investment becomes an option, as does buying publicly quoted shares.

You must have a clear idea in your mind about how much you plan to invest and in what form. If you are saving on a regular basis, consider how long this will be for. Bear in mind that regular savings products have advantages and disadvantages. On the one hand, they tie you in and there can be strict penalties for early encashment or withdrawal. On the other, they force you to be disciplined and they take away the tricky decision of how to invest your money. You should also think about the cost of such plans.

How long can you tie your money up for?

Is there a date you need your money back? In other words, are you investing for something specific or just to build your overall wealth?

Investments have varying degrees of accessibility or **liquidity**. An investment that allows you to get at your money immediately is considered 'highly liquid'. Cash held in a deposit account or publicly quoted shares, for instance, are both liquid. Property and pension plans are not.

How long you stay with any particular investment will partly be determined by the investment vehicle itself (a ten-year savings plan is – unless you break the terms – a ten-year savings plan) and partly by events (there may be a good reason to sell your investment).

What type of return are you looking for?

Returns vary enormously. The graph below shows how, up to 2004, €1,000 would have grown over almost 20 years had you invested it in different ways. Since 2004, this graph has practically reversed, with bonds as the main winner, while in the last 7 years we have enjoyed the third-longest and strongest bull market (up 200% since March 2009). This illustrates how diversification is a sound philosophy.

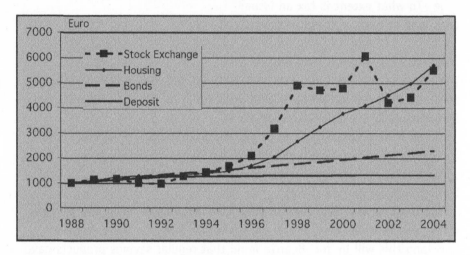

How much risk are you willing to accept?

In general, the higher the return, the greater the risk. The highest possible returns are to be made from investments such as **commodities** and **spread betting** – but in both cases you can actually lose substantially more than your original investment. The lowest returns are to be made from investments such as bank deposit accounts and An Post savings plans – where your money can be considered 100% secure.

In formulating your overall investment strategy, you need to consider your approach to risk. Are you willing to accept some risk in order to boost your return? How much? Email consultation@moneydoctors.ie for a risk questionnaire.

To what extent is tax an issue?

If you are a higher-rate taxpayer, or expect to be, then you need to consider to what extent tax saving is an issue for you. Bear in mind that there are a number of highly tax-effective investment options available – though all carry above-average risk. Remember, too, that capital gains are taxed at a much lower level than income – which may make this a more attractive option for you (see Chapter 26).

A proven investment strategy

The saying 'don't put all your eggs in one basket' is extremely sound advice when it comes to building wealth. In fact, it forms the basis of the only investment strategy I believe can be relied upon: **diversification**. If your investment strategy is too safe, then you won't enjoy decent growth. If your investment strategy is too daring, then you risk losing everything you have been working towards. The solution? Diversify your investments so that your money is spread across a range of areas. This leaves you two simple decisions:

- In which areas should you invest your money?
- How much should you invest in each area?

As already mentioned, you should start by diversifying into the three most important areas of investment – your emergency fund, your pension and buying your own home. Having done this, I would suggest putting your money into the following five areas:

- Pooled investments
- A 'basket' of directly held stocks and shares
- Investment property
- Higher risk and tax-efficient investments
- Alternative investments such as art, antiques, gold and other precious metals

Within each area there is much scope for choice, allowing you to vary the amount you invest, the length of your investment, the degree of risk and so forth. You must decide for yourself what mix of investments best suits your needs.

The information on the next pages will give you a feel for the various opportunities available. Your next step will depend largely on how active a role you want to play. One option is to investigate each area thoroughly yourself. Another option is to allow an authorised adviser to handle it all for you. My own suggestion would be to go for a combination of the two. Educate yourself, keep yourself informed, but let an expert guide and support you.

When long-term means long-term

One of the biggest mistakes investors make is that they forget their own financial objectives. If you are investing for long-term capital growth – a good, solid gain over, say, 20 years – then if you change your strategy halfway through you must resign yourself to a poor return and even losses. This is true regardless of the investment vehicle you are using.

If a change of strategy is unavoidable, try to give yourself as long as possible to enact it.

There are various areas where investors seem particularly prone to chopping and changing. Long-term savings plans, such as endowments, is one. The stock market is another. Leaving aside some sort of personal financial crisis, the usual reason is despondency over a perceived lack of growth or falling values. If you have chosen your investments well, you shouldn't be worrying about a few lean years or an unexpected dip in values. If you are concerned that you have made a bad investment decision in the first place, take professional advice before acting. **The biggest losses come when an investor panics**.

POOLED INVESTMENTS

A pooled investment – sometimes known as an investment fund – is a way for individual investors to diversify without necessarily needing much money. Your money is pooled with the money of all the other participants and then invested. Each pooled investment fund has different, specified objectives. For instance, one might invest in the largest Irish companies, another in UK companies, a third in US gilts and a fourth in European property. In each case the fund managers will indicate the type of risk involved. They will also provide you – on a regular basis – with written reports or statements detailing how your money is performing.

Since it would be impossible for all but the richest of private investors to mimic what these pooled investments do, they are an excellent way to spread your risk. A typical fund will be invested in a minimum of 50 companies and will be managed by a professionally qualified expert.

Fund managers make their money from a combination of commission and fees:

- There is often an entry fee of up to 5% of the amount you are investing.
- There will definitely be an annual management fee – usually 1% of the amount invested, though the more successful ones charge 2%+.
- If you want to sell your share in a pooled investment, you may also be charged a fee.

It is sometimes suggested in the media that fund managers are rewarded too highly. My view is that if a fund is meeting its objectives, then it is only fair that the fund managers recoup their costs and earn a fee for their expertise. I wish journalists would put more effort into reporting performance figures and less into complaining about whether a manager is charging 0.85% a year or 0.93%!

A couple of other points before we look at all the options in a little bit more detail:

- The funds described below are all medium- to long-term investment vehicles. In other words, you should be thinking about leaving your money in them for an absolute minimum of five years – and more like ten years or even longer.
- Although past performance – as it always says in the small print – can be no guide to future performance, it is still useful to know. One thing to check is who is making the actual investment decisions and how long they have been doing it for. If the individual manager of a fund has changed recently then the past performance may not be so relevant.

I include several different types of investment in this category:

- tracker bonds
- unit trusts and other managed funds
- with-profits funds
- stock market 'baskets' (or guaranteed stock market active funds)

All of these are what I would describe as 'tailor-made investment vehicles'. That is to say, they have been specifically designed to meet the needs of ordinary, private investors. This is in direct contrast to, say, un-tailored opportunities – such as a publicly quoted share or an investment property – which aren't aimed at any specific group of investors.

Tracker bonds

These funds guarantee to return your initial investment plus a return based on a specific stock market index or indices. For example, it might give you all your money back after five years plus 80% of any rise in the FTSE 100.

Unit trusts

Your money is used to purchase 'units' in an investment fund. The price of the units will depend on the underlying value of the investments. For instance, if the unit trust specialises in European technology shares, then the value of the shares it holds will determine the price of the units. You can sell your units at any time, but you should be wary of buying and selling too quickly as charges and fees can eat up your profit.

Unit-linked funds

As above, but with the added element of a tiny bit of life insurance so that they can be set up and run by life insurance companies.

Managed funds

Again these are, in essence, unit trusts. A managed fund makes a wide spread of investments, which theoretically reduces risk – though you should not assume that this is the case. Most are categorised (ESMA is the European Securities Marketing Authority who categorise every stock, share and company in the world into 7 categories – the higher the number, the higher the risk). Fund #1 (cautious) includes government bonds and cash funds, while Funds #5–#7 (aggressive) includes tech and energy stocks, emerging markets, BRIC countries, etc.

Specialised funds

These funds concentrate on very specific market opportunities – such as oil shares or companies listed in an emerging market. This is obviously riskier, but if the underlying investment performs well, then you will make above-average returns.

Indexed funds

An indexed fund aims to match the overall market performance. For instance, you might have a fund that plans to achieve the same return as the UK's leading 100 shares (FTSE 100) or Europe's top index, Eurostoxx 50.

With-profit funds

These funds are run by insurance companies and guarantee a minimum return *plus* extra bonuses according to how the fund has performed over the longer term. These bonuses might be added annually (annual bonus) or when the fund is closed after the agreed period of time (terminal bonus). The terms, conditions, objectives and charges for these funds vary enormously.

Stock market 'baskets'

Investors or their advisers choose a number of stocks, which can range from blue chip shares (such as the big corporates and retail groups) to downright risky stocks. Depending on how risk-averse you are, a percentage of your 'basket' will be conservative solid choices, while a smaller percentage will be a little bit of a gamble. **Diversification** is again the buzz word – the greater the spread or choice of stocks, the softer the fall if there is to be a fall.

SPECIALISED STOCK MARKET STRATEGIES

Futures, options, hedge funds, exchange-traded funds, derivatives, contracts for differences (CFDs) and the like constitute the specialised investment sectors of the stock market. Good solid advice is essential if you wish to participate in this area.

ALTERNATIVE INVESTMENTS

There is a large number of alternative investment options, all of which come with varying amounts of risk. Some, such as gold or other precious metals, are easy to buy and sell. Others, such as art, may have a limited market, making them difficult to find a buyer for when you want to dispose of them. Alternative investments include:

- paintings and other art
- antique furniture and other objects
- debentures at Wimbledon
- rock'n'roll memorabilia
- gold and other precious metals
- diamonds and other precious gems
- wine
- jewellery
- collectibles such as rare stamps, coins, classic cars or watches.

In general, alternative investment is 'direct' – this is to say, you purchase the actual items. Specialist knowledge is vital if this is to be a genuine investment. You should not consider alternative investments until you have a reasonably high net worth and a portfolio of more conventional investments, since the risks can be high.

MONEY DOCTORS WEALTH WARNING

Think carefully before you buy an annuity

If you have a lump sum to invest and you are aged at least 65, one option is to purchase an annuity. The key advantage of an annuity is that it guarantees you an income for the rest of your life. The key disadvantage is that, once purchased, you cannot get your lump sum back. Furthermore, when you die the income stops and nothing will normally be returned to your estate.

Annuities are purchased from life assurance companies, and the return is linked to your age. The younger you are, the lower the return you can expect to receive. It's possible to take out a 'joint-survivor annuity' if you're married. With these, when either you or your spouse dies, the income continues at a reduced rate until the death of the other. Joint-survivor annuities produce a lower return, or income, than single-life annuities.

At the moment, annuity rates, like interest rates, are relatively low. If you were a male, aged 65, and you wanted to generate a guaranteed income of €1,000 a month, you would need to invest €400,000. However, if you were aged 75, you would only need to invest €270,000.

Annuity rates differ from insurance company to insurance company, and from day to day. It is possible to arrange for your annuity rate to be linked to inflation, and some companies will also guarantee you a minimum return if you die within five years of purchasing the annuity. Finally, you should be aware that the income from an annuity is subject to income tax.

If you've got a limited amount of capital and you're worried about supporting yourself through your retirement years, an annuity could well be the perfect solution. However, I would advise getting professional help to make sure that you purchase the best-value annuity for your needs.

A low-risk, medium-term investment option
For a low-risk, medium-term investment option, consider **guaranteed bonds**. These offer above-average returns in exchange for you locking your money in for an agreed period. Some offer limited penalty-free withdrawals or provide a regular income for the term of the bond.

Investing in stocks and shares

Direct investment in the stock market is not for everyone. The risk associated with buying individual shares is obviously much greater than when buying into a diversified portfolio of shares – which is essentially what you are doing with a pooled or investment fund. Yes, if the share price goes up, you can make a small fortune. But if the price falls or the market crashes, your shares will be worth a fraction of what you paid for them.

For an investor with limited funds, buying shares is probably not a sensible option. However, once you have started to build your capital wealth, you should definitely consider adding individual share holdings to your portfolio of investments:

- Over the longer term, the stock market has shown a greater return to investors than any of the alternatives, including property.
- Irish investors are not limited to the Irish stock market – you may buy shares anywhere in the world.

- The charges for buying and selling shares have dropped dramatically, making it feasible to buy and sell in much smaller quantities.
- There are excellent sources of advice on which shares to buy and sell.
- Shares have widely varying degrees of risk.
- One of the big advantages of share ownership is that you literally own part of the company itself and its assets.
- Share ownership should bring you a regular income in the form of dividends plus capital appreciation (if the company is doing well).

Private investors have a choice of doing their own research and making their own decisions or seeking professional help from a stockbroker. Either way, if you are tempted to start buying and selling, you should arm yourself with as much information as possible. Remember, it is ultimately your decision what happens to your portfolio. You should always keep a close watch on what is happening to any company whose shares you have bought, the sector it operates in and the market as a whole. I would particularly recommend the internet for information purposes.

How to read the financial pages

If you do decide to buy stocks and shares, you can keep track of their performance by reading the stock market pages in your daily newspaper. Next to the name of your company you'll find the following information:

High: This is the highest price your particular company share has reached in the past 12 months.

Low: This is the lowest price your share has reached in the past 12 months.

Share price: This is the average price paid for your share at close of business on the previous day.

Rise or fall: This is usually represented by a (+) or (-) symbol, and it lets you know how much your share increased or fell by in the previous day's trading.

Dividend yield: The dividend yield is the relationship of a share's annual dividend to its price. The figure will be before tax. For instance, if the dividend yield was 5.8%, and if you'd purchased €100 worth of shares at the current price, you would receive an annual income of €5.80 before tax.

P/E: This stands for **price/earnings ratio**, and is one of the methods used to value a share. The price/earnings ratio is calculated by dividing the company's share price by the after-tax earnings due to each share over the company's most recent financial year. A high price/earnings ratio means that the market is confident in the company's future. But, by the same token, it could mean that the shares are over-priced. A low price/earnings ratio implies a lack of market confidence in the shares, but perhaps the potential for an investor to pick up a bargain.

Dividend payments

When you own shares in a company you are entitled to a portion of the profits – pre-supposing that there are profits to be shared. This portion is called a dividend, and it is paid twice a year. The first payment is called an 'interim dividend' and the second is a 'final dividend'. Several weeks before the dividend is due to be paid, the company directors will announce how much it is to be. A few weeks after this, they will 'close the register of shares'. Although you can still buy and sell the shares, if you do so while the register is closed, you won't be entitled to the forthcoming dividend. During this period, the company shares will be marked 'XD' – 'ex-dividend' – in the newspapers.

Shares and tax

Irish shares are liable to two different types of tax. First, you'll have to pay **income tax** on any profits (in other words, 'dividends') you receive. In fact, when you receive a dividend from an Irish company, they will already have withheld tax at the standard rate of 20%. If the amount of tax withheld exceeds your liability for that particular year you can claim a refund. However, if you are in fact a higher-rate taxpayer, you'll have to pay the difference between the standard rate and the higher rate when completing your annual tax returns. Second, when you sell your shares, if you've made a gain, you'll be liable for **capital gains tax** at 33%.

Choosing a stockbroker

The only way to buy and sell shares is through a registered stockbroker. You will pay either a flat fee or a commission, depending on whether the stockbroker is also advising you and/or the size of the transaction.

If you don't need advice when buying or selling, then you require an **execution only** service. In this instance, your main concern should be to keep costs to a bare minimum. Online services tend to be the cheapest, but it is well worth checking with your bank and the leading stockbrokers just to make sure.

Stockbrokers will be happy to provide you with an advisory service. You'll pay a higher level of commission for this (up to an average of 1.25%), but, of course, you'll benefit from your stockbroker's knowledge of the market.

There is no official minimum value regarding the volume of shares you can purchase. However, there is a minimum level of charges, usually around €25, so it probably doesn't make much sense to buy less than €1,000 worth of shares at a time.

If you want a list of Irish stockbrokers, then contact:

The Irish Stock Exchange
28 Anglesea Street, Dublin 2
Tel: (01) 617 4200

MONEY DOCTORS WEALTH CHECK

Why not start an investment club?

If you'd like to dabble in the stock market but only have a relatively small amount of money to invest, why not start an investment club? This is when a group of friends or work colleagues pool their resources and make buying and selling decisions together. My experience of investment clubs is that they regularly out-perform the stock market, because those involved take a real and detailed interest in every investment decision. However, you need time and patience.

Bonds

A bond is a long-term, fixed-interest investment. Bonds are issued by public companies and by governments as a way of raising money. They are, in effect, loans by you to a company or a government. Government bonds are usually referred to as **gilt-edged** securities or, for short, 'gilts' (see below). Bonds have a face value and term – expressed as a **maturity date**.

For instance, if you had purchased a 15-year €100 bond in a Dutch health insurer in 2002 for a face value of €99.10 – the discount is 90c – at a yield of 6.375% (the coupon), you would receive an annual income of €6.38 until the bond reaches its maturity date in 2017 if it is not 'called in' beforehand. On maturity, you are guaranteed to receive €100.

What if you want to cash in your bond sooner? There is a thriving market for second-hand bonds. For instance, the example I mentioned above is currently worth €122.37 with a yield of 3.925%. The second-hand value of a bond will be linked to its underlying security, its rate of interest, and the length of time until it matures.

Gilts

These are government stock, used over the years, rather like an IOU, to raise money to fund spending. They offer investors a fixed rate of interest for a set period of time in exchange for the use of their savings. The interest is paid without DIRT being deducted – making them very tax-efficient for some non-taxpayers. As interest rates in general fall, government stock tends to rise in value. Gilts are a totally secure and relatively inexpensive way to invest.

PROPERTY

It is easy to understand why so many private investors are attracted to residential and even commercial property:

- Property values have risen and fallen dramatically over the last 30 years.
- It is possible to fund up to 75% of the purchase price with relatively inexpensive loans.
- Rental income from property can cover all the expenses – interest, maintenance, tax and so forth.
- Your investment is in bricks and mortar – something solid – that you can actually see.
- If you make a gain when you sell the property, you will pay substantially less tax – because it is not 'income' but a capital gain, and is thus taxed at a lower level, currently 33%.

Property prices have fluctuated dramatically over the last 20+ years. If you had borrowed €180,000 to buy a €200,000 property some 20 years ago, you would have seen your €20,000 deposit turn into €341,200 profit by 2007! Not so much in the last 10 years!

Clearly, property prices rise and fall, so you would be unwise to assume that this is a one-way bet. If the market does fall, you may find it hard to sell a property and take out your money – as we witnessed from 2008 on. However, in the last three years, Irish property prices rose by up to 25% in certain areas. Also, the supply of property to rent has risen so much that in some areas it is now harder to find and keep tenants.

On the other hand, as the old saying goes, 'they aren't making any more of it', and as planning restrictions become tighter, there is every reason to believe that property will continue to be a highly attractive investment in the future. The golden rule, in my opinion, is to pick a location and type of property that is always easy to rent, near public transport and requiring little maintenance.

MONEY DOCTORS WEALTH CHECK

Tax treatment of rental income

Your rental income is treated the same way as income earned by self-employment. You are allowed all your expenses, including:

- wear and tear on furniture, currently an eighth of the cost for each of the following eight years;
- any charges made by a management company or letting agent;
- maintenance, repairs, insurance, ground rent, rates, RTB and so forth; and
- the cost of any other goods or services you supply to your tenants (such as cleaning).

With regard to relief on interest payable on loans borrowed to purchase, improve or repair a rented property this is allowable (only 80% of the interest) except – roughly – from the period 23 April 1998 to 1 January 2002. If you bought rental property during this period, you should seek professional advice or contact the Revenue Commissioners to clarify your position. Do note that not all your property expenses will be allowable for tax relief in the year in which they are incurred. For instance, the cost of 'wear and tear' will be spread over several years. For more information about tax treatment of property see Chapter 24.

TAX-EFFICIENT INVESTMENT OPTIONS

Financial experts often comment that 'you should never let the tax-saving tail wag the investment dog'. In other words, you shouldn't invest in anything simply to enjoy the tax savings, but should always consider the underlying value of the opportunity.

When it comes to **property investment**, there were a number of tax incentives designed to make certain types of property more attractive. Most of these have been phased out now.

In Budget 2012, a new **Employment and Investment Incentive** scheme (EII) was introduced to replace the BES Scheme. This is still in operation.

THE MONEY DOCTOR SAYS ...

- Don't put all your eggs in one basket. Divide your savings and investments into different parts, so that if one area doesn't perform as hoped your overall financial objectives can still be met.

• Remember, the stock market has outperformed all other investments over the long term. You can take advantage of this by investing in a pooled fund such as a unit trust, or by investing directly in a broad selection/portfolio of shares.

• You must keep reviewing your investment decisions, even if you get a professional to help and advise you.

• Investment is for the long term – anything from five years upwards. Most managed funds have penalties that decrease over the first 5 years. Don't allow short-term rises and falls to distract you from your long-term strategy.

MONEY DOCTORS WEALTH WARNING

As always, if you get professional help, make sure it is unbiased and doesn't only represent one or two firms. Some so-called 'experts' will sell you their solution without listening to your objectives. Email consultation@moneydoctors.ie for more information on investments.

PART 7

PLANNING FOR A RICHER RETIREMENT

Until 20 or 30 years ago, the word 'retirement' was associated with a certain age. Women, if they worked, retired at 60, and men at 65. Life expectancy was shorter and money was scarcer.

Today, retirement has taken on a whole different meaning. With a bit of careful planning, it is now common for people to give up work and 'retire' from their late 40s onwards. There is also a strong trend towards second and even third careers.

So when we talk of retiring, yes, we mean giving up work, but we also mean having enough money to do what we want.

Thankfully, successive governments have encouraged the trends I am describing, and have rewarded those who save for their retirement with very, very, very tasty tax breaks. There are also some relatively new pension structures that offer incredible flexibility.

In this section, you will learn how to ensure that when you retire (whenever that may be), you have sufficient wealth to lead a comfortable life. Specifically, you will discover how to:

- *decide what sort of pension you will need;*
- *assess your current pension prospects;*
- *understand the various options open to you;*
- *arrange a pension that will ensure a comfortable retirement;*
- *retire early; and*
- *find someone you can trust to steer you through the pensions minefield.*

I must emphasise that no one should be complacent about retirement planning. Even if you have a pension, you must review it on a regular basis. You could be a long time retired, anything from 20 to 40 years, so you need to get it right.

17

RETIREMENT BASICS

In this chapter we will look at why pension planning is so important, and learn about what I call 'retirement basics' – such as understanding what your existing entitlement (if any) is – together with general planning advice.

WHY YOU SHOULD MAKE PENSION PLANNING YOUR NUMBER ONE PRIORITY

The only people who don't have to worry about retirement planning are those lucky enough to belong to a really first-class pension scheme (one with generous, cast-iron benefits) and those who are so rich that money will never be a problem.

For the rest of us, pension planning should be a top priority – more of a priority, in fact, than almost any other financial decision we take. Frankly, it doesn't matter if you haven't bought your own home or invested a single penny of your money, provided you have a good pension plan. This is because, thanks to longer life expectancy, many people will spend anything from 20 to 40 years in retirement.

Typically, as we get older and progress in our careers, we earn more money. However, on retirement, we are no longer earning an income, and must rely either on our savings or on state benefits. Our earnings are usually at their highest just before we retire. And unless we have made proper provision, they will be at their lowest just after we retire. This can result in a massive drop in lifestyle at the point of retirement.

This is where the concept of **income equalisation** comes in – that is, reducing your disposable income when you are earning good money to help increase your income when you are not earning. We reduce our disposable income now by putting money into a pension scheme that can be used to increase our retirement income. It is still likely that when we retire, our income will fall, but with this type of planning the transition will be far less of a shock to the system.

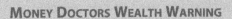

IT IS NEVER TOO EARLY OR TOO LATE TO BEGIN

It is not impossible that your retirement may turn out to be a longer
period than your working life, and so it isn't surprising that pension
experts stress the importance of starting to plan early.

Nevertheless, if the number of men and women in their 40s, 50s
and even their 60s consulting the Money Doctor on pension planning
is anything to go by, a huge percentage of the population don't start
thinking about their retirement until it isn't that far away.

Obviously, the later you leave it, the more of your income you will have
to devote to building up a decent pension fund and the less well off you
can expect to be when you stop working. It is never too late to begin, but
this doesn't mean you should go to the wire. Every single day counts.

START BY TAKING STOCK

The first step towards a comfortable retirement is to take stock of where
you are now in pension terms:

- Are you part of one or more company or occupational pension
  schemes already?
- Are you entitled to a state pension by virtue of your employment?
- Are you entitled to a non-contributory old age pension?
- Do you need more than a third of the average industrial wage to
  live on? Because that is roughly what the state pension will give
  you!
- Have you started a pension plan in the past?

If you answer 'yes' to any of these questions, you need to find out what your existing pension is going to be worth to you.

You also need to consider what other assets you have. Will your home be paid for by the time you retire? Have you any other savings or investments? By the same token, are there any other debts that you will need to discharge before retirement?

WHERE DO YOU GO FOR THE ANSWERS TO THESE QUESTIONS?

The easiest thing to do is to get a qualified professional to do the work for you – in other words, either an accountant (if they specialise in this area) or an independent, regulated financial adviser. The alternative is to approach all the relevant parties yourself. That is to say:

- your current employer and any past employers;
- the managers of any pension scheme you may have started in the past;
- the Department of Social Protection (check your telephone directory for the relevant department or Chapter 5 of this book); and
- the Financial Services and Pensions Ombudsman.

If you are unhappy with any aspect of the way a non-government pension scheme has been administered, then you should contact:

Financial Services and Pensions Ombudsman
36 Upper Mount Street, Dublin 2
www.fspo.ie

THE MONEY DOCTOR SAYS ...

If you are self-employed or you are not in an employer-sponsored pension scheme then, unless you take action, you'll have to rely on the state. You can guess how well off that will leave you.

HOW MUCH WILL YOU NEED WHEN YOU RETIRE?

The whole concept of retirement has been turned on its head in recent years. As a population we are:

- giving up work sooner – often in our late 40s or 50s;
- living longer and healthier lives; and
- leading more active lives in retirement.

We also expect a much higher standard of living. As a result we need more money in retirement than our predecessors did. Here are some things you will need to consider:

- Will you need a lump sum on retirement to pay off debts or to invest for a regular income?
- Will you still have unavoidable expenses (such as children's education) to pay for? Perhaps your mortgage will continue until you are 70 or 75?
- How much of an income will you need? Could you manage on half of what you earn now? Could you manage on a quarter?
- What changes would you have to make in your lifestyle if the only money you had coming in after retirement was the state pension?
- Do you have anyone else to provide for? Your spouse, for instance? What will happen if you die before they do?

Our civil servants receive an index-linked income of up to half of their final pay, a tax-free sum of up to one and a half years' salary, and a half-pension for their spouses after they die. Only a very tiny percentage of private-sector schemes offer this type of benefit.

If you work in the private sector and want to receive this sort of benefit from the age of 65, you would have to put about 15% of your income into a pension fund from the age of 20.

THE GOOD NEWS

There are three excellent reasons why you shouldn't despair, regardless of whether you have any sort of pension in place already:

- The government realises that it is vital to encourage you to save for your retirement so they will give you *huge* tax incentives to do so. For every €1 invested in a pension, you will receive 20c or 40c back depending on your tax margin. Plus, all growth in the fund is tax-free, and 25% of the fund can be taken as a tax-free lump sum (or €200,000, whichever is the lesser).
- Good planning at any age can optimise your retirement income.
- By taking action now, you can alter your position dramatically. Only people who continue to ignore the risks they are running face the possibility (one might say certainty) of an impoverished retirement.

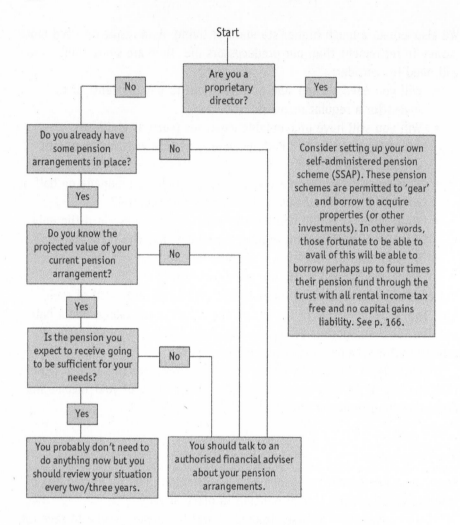

Start

Are you a proprietary director?

No / Yes

Do you already have some pension arrangements in place? — No

Yes

Do you know the projected value of your current pension arrangement? — No

Yes

Is the pension you expect to receive going to be sufficient for your needs? — No

Yes

You probably don't need to do anything now but you should review your situation every two/three years.

You should talk to an authorised financial adviser about your pension arrangements.

Consider setting up your own self-administered pension scheme (SSAP). These pension schemes are permitted to 'gear' and borrow to acquire properties (or other investments). In other words, those fortunate to be able to avail of this will be able to borrow perhaps up to four times their pension fund through the trust with all rental income tax free and no capital gains liability. See p. 166.

WHAT TO DO IF YOU WORK IN THE PRIVATE SECTOR

If you work for someone else, you will be in one of two situations – either:

- you are in a company or occupational scheme; or
- you aren't in any scheme at all.

If you are in a company or occupational pension scheme, then you will need to ascertain how good the scheme is, the sort of pension you can expect, what other benefits you may be entitled to and whether it is possible to increase your pension by making **additional voluntary contributions** (AVCs). If, on taking expert advice, the existing pension scheme doesn't appear to be that good, then concentrate on those AVCs.

Don't forget any schemes you may have been in during your previous employment.

All employers are now obliged to operate a scheme under recent legislation – **personal retirement savings accounts** or PRSAs – or at least to have a direct debit provision from your salary to such an investment. If you aren't in your employer's scheme, you should consider joining.

If you have no pension arrangements at all, and you don't want to do something through your employer, then you need to start a scheme of your own. Your own pension scheme might be a personal pension plan or a PRSA. I'll be looking at these options in greater detail in the next chapter.

WHAT TO DO IF YOU WORK FOR YOURSELF

If you work for yourself, you are going to have to provide your own pension. The big advantage of this is that you can design a pension plan that matches your needs perfectly:

- It will be flexible, allowing you to invest on a regular basis or with lump sums.
- You'll have the choice of investing your money in an established fund or starting your own if you are a company owner, proprietary director (i.e. have at least a 5% shareholding in your company) or a senior company employee (e.g. a **small self-administered pension scheme** – SSAP) or self-directed trusts.
- If you own your own company you could even consider setting up a company scheme.

THE MONEY DOCTOR SAYS ...

- You are probably, to quote a line from the television programme *Blackadder*, 'perfectly happy to wear cotton without understanding how the weaving process works'. By the same token, you shouldn't feel that you need to understand pensions legislation in its entirety to make your retirement plans!
- Action is imperative. If you have a really good pension plan, allowing you to retire early, you don't need any other investments (not even a house).
- The sooner you act, the better it will be, but it is never too late to start. Extra tax benefits may apply the older you are. It's certainly never too late to enquire: consultation@moneydoctors.ie.

18

PENSIONS MADE EASY

This chapter contains detailed instructions on retirement planning – all the information, advice and tips you need to make your own decisions about what you need and want.

A QUICK GUIDE TO PENSION SCHEMES

My youngest daughter's favourite expression is 'too much information'. This may be your reaction when faced with trying to understand the pension system. Little wonder, when you consider how complicated the various options are. Opening a book on the subject at random (a book aimed at ordinary consumers, by the way), my eyes fell on the following sentence:

> Where a 5% Director chooses the New Retirement Options, they must first ensure that the total fund accumulated would not result in a situation where the maximum benefits would be excluded had they gone down the traditional annuity purchase route.

My own view is that you should inform yourself, in the same way that you would inform yourself before making any major purchase. However, unless you find the topic fascinating, don't waste your time grappling with the minutiae. Instead, let an independent and authorised expert advise you. Here, then, is my quick guide to pension schemes.

CATEGORIES OF PENSION SCHEMES

A pension scheme, or retirement plan, is a way of saving money specifically for your retirement. What differentiates it from an ordinary savings plan is that you will receive substantial help from Revenue but, in exchange, access to your savings will be restricted. How restricted? Well, it will vary, but typically you won't be able to touch any of the money you have saved until you reach a minimum age (and this will vary according to the scheme and even the sort of job you have), and even then you won't be able to get your hands on all of it as a tax-free lump sum.

There are three basic employment categories and the pension options can be defined as follows:

- employee schemes
- self-employed schemes
- directors' schemes

Employee schemes

- **Occupational pension schemes:** Money invested in these schemes is locked away until you actually retire. At this point, there will be restrictions on how you take the benefits. For instance, you'll only be allowed a limited amount as a tax-free lump sum, and the rest has to be taken as an income.
- **Defined benefit:** This is the Rolls Royce of schemes, and extremely valuable. It can be either a contributory or non-contributory scheme – invariably, the employer will make contributions to the scheme. With this type of pension, the employer guarantees you a certain percentage of your final salary, as a pension for life, for every year you have been working for them. Depending on the particular scheme, this can be up to 66% of the annual average of your last three years' income. You can also elect to take part of your benefits as a tax-free lump sum of up to one and a half times your salary. The beauty of defined-benefit schemes is that, irrespective of fund performance, you are guaranteed to receive the promised pension. It is the trustees of the scheme who have to worry about how they are going to fund what could be a very expensive company cost. More and more employers are opting out of the defined-benefit pension because of cost, a trend exacerbated by the poor pension fund performances of the late 1990s and first part of this century. Defined-benefit schemes undoubtedly provide the best pension benefits. However, you should note that benefits are based on how long you have been working for that company. If you have a relatively short number of years' service, you can still top up your pension benefits by making some additional voluntary contributions (AVCs). Remember that over 70% of defined benefit schemes in Ireland are insolvent, so ensure that *your* company will be able to meet its future commitments.
- **Defined contributions:** Your pension is based on the growth of your monthly contributions (again the employer will usually also make contributions to your pension) up to maturity on retirement age. Unfortunately, there is no guarantee of how much you will receive on retirement, as values may fall as well as rise. Your fund is purely down to how fund managers perform and how much

you have invested. It is vital therefore that you be fully briefed and communicated with on a regular basis so that you can take corrective action if necessary. That corrective action may be an AVC.

- **Additional voluntary contributions (AVCs).** Depending on your own existing pension contributions and your age, you could put up to 40% of your annual income into an AVC. You can offset the entire 40% against your income tax liability, making this procedure a very tax-efficient one. Furthermore, most employers will deduct your AVCs directly from your wages. There is also greater flexibility about how and when you take the benefits, and you won't have to pay for setting up a scheme of your own. If your employer's pension scheme has a good investment performance or guaranteed benefits, then putting more money into it via an AVC can make excellent financial sense.

    Check with an authorised adviser for specific details, as there are many regulations and you want to ensure you're making the right decision.

If no occupational pension scheme is available to you through your employer, you have the same options as someone who is self-employed (see below). The one exception is that your employer is required, by law, to provide you with a payroll deduction facility to a nominated PRSA provider.

Self-employed schemes
Personal Retirement Savings Accounts (PRSAs)/personal pensions – with the 2002 introduction of PRSAs, pensions became more accessible and less expensive to start. PRSAs have maximum charges of 5% of each premium paid plus 1% a year of the accumulated fund. The affordable pension is here to stay. Benefits include:
- It's low-cost.
- There is generous tax relief at your marginal rate. Depending on your age, this can be on contributions of up to 40% of your income.
- It's easy to understand – you decide how much you want to invest, and where you want the money invested.
- It's portable – you can bring the pension with you from employment to employment.
- It's flexible – you can adjust your annual contributions depending on your circumstances, and there is flexibility in how you use the fund on retirement.

- When you retire, you can have up to 25% of the fund as a tax-free lump sum (useful for paying off a mortgage), up to a maximum of €200,000.
- It's suitable for people who work for themselves, have no company scheme or change their employment frequently.

In theory, a PRSA is a simplified version of a personal pension plan. In practice, the rules governing PRSAs are just as complicated. You should seek independent advice.

Directors' schemes

If you are a director, you can avail of a **director's executive pension** (if you have 5% or more shareholding in your company). In fact, the advantages offered by company schemes are so good that if you are self-employed (a sole trader), it may be worth your while to form a limited company in order to take advantage of them. If you do own your own company, then setting up a company pension scheme will probably be the best route for you. The limits for which Revenue will give tax relief on pension contributions are significantly higher for a company investing in a company pension scheme than for an individual investing in a corresponding PRSA or personal pension.

Company schemes can be arranged to benefit as many employees as you want, or just you, or selected members of your staff, as you prefer. This route is particularly good for anyone who has left it late in life to plan for his or her retirement.

- As there is no benefit in kind on contributions to a company pension scheme, your company will be able to put substantial tax-free money into your pension.
- There is greater flexibility with regard to your retirement date.
- You have more control over where your contributions are invested.
- You can take a portion of your fund tax-free – so there are tax breaks on the way in and the way out!

Small self-administered pension schemes (SSAPs) or self-directed trusts

Under most pension arrangements, it is left up to fund managers to determine what the pension funds actually invest in. If you want more direct control on the actual assets that make up your pension fund you can set up an SSAP. Here you appoint a **pensioner trustee** to run your pension, but you dictate what it invests in. For example, if you want to invest in shares you can pick the individual shares as opposed to just a managed fund.

Recent legislative changes have also brought in for the first time a provision that allows pension funds to borrow for property acquisition. This means that you can borrow within your pension fund to buy an investment property (at arm's length – not your own company's offices, your holiday hot spot or your granny's flat), and both the rental income contributions and your own monthly contributions will be paid into your pension fund tax-free; at the same time, your fund (i.e. your property) should be appreciating as you are making those contributions. There are the added benefits that no capital gains tax liability is incurred and your estate keeps the asset (i.e. your property) after you die.

I predict that for company executives, SSAPs/self-directed trusts will grow considerably over the coming years as a result of the introduction of that one provision, allowing pension funds to borrow or gear perhaps up to four times the fund value to buy investment property.

SSAPs are not just confined to property either. Shares, investments and even complex financial instruments (e.g. hedge funds) can be incorporated into SSAPs. Email the Money Doctor for a free brochure on self-directed trusts at info@moneydoctors.ie.

BIG TAX RELIEF – THE REVENUE COMMISSIONERS ARE ON YOUR SIDE

I have made repeated mention of the huge tax incentives offered to those who invest in a pension. These include:

- There is tax relief at your marginal rate of tax. So if you are paying tax at 40% when you put €100 into your pension fund, it will only cost you €60. Put another way, pension funds almost double the value of your savings before the money has been invested in anything. Even at 20% taxable, the fund would have to drop by 20% before you would lose out.

- Investments grow tax-free. If you put money into your own company scheme, it is a legitimate business expense for tax purposes, and profits within the pension fund are tax-free (e.g. dividends and interest).

- Put another way, if a gross premium of €5,000 were paid for 20 years, the value of the premiums would be €100,000 at the end of the period. Thanks to the tax element, the net cost **from after-tax income** (if the tax remains at 40%) is €60,000. To achieve the same return on investing, the net income would need an annual compound return of 6%! This is the value of the government's contribution and it is given **for free**.

- While it is in a pension fund, no income tax or capital gains tax is payable on your investment.
- All pension schemes allow you to take out a certain portion of your fund tax-free when you retire.
- PRSI is not payable once you are 66.

There are limits on the amount you can invest into a pension fund and still get the tax relief. Check with your authorised adviser for details or go to consultation@moneydoctors.ie.

WHAT HAPPENS TO YOUR PENSION CONTRIBUTIONS?

If you are part of an occupational pension scheme, your money will be invested by the scheme's managers. If it is a big scheme, they may invest it directly themselves. Most companies, however, use the services of professional fund managers, who invest in everything from stocks and shares to property and commodities. Performance will be determined by how well the scheme is managed, and if you are in a 'defined contribution' scheme, you need to pay close attention to this. For employer-sponsored schemes (e.g. occupational pension schemes) trustees play an important role, as they look after the investment decisions on advice from fund managers.

If you set up your own personal pension plan or your own company sets up a company scheme, then you have much more control over how your contributions are invested. Most opt for equity funds – where your money is pooled and invested in stocks and shares. Such funds will have varying returns and different levels of risk. As you near retirement, you will be less likely to place your fund in a higher-risk investment than you would in your early 30s.

MONEY DOCTORS WEALTH WARNING

Don't buy a pension from someone who can't offer you choice

All the financial institutions involved in the retirement market, and I'm speaking chiefly about life insurance companies and banks, employ salespeople whose job it is to promote their own company's pension products.

One such example is that of a young solicitor who was persuaded to take out a bank assurance pension plan at a premium of more than €500 per month, based on her expectation of a certain income on retirement. After a couple of months she cancelled the policy, because she hadn't been asked one of the most important questions: 'Can you afford to pay this amount each month into a pension scheme?'

While it is important to aim for a similar level of income to retire on, it is equally important to be able to afford it and have a life in the meantime.

Ideally, you should not choose a pension from someone who only represents one company. You should always deal with someone independent who is authorised to tell you about every single option available to you. Pension fund performance and management fees vary enormously. Buying without comparing the whole market could cost you a great deal of money.

WHAT IS IT GOING TO COST?

Almost without exception, the pension industry gets paid on **commission**. This commission comes out of your monthly payments. The amount will vary according to the type of pension scheme you join or set up. Many schemes (though not all) will involve an initial, one-off fee, followed by an **annual management charge**. To give you an example, for a standard PRSA the maximum annual management charge is 1% of the accumulated fund, whilst the initial set-up fee is capped at 5% of the premiums. When you take out a pension, your authorised adviser will explain, in full, what charges you are paying.

Having a pension is one thing, but having a pension that is going to provide you with the income you think you will need is another. One example of this was a shop-owner who sought advice on investing a lump sum. One suggestion was to look at investing this in a pension. However, he indicated that he was alright here, as he had already put a pension in place. It transpired that this 45-year-old shop owner was currently earning €50,000 a year and had just taken out a pension plan for €400 a month. He was shocked to learn that if he kept contributions at this level, and took the state contributory pension into account, he could expect to have a total after-tax retirement income of around €750 a month (in today's terms) at age 65 – a fraction of what he currently earned.

You get what you pay for. One way of looking at it is to look at what level of income you think you need and finding out how much it would cost to provide this. You may not be able to afford the cost now, but at least you will know what to expect.

Below is a table showing the approximate costs of funding a total after-tax income of €1,250 per month and €2,500 per month in today's terms should you retire at 65. These figures assume that you will be entitled to the state contributory pension. These figures are meant as a guide only, and make a number of assumptions. You should discuss your own particular circumstances with a financial adviser or get in touch at consultation@moneydoctors.ie.

	Aged 25	Aged 30	Aged 35	Aged 40	Aged 45	Aged 50	Aged 55
€1,250pm	€191pm	€255pm	€347pm	€482pm	€673pm	€1,001pm	€1,681pm
€2,500pm	€341pm	€457pm	€623pm	€864pm	€1,207pm	€1,790pm	€3,019pm

(The above figures are before tax relief and assume that contributions are increased by 5% a year, inflation is 5% a year and the state pension increases by 5% a year. It also assumes that the funds the pension is invested in increase by 6% a year and that tax rates on retirement are similar to today.)

WHAT BENEFITS SHOULD YOU BE LOOKING FOR?

How do you judge a pension scheme? Here are some tips:
- If it is a defined benefit scheme, you should judge it primarily on what percentage of your salary you'll receive once you retire. Remember, these are the only schemes where the benefit is guaranteed based on service and salary. (Public sector employees receive one eightieth for every year of service, so 40 years will return half their annual salary. Should they bolster this?)
- Depending on the pension plan you have, you will be given a certain portion, by way of a tax-free lump sum, of the fund's value. Establish how much.
- Death-in-service benefit: Essentially, this is life cover giving your beneficiaries a lump sum and/or income should you die before retirement age.
- Death-in-retirement benefit: This gives your beneficiaries a lump sum and/or an income if you die after you have retired. Generally covers the first 5 years.

- The minimum retirement age for occupational pension schemes is 60, but if you own your company you can take a well-earned rest at age 50.
- How much will your pension income increase each year after you have started claiming it? Will it increase in line with the cost of living? More than the cost of living?
- Are there any special benefits offered to your spouse or other dependants?

WHAT HAPPENS WHEN YOU RETIRE?

This will depend on your employment status and scheme.

- For **defined-benefit** schemes, you will receive a tax-free lump sum and a guaranteed annual income, usually index-linked and based on your service.
- For **defined-contribution** schemes, the accumulated fund on retirement is used to buy an annuity income based on how much is in the fund after taking out an allowable portion as a tax-free lump sum.

An annuity is a guaranteed fixed income for life (mostly guaranteed for the first five years on retirement, after which the insurance company keeps the fund). The Finance Act 1999 introduced a new alternative: Approved Retirement Funds (ARFs), which allow pension-holders to retain greater control, choice of investments and flexibility – plus, importantly, the ability to pass on any residual balance in the fund to their estate on their death.

The Finance Act 2006 introduced a new requirement to draw income from ARFs called 'imputed distribution':

- 1% in 2007
- 2% in 2008
- 3% in 2009
- 5% in 2010
- 6% in 2012, where the total value of ARF(s) exceeds €2 million
- From 2015, the rate for those aged 61 to 70 is 4% (6% for funds greater than €2 million) and the rate for those aged 71 and over is 5% (6% for funds greater than €2 million).

The Finance Act 2011 saw the extension of the ARF option to members of defined contribution plans (AVCs and PRSAs), so they are not now confined to buying an annuity on retirement.

THE MONEY DOCTOR SAYS ...

- The tax benefits of having a pension are enormous. For a taxpayer on the higher rate of tax, putting €100 into a pension currently costs only €60. This is a bargain by anyone's standards.
- If your pension incorporates life cover you may receive extra tax relief.
- The pension end-game is important. Make sure that whatever contributions you make to a pension plan are sufficient to meet your monthly needs when you retire.
- Please, please take independent professional advice. I am repeating myself, I know. But only someone who is authorised to advise you on every pension available is going to guarantee you the most appropriate pension for your needs. Email consultation@ moneydoctors.ie.

From 2022 – though this is still to be formally decided – auto-enrolment is due to be introduced. This means that all employers will be obliged to set up pensions for their employees, and all employees will be obliged to contribute. In my opinion, it is about time. Contact Money Doctors for more information on this for your company.

PART 8

WHY PAY MORE TAX THAN YOU HAVE TO?

Would you like to slash your 2020 tax bill quickly and easily, without having to plough through a lot of incomprehensible jargon? Then this section is for you. Because in plain English – using plenty of examples and case histories – I am going to explain how, as a taxpayer, you can:

- *make certain that you don't pay a single cent more tax this year than you have to;*
- *reclaim any tax you may have overpaid in previous years; and*
- *plan your finances so that future tax bills are kept to a bare minimum.*

MONEY DOCTORS WEALTH CHECK

For the hottest tax tips email info@moneydoctors.ie

Tax rules sometimes change during the year, and the Money Doctors' team of tax advisers are always searching for new ways to save you tax. So for the hottest tax tips email info@moneydoctor.ie today.

19

TAX BASICS

GETTING TO GRIPS WITH THE TAX SYSTEM

There are really only two things you need to know about Irish tax to start beating the system. Firstly, most people are hit hardest by just three taxes, so it is these that you want to concentrate on reducing or – better still – avoiding completely. They are:

- income tax;
- capital gains tax (CGT); and
- capital acquisition tax (CAT).

(Of course, there are many other taxes, such as stamp duty and deposit interest retention tax (DIRT), and, believe me, I am not going to ignore them. But the first three will probably offer you the biggest scope for juicy savings.)

Secondly, the beauty of the Irish tax system is that it consists almost entirely of exceptions. There are, literally, hundreds of different reasons why you might not have to pay a particular tax. So, cutting your tax bill is simply a matter of either:

- studying these reasons to see which ones apply (or could be made to apply) to your own circumstances; or
- looking at your circumstances and seeing how they might be altered to give you a tax advantage.

Let me give you a quick example. In theory, if you are single, the first €34,550 of your 2018 income should be taxed at 20%, and anything over this sum should be taxed at 40%. In practice, there is a minimum income (**income exemption limit**) you have to receive before you pay any tax at all (this could be as high as €36,000 depending on your age and circumstances), and once your income exceeds this level there are all sorts of allowances, credits and other ways to reduce the amount you actually have to part with.

How old you are, where you live, your marital status, the source of your income, any borrowings you may have, your health, the health of your family ... all of these factors and many, many others can be used to slash your tax bill.

It is not inconceivable that you could have an income of as high as €75,000 and not actually have to pay a single cent in tax – except for USC!

KEEPING IT LEGAL

The difference between legal tax saving – which is called **tax avoidance** – and illegal tax saving – which is called **tax evasion** – was once described as being 'the thickness of a prison wall'. It is perfectly legal to use our tax laws in any way you can to reduce the amount of tax you pay. Naturally, all the tax-saving suggestions in this book are 100% legal.

GET TO KNOW YOUR TAX LIABILITIES, AND THE REVENUE COMMISSIONERS IN THE PROCESS

The following are the taxes that affect individuals:

Income tax

This, as its name implies, is a tax on annual income. How much you have to pay is linked to:
- how much you earn;
- your personal circumstances; and
- what tax credits and allowances you are entitled to.

If you are an employee, you pay your income tax monthly. If you are self-employed, you pay it annually. Either way, there are dozens of income tax-saving tactics available.

Capital gains tax (CGT)

If you buy something at one price and either sell it later for a higher price or give it away when it is worth more than you paid for it, then you will have made a capital gain. This gain may be taxed – depending on all sorts of factors, including:
- how big the gain is;
- what sort of gain it is;
- the rate of inflation; and
- allowable expenses.

CGT is paid annually. As with income tax, there are plenty of ways to reduce your liability. See Chapter 26.

Capital acquisition tax (CAT)

This is a tax on gifts and on inheritances. The person receiving the gift or inheritance pays it. Whether tax has to be paid will depend on a variety of factors, including:
- the amount of money or the value of the property involved;
- the relationship between the parties involved; and
- the nature of the gift or inheritance.

Once again, it is paid annually and, once again, there are any number of ways to avoid and/or reduce your liability. See Chapter 27.

Stamp duty

If you are buying a property you will be liable for stamp duty, which is a one-off tax. You'll also have to pay stamp duty – at a considerably lower level – on your mortgage deed. For individuals, it is very hard to legally reduce or avoid this form of taxation. See p.123 for current rates.

Pay Related Social Insurance (PRSI)

Whether you are employed or self-employed, you must pay PRSI at 4% on your gross income. However, those earning less than €38 per week will have no liability to make a PRSI contribution. There is little scope for legally avoiding PRSI. However, PRSI is no longer payable once you reach the age of 66.

Value Added Tax (VAT)

This is a tax on your spending. It is charged at different rates, from 0% to 23%, depending on what you are buying. Businesses and the self-employed have some opportunities for avoiding or reducing their VAT liability – individuals are limited in their options.

DO YOU HAVE TO FILL IN A TAX RETURN?

One question I frequently get asked – especially by those in retirement, in regular employment or receiving welfare payments – is whether or not they are legally obliged to complete an annual tax return. Let us consider who must fill out that dreaded form whether they want to or not. Into this category falls:

- anybody who works for themselves, whether full- or part-time;
- anyone with a second income, even if it's from casual work like cleaning or babysitting;
- all company directors;
- anyone in receipt of income that hasn't already been taxed – for instance, a private pension or dividends from an overseas investment;
- anyone who has made a capital gain;
- anyone with rental income from a property;
- anyone who has received or made a gift; and
- anyone who has received money of any sort that may be liable to tax here in Ireland.

The fact that you may be paying PAYE does not exclude you from having to complete a tax return. Indeed, even if you're on PAYE, it may be to your advantage to complete a tax return as it could reduce your tax bill for the year.

So who doesn't have to complete a tax return? If you fall into any of the following categories, you are off the hook:

- You have a relatively low income (See p.184 for details);
- You have absolutely no income; or
- You pay your tax through the PAYE system, and haven't received any other money that might be liable to tax.

MONEY DOCTORS WEALTH CHECK

Take advantage of the taxperson

Many people forget that the Revenue Commissioners are there to serve you. They publish a wide range of brochures designed to assist taxpayers, and you'll also find an enormous amount of information online at their website (www.revenue.ie). Your local tax office will be delighted to answer questions for you – you can find details of their information helpline in the 'Useful Addresses' section (Appendix 8). The Revenue Commissioners also have a highly efficient online service called, oddly enough, the Revenue On-line Service or ROS. This internet facility allows you to file your tax returns, make payments, and access your personal revenue data any time, night or day. Registering is a simple process, and the software is easy to use and compatible with every type of computer. When completing a tax return you will also find that it saves you a vast amount of time since you won't have to wade through all the relevant sections looking for the questions you need to answer. However, it is not yet available to everyone.

20

INCOME TAX BASICS

THE FIRST STEPS TOWARDS REDUCING YOUR INCOME TAX BILL

'Income tax', claimed Will Rogers, 'has made more liars out of the American people than golf.' Being a patriotic soul, I like to think that we Irish people are above such deceit. Not that we mightn't be tempted when it comes to income tax – if only because the thing is so wretchedly confusing.

The Revenue Commissioners (who appear to be allergic to plain English) hardly help by defining income tax as being the tax:

> payable on your taxable income, i.e. your total assessable income tax for a tax year, less deductions for any non-standard rate allowances (not tax credits) to which you may be entitled.

Then, as if this wasn't sufficiently obscure, they divide 'income' into several different categories which they call, unhelpfully, 'schedules'. The schedules are then divided into 'cases'. And so it goes on.

Unfortunately, if you are going to make a serious attempt to reduce your income tax bill, you really need to understand how the Revenue Commissioners are actually taxing you. Therefore, the first part of this chapter is devoted to a basic, jargon-free guide to income tax. However, once the terms of engagement, as it were, have been explained, we will get straight down to all the different ways in which you might cut – or even avoid altogether – your income tax liability.

WHAT SORT OF INCOME DO YOU HAVE?

In order to differentiate between the different types of income people receive, the Revenue Commissioners classify income under a number of different headings or 'schedules'. Since accountants and other financial professionals refer to these schedules all the time, it's quite useful to know what they are:

Schedule C relates to organisations like banks that have deducted income tax from certain payments. You almost certainly won't have to worry about this.

Schedule D is divided into five separate classes referred to as 'cases'.
- Case I relates to profits from a trade.
- Case II relates to profits from a profession.
- Case III refers to interest not taxed at source, and all foreign income.
- Case IV refers to taxed interest income not falling under any case schedule.
- Case V refers to rental income from properties in Ireland.

Schedule E basically covers all the money earned from regular employment, technically defined as 'income from offices or employments, together with pensions, benefits in kind, and certain lump sum payments arising from an office or employment'.

Schedule F covers dividends and other distributions from Irish-resident companies.

Whenever you deal with the Revenue Commissioners in relation to income tax, you'll find that they make reference to the above schedules and cases. It is always worth checking that they have your income correctly classified – if they don't, you may be paying too much tax.

A QUICK EXPLANATION OF INCOME TAX RATES

For many years, income tax has been levied at different rates according to the amount of income involved. There are currently two different rates in Ireland – **20%** and **40%**. Which rate of tax you'll pay will depend on your circumstances and income. For instance, for 2019 if you are a single person the first €35,300 of your income will be taxed at 20% and the balance at 40%. It is worth remembering that these tax rates can change from year to year.

The table overleaf shows the tax bands and rates for 2019. As you will see, taxpayers are divided into four different groups:
- single people and widow(er)s;
- one-parent families;
- married couples where only one spouse is working; and
- married couples – where both spouses are working.

Rates of income tax

Single/widowed without dependent children	€35,300 @ 20% Balance @ 40%
Single/widowed qualifying for single person child-care credit	€39,300 @ 20% Balance @ 40%
Married couple (one spouse with income)	€44,300 @ 20% Balance @ 40%
Married couple (both spouses with income)	€44,300 @ 20% (with increase of €26,300 max.) Balance @ 40%

Universal Social Charge (USC)

An income levy was introduced in the budget of October 2008 and increased in the supplementary budget of April 2009. In the budget of December 2010, this was abolished and replaced with one part of the Universal Social Charge (see page 337). If your income is less than €12,012, you pay no USC. Once your income is over this limit, you pay USC on *all* of your income.

USC rates (2019)

On the first €12,012	0.5%
On the next €7,862	2%
On the next €50,170	4.5%
On the balance (over €70,044)	8%
Self-employed income over €100,000	11%

Some good news for anyone on a low income

If your income falls below a certain level, you are completely exempt from income tax. The chart below sets out the maximum amount of income you can receive this year – according to your circumstances – without paying a single cent in tax. It's worth noting that if you earn income over the amounts set out below, you will be eligible for something called 'marginal relief', which is explained below.

Low income exemption limits for 2019	
Single/widowed, 65 or over	€18,000
Married, 65 or over	€36,000

Additions to exemptions limit for dependent children (€)	
1st and 2nd child (per child)	€575
Each subsequent child	€830
Marginal relief tax rate	40% of the amount by which the total income exceeds the exemption limit.

Taking advantage of marginal relief

Supposing you are on a relatively low income, earning just slightly more than the amount necessary to avoid tax completely? As it would be unfair to tax you too heavily, you are entitled to marginal relief. Any individual or married couple whose total income from all sources is slightly over the exemption limit may qualify for marginal relief but it will only be granted if it is more beneficial to the claimant than their tax credits. It restricts the tax payable to 40% of the difference between your income and the appropriate exemption limit. The exemption limits vary depending on age, marital status and the number of qualifying dependent children. As this is quite complicated, let me explain it with an example:

Marginal relief advantageous

Over 65 married with two children

	€		€
Total income	36,000	Total income	36,000
Tax @ 20%	7,200	Less: Exemption	36,000
Less: Tax credits	5,440	Excess	nil
Tax due	1,760	Tax @ 40%	nil

PERSONAL CREDITS AND TAX ALLOWANCES

Although you are liable to pay income tax at the rates outlined, you are entitled to claim all sorts of personal tax credits and allowances, which help to reduce this bill substantially. You'll find a complete guide to all the income tax credits and allowances in the next chapter.

PRSI – ANOTHER FORM OF INCOME TAX

The initials PRSI stand for **pay-related social insurance**. Because it is calculated as a percentage of your income it is effectively a form of income tax.

The purpose of PRSI is to raise money to provide all sorts of social welfare benefits – these range from invalidity pensions to redundancy pay to maternity benefit. Your ability to claim social welfare benefits is linked to your having paid PRSI.

- How much PRSI you have to pay will depend on your job. There are three key categories: private sector employees, public sector employees, and the self-employed.
- Your entitlement to benefits is normally based on your contributions made two years before the year in which you claim! In other words, what you paid in 2016 will determine what you can claim in 2018.
- The level of PRSI you have to pay is calculated as a percentage of your gross income.
- You can volunteer to pay PRSI, or pay it at a higher level, if this is to your advantage.

It's worth noting that the employee and employer normally share PRSI contribution costs. Most employees, of course, pay their PRSI through the PAYE tax system.

A summary of the benefits to which you are entitled under PRSI is to be found in Chapter 5. To claim a **social insurance benefit** it is necessary to have made a minimum number of PRSI contributions. Confusingly, the word 'contribution' means not just the PRSI you've paid, but also your PRSI credits. PRSI credits are awarded to someone who would normally have been making a contribution, but for various reasons did not do so. For instance, you receive PRSI credits during any weeks when you receive a disability benefit or unemployment benefit. You also receive credits when you first start working.

If there were an Olympic category for 'most complicated tax in the world', PRSI would probably win the gold medal. If you need help with your PRSI, I suggest talking either to an accountant or contacting the Department of Social Protection or the Revenue Commissioners.

21
ALL ABOUT INCOME TAX CREDITS

HOW TAX 'CREDITS' AND 'ALLOWANCES' CAN HELP YOU SAVE MONEY

Depending on your circumstances, you can probably reduce your income tax bill by claiming certain tax credits and allowances. So what is the difference between 'credits' and 'allowances':

- A tax credit is money off your actual tax bill. So, if you have a tax bill of €1,000 and tax credits of €800, you only pay €200 in tax.
- A tax allowance reduces the amount of income on which tax is payable. How much it will be worth to you will depend on the rate of tax you pay. For instance, if you pay income tax at 20%, a €1,000 tax allowance will save you €200 of tax.

The old system of tax allowances has largely been replaced by tax credits.

Every year, you are sent an annual **tax certificate**, referred to, somewhat long-windedly, as the 'notification of determination of Tax Credits and standard rate cut-off point'. This sets out full details of all your tax credits, together with the income level at which you will start to pay the higher rate of tax.

HOW TAX CREDITS WORK IN PRACTICE

Before going into detail about all the different personal tax credits that exist, let's look at how they work in practice.

In 2019, John O'Brien, a single taxpayer on PAYE, pays tax at 20% on the first €35,300 of income and 40% on anything above this sum. His tax credits amount to €3,300. Here is how his tax credits reduce his tax liability on his income of €40,000.

Income €40,000		
Tax on the first €35,300 @ 20 %		€7,060
Tax on the remaining €4,700 @ 40%		€1,880
Total tax before tax credits		€8,940
Deduct tax credits		
Single tax credit	€1,650	
PAYE tax credit	€1,650	€3,300
Tax payable		€5,640

CHECK YOUR TAX CREDITS EVERY YEAR

Do remember to check that you're claiming all your tax credits every year. You can also go back to the Revenue Commissioners and claim tax credits that you failed to take advantage of over the previous four tax years.

A COMPLETE GUIDE TO PERSONAL TAX CREDITS AND ALLOWANCES FOR 2019

Over the next few pages you'll find brief details of all the different tax credits and allowances for which you may be eligible.

Single person's credit

You can claim this if you're single, if you're married but decide to opt for single/separate assessment or if you're separated and you and your former partner have not opted for joint assessment. It is worth €1,650 for 2019.

Married persons' credit

This is double the single credit, and it's granted to married couples who have opted to be assessed together. It can also be claimed by separated couples where one partner is maintaining the other and is not entitled to claim tax relief on the maintenance being paid. For more details on tax relief for separated and divorced couples see chapters 32 and 33. The married persons' credit is worth €3,300.

One-parent family credit

If you have a dependent child and you are unmarried, widowed, separated, divorced or deserted (that is, your spouse has left but you are neither separated nor divorced), then you can claim the one-parent family tax credit of €1,650. This is in addition to your normal personal tax credit.

Widowed parent credit

A special credit is granted to widowed parents for the first five years following the year of bereavement. For the year 2019 the credit is: €3,600 in the first year; €3,150 in the second year; €2,700 in the third year; €2,250 in the fourth year; and €1,800 in the fifth year.

Special age credits

If you are over 65, or if your spouse is over 65, you receive an extra credit. If you are single or widowed this is worth €245, or for a married couple €490.

Home carer's credit

If you care for someone who's elderly (defined as being over 65) or incapacitated, you may be eligible to claim an additional credit of up to €1,500. The home carer credit is only available to married couples where one spouse cares for one or more dependent people. You can't claim if you are looking after your own spouse. The maximum income of the home carer to claim maximum relief is €7,200. A reduced tax credit applies where the income is between €7,200 and €10,200.

A new childminding relief was introduced in 2006. Where an individual minds up to three children (other than their own children) in the minder's own home, no tax will be payable on the childminding earnings received provided the amount is less than €15,000 per annum. If the childminding income exceeds this amount, the total amount will be taxable, as normal, under self-assessment. An individual will be obliged to include their childminding income in their annual tax return.

Incapacitated child credit

If you are looking after an incapacitated child, you're entitled to claim a tax credit of €3,300. Note that the child must be under the age of 18 or, if over the age of 18, must have been incapacitated before reaching 21 years of age or while still receiving full-time education.

Dependent relative credit

If you can prove that you maintain, at your own expense, a relative who cannot live independently (or a widowed mother, whether incapacitated or not), you can claim a tax credit of €70 per year provided the relative's income does not exceed €14,504 per year.

Incapacitated person's allowance

An allowance of €75,000 is available to any taxpayer who is incapacitated and has to employ someone to look after them. The same allowance is available to any taxpayer who is employing someone to look after an incapacitated spouse. In fact, the allowance is available where a family employs a carer to look after a totally incapacitated person. Clearly, to take advantage of this allowance you need to have an income, and because it's an allowance (as opposed to a tax credit), the value of the benefit will be determined by your marginal – or top – rate of tax.

Blind person's credit

If you are blind, you can claim a tax credit of €1,650. If both you and your spouse are blind then you may both claim, bringing the total credit up to €3,300. An additional allowance of €825 is available to any blind person who uses a guide dog. This allowance can be claimed on your tax return under the heading of Health Expenses and at the standard rate of 20%.

PAYE credit

If you pay tax by the PAYE system you're entitled to a PAYE credit of €1,650. If you're married, and both you and your spouse are on PAYE, then there is a doubled credit. However, you should bear in mind that you cannot claim the PAYE credit if you are the director of a company and control, either directly or indirectly, 15% or more of the shares. You can't claim it, either, if you employ your spouse (either as an individual or as a partner in a firm).

Medical insurance

If you take out medical insurance, the premium you pay will already have been discounted by the standard rate of tax (currently 20%). The insurance company will receive this tax relief directly from the government so there is no need for you to make a separate claim. It is worth noting that you can enjoy this tax relief even if you don't pay tax!

Permanent health insurance

If you are worried about a drop in your income as a result of an accident or illness, and you take out permanent health insurance to protect you against this eventuality, your contributions will be tax deductible. However, the amount of relief you can claim must not be more than 10% of your total income for the year of assessment. Any benefit you claim under a permanent health insurance policy will be liable to income tax.

Medical expenses relief

If you have to spend money on medical care, or non-routine dental treatment, then you can claim tax relief at the standard tax rate.
- You can claim for yourself, your spouse or any other person for who you claim tax allowances.
- The allowance can be shared among a number of people. If, for example, several children are paying for their parent to receive treatment, each can claim.

- When it comes to medical expenses, most things are eligible for tax relief – from a visit to a doctor to hearing aids, and from physiotherapy to the cost of gluten-free food for cœliacs. There are a few exceptions, including routine dental treatment, having your eyes tested and the purchase of spectacles and contact lenses.
- Note that all expenses in relation to maternity care are fully allowable.
- For nursing home expenses, relief is available at your marginal rate of tax.

Third-level college fees

You may be able to claim tax relief on tuition fees for approved:

- Undergraduate courses;
- Postgraduate courses;
- Information Technology (IT) courses; and
- Foreign language courses.

You can claim tax relief as long as you have actually paid the fees, either on your own behalf or on behalf of another person in private or publicly funded third-level colleges.

For the 2012 tax year and thereafter you can claim the Student Contribution as part of the tuition fees tax relief. The maximum annual relief for tuition fees including the Student Contribution is €7,000 per person per course.

If you are claiming for a full-time student, there is no tax relief on the first €3,000 of all tuition fees for the 2018/19 academic year. If the claim refers to a part-time student, there is no tax relief on the first €1,500 of tuition fees for the 2018/19 academic year.

If you are claiming for more than one student, you will get full tax relief on the Student Contribution for the second or subsequent students. Tax relief is given at the standard rate and there is no limit on the number of individuals for whom you can claim.

Loan interest relief

If you're paying interest on a loan, you may be able to claim tax relief. Various types of loan are eligible, including:

- mortgages in relation to your main home;
- bridging loans;
- loans taken out for business purposes;
- loans borrowed to pay death duties; and
- borrowings used to acquire shares in your own business.

Mortgage interest relief is now granted 'at source' – your lender will claim it on your behalf and reduce your monthly payments accordingly. You should be aware that mortgage interest relief is available on money borrowed for the purchase, repair, development or improvement of your sole or main residence situated in Ireland.

You can also claim the relief if you borrow money to 'purchase a residence for a former or separated spouse or a dependent relative where the accommodation is being provided by you rent-free'. The amount of relief you can claim will be determined by your personal circumstances. Only first-time mortgage holders can claim tax relief, for the first seven years of the mortgage, up to a limit of €20,000 for married couples or widow(er)s or €10,000 for a single person. Tax relief at source no longer applies for those who purchased their homes after 1 January 2013.

Relief on deeds of covenant

If you make a legal commitment – known as a deed of covenant – to pay money for a period of time to someone who is aged 65 or over, or permanently incapacitated (providing the latter isn't to a son or daughter under 18) you will be able to claim tax relief. A deed must be capable of exceeding a period of six years to qualify for tax relief.

Pension contributions

If you're making payments into an approved personal pension scheme (here the word 'approved' refers to Revenue Commissioners' approval!), income tax relief will be available to you at your marginal (top) rate of tax. The amount of relief is restricted to a percentage of your income. Unused allowances in any one year can be carried forward to the next. The percentage of your income that you're allowed to put, tax-free, into a pension scheme increases as you get older. For 2017 it works as follows:

- If you're under the age of 30 you can put up to 15% of your income into your pension scheme tax-free.
- If you're aged between 30 and 39 you can put 20% in.
- If you're aged between 40 and 49 you can put 25% in.
- If you're aged between 50 and 54 you can put 30% in.
- If you're aged between 55 and 59 you can put 35% in
- If you're aged 60 and over you can put 40% in.

However, there is a cap of €115,000 on the income taken into account.

Investment relief

The **Employment Investment Incentive Scheme (EIIS)** is a tax relief incentive scheme that provides tax relief for investment in certain corporate trades. The scheme has replaced the Business Expansion Scheme (BES).

Seafarer's allowance

If you are a seafarer and you're away on a voyage for at least 161 days in a tax year, then you are eligible for a special allowance of €6,350. Note, however, that this allowance can only be offset against seafaring employment.

22

PAYE

HOW TO MAKE THE PAYE TAX SYSTEM WORK IN YOUR FAVOUR

Even if you're in salaried employment and your income tax is deducted automatically using the Pay As You Earn (PAYE) system, there are still plenty of things you can do to keep your tax bill to a bare minimum. In addition to explaining how PAYE operates, this chapter examines some of the tax-saving opportunities open to those who pay tax by this method.

THE INS AND OUTS OF PAYE

It is easy to understand why the Revenue Commissioners like the PAYE system. It allows them to collect tax as it falls due, rather than once a year. But it has two advantages for the taxpayer as well. Firstly, your employer and the Revenue Commissioners handle all the administration involved with your tax bill. If you were self-employed, this could cost you thousands of euros a year. And secondly, you don't have to worry about being faced with a tax bill every year.

PAYE is operated by employers in conjunction with the Revenue Commissioners. The system is simplicity itself:

- Your employer provides your details to the Revenue Commissioners.
- Before the beginning of each tax year (usually in December), the Revenue Commissioners issue a 'Notification of Determination of Tax Credits and Standard Rate Cut-off Point'. This sets out any tax credits due to you, details your rate or rates of tax, and incorporates your **standard rate cut-off point** – something I'll explain in a moment.
- Using the information supplied by the Revenue Commissioners, your employer calculates how much tax to deduct from your salary.

So what is the standard rate cut-off point? Basically, it's the amount of money you can earn at the standard rate – currently 20%. This is determined by your personal circumstances – whether you are married, single or widowed. You may also have allowances that are allowed at the higher rate of tax, such as a contribution to an approved pension scheme. Where this is the case, your standard rate cut-off point will be higher.

The formula for working out PAYE is:

- The standard rate of tax (currently 20%) is applied to your gross pay up to the standard rate cut-off point for the period in question.
- Any income over and above that amount in the pay period is taxed at the higher rate (currently 40%).
- The sum of these two amounts is called the **gross tax payable**.
- Any tax credits you're entitled to are then deducted from the gross tax payable, to arrive at the **net tax payable**.

MONEY DOCTORS WEALTH CHECK

It is in your interest to keep the taxperson up to date

If the Revenue Commissioners don't have all your personal information, they may make a mistake regarding the various tax credits and allowances to which you are entitled. You can use the information in the previous chapter to compile a list of credits and allowances that you believe you can claim, and you should then complete a Form 12A: 'Application for a Certificate of Tax Credits and Standard Rate Cut-off Point' and send it to your tax office.

This form is available on request or can be downloaded from www.revenue.ie. When you receive your 'Notification of Determination of Tax Credits and Standard Rate Cut-off Point', double-check that it lists all the tax reliefs you wish to claim.

EMERGENCY TAX

If your employer doesn't have the information needed to calculate the correct amount of tax to deduct (a 'Notification of Determination of Tax Credits and Standard Rate Cut-off Point'), you will automatically be put onto PAYE **emergency tax**. As emergency tax only incorporates minimal tax credits, you will be paying too much tax! You should contact your local tax office to resolve the situation.

GETTING YOUR TAX BACK! PAYE REFUNDS

There are various circumstances under which you may be entitled to a PAYE tax refund. For instance:

- If you become unemployed: In this situation you should write to your Inspector of Taxes and ask for a **Form P50**. You should complete and return this, along with Parts 2 and 3 of your **Form P45** (the form your last employer should have given to you prior to you leaving).

- If the Revenue Commissioners have made an error and overtaxed you due to some factor of which they were unaware.

After the end of the tax year (31 December), your employer should give you a **Form P60**, which sets out the amount you earned in that year together with any tax that has been deducted. Check this form to make sure that all the allowances, deductions and credits to which you are entitled have been claimed. If you believe there is an error, you should advise your employer and your local Inspector of Taxes to request a refund.

MONEY DOCTORS WEALTH CHECK

Double-check you are claiming everything

Below is a list of all the tax credits and allowances you may be entitled to (full details are to be found in the previous chapter). Why not take a moment or two to check through it now, to make doubly sure that you aren't paying a cent more tax than you have to?

Tax credit 2019	(€)
Single person	1,650
Married person	3,330
Widowed person (w/o dependent children)	2,190
Widowed person (qualifying for one-parent family tax credit)	1,650
Widowed person (in year of bereavement)	3,300
One-parent family (widowed person)	1,650
One-parent family (other person)	1,650
Age tax credit (65 years plus & single/widowed)	245
Age tax credit (65 years plus & married)	490
Home carer's credit (max.)	1,200
Incapacitated child (max.)	3,300
Dependent relative (max.)	70
Employee's tax credit	1,650

MAKING SURE YOUR EXPENSES ARE TAX-FREE

One of the areas in which the Revenue Commissioners are extremely strict is that of expenses paid to employees. They don't want employers to disguise a benefit (effectively extra salary) as a legitimate expense. The Revenue Commissioners' guidance rules say that any expense 'must have been wholly, exclusively and necessarily incurred for the purpose of performing the duties of your employment'. (Interestingly, if you're self-employed, the 'necessarily' criterion doesn't apply.)

So what is, and isn't, allowable? If you have to buy special equipment or clothing, for instance, it is unlikely that the Revenue will argue with your claim. By the same token, they are unlikely to take issue if you use a company-owned computer at home or claim part of your telephone bill if it is used for work calls. In general, what you can legitimately claim will very much depend on the nature of your employment. For instance, if you work in a publishing company, any books you buy will almost certainly be allowable, as might trips to the theatre or cinema. If you're an engineer, this is unlikely to be the case!

If the Revenue Commissioners believe that you are making a claim for something that is not wholly, exclusively and necessarily incurred for the purpose of performing the duties of your employment, they will tax it! This tax is called **benefit in kind**. Cars supplied by your employer are subject to benefit in kind (see Chapter 25). Your employer will be required to value the benefit and to stop tax and PRSI at source through the PAYE system. So, for example, if your employer were to send you away on a one-week holiday to recuperate from overwork, you would pay tax on the cost of that holiday as if you had been paid it as extra salary.

23

INCOME TAX FOR THE SELF-EMPLOYED

HOW TO REDUCE YOUR INCOME TAX BILL IF YOU WORK FOR YOURSELF

If you are self-employed – or thinking of becoming self-employed – this chapter is essential reading. You will find out:

- how the tax system operates in relation to your earnings;
- ways to reduce your share of the tax burden; and
- how to avoid the unwanted attention of Revenue, while making some worthwhile tax savings.

Let's start by explaining the basic ground rules, and what is meant by the self-assessment system and preliminary tax.

SELF-ASSESSMENT SYSTEM

If you are a director in your family company, or if you're in salaried employment (in other words on PAYE) but have income from other sources, you'll have to pay tax under the self-assessment system. Self-assessment means that you have to complete your own tax return, decide how much tax you owe, and pay it to the Revenue Commissioners at the specified time. You can, of course, get a professional accountant to do all of this for you.

The latest date by which you can complete your income tax return (**Form 11**) for the Revenue Commissioner is 31 October following the year of assessment. In other words, your 2018 tax return must be submitted no later than 31 October 2019, or mid-November 2019 if using the Revenue Online Service (ROS).

PRELIMINARY TAX

When you submit your income tax return you must also pay something called preliminary tax. Preliminary tax is the amount of income tax you think you're going to owe for the year in which you pay it. In other words, on 31 October 2018 your preliminary tax will be the amount of tax you think you'll owe for 2018. The amount you'll actually have to pay is the lower of either 90% of your final liability for 2018 or 100% of your liability for 2017. Let me give you an example:

> Supposing you had a good year last year, but are having a bad year this year. Last year you had to pay €10,000 tax, but this year you only expect a liability of €1,000 tax. Your preliminary tax bill would, therefore, be 90% of this year's liability – or €900.

> Since your preliminary tax is only an estimate of the tax you owe, you will naturally either have to pay the difference or ask for a refund. This is done at the same time. Supposing, for instance, you've paid €1,000 preliminary tax on 31 October 2017. Your final tax bill for the year, however, turned out to be €1,500. The €500 extra will fall due no later than 31 October 2018.

In other words, on or before 31 October every year you submit a return and pay preliminary tax plus the balance of the previous year's income tax. If you're owed money by the Revenue Commissioners from the previous year, you can deduct it from the amount you're paying. This is known as **Pay and File**.

THE MYSTERY FACTOR!

As if this isn't complicated enough, there is an added factor that makes it all the more confusing: you can choose the dates of your financial year. The tax year, of course, runs just like the calendar year, from 1 January to 31 December. However, the Revenue Commissioners allow you to pick your own accounting period. So while your 2018 tax return could refer to the period 1 January 2017 to 31 December 2018, it could alternatively refer to the 12 months ending on 2 January 2018.

A quick aside about accounting dates

It may seem like a tiny detail to you – considering the enormity of being self-employed and running your own business – but your accounting date can have important implications. For instance, if you run a seasonal business, you're unlikely to want your accounting period to end during a busy period. Also, while you can choose an accounting period that gives you the longest possible time to pay your tax, if you aren't good at putting money away to meet your tax liabilities all you're doing is postponing your problem and making it worse.

As hardly anyone starts a new business on 1 January, what many self-employed people do is submit their first set of accounts for a period of less than 12 months. For instance, if you started your business on 1 July you might submit your first set of accounts to cover the period 1 July to 31 December. Your second tax return would then run from 1 January the following year.

You are entitled to change your accounting period any time you want. However, this can trigger an additional tax charge, so you need to think carefully before you do so.

MAKE YOUR PAYMENTS ON TIME ... OR ELSE

The Revenue Commissioners do not take kindly to income tax returns being submitted late. They take a similar line if you fail to pay any tax you owe on the date it is due. If you don't submit your tax return by 31 October, the Revenue Commissioners will add a surcharge to your tax bill:

- A surcharge of 5% of any tax due can be imposed if you are up to two months late.
- If you are more than two months late, the surcharge can rise to 10% of the tax due.
- In addition to the surcharge, you will be charged interest at the rate of roughly 1% per month on any outstanding tax.

If you are going to have trouble making a tax payment, let the Revenue Commissioners know in good time. Remember, it is almost certainly cheaper to borrow the money from a bank than to suffer heavy late payment surcharges and interest.

Revenue Online Service (ROS)

ROS, the Revenue Online Service, has been available to self-employed taxpayers for some time. Once registered, ROS enables you to view your current position with Revenue for various taxes and USC, to file tax returns, fill out forms and make payments for these taxes online in a variety of ways.

The service is highly efficient and avoids the pitfalls of postal delays for returns sent close to the due date.

Furthermore, self-employed taxpayers filing their annual return (**Form 11**) through ROS are given an extra approximately two weeks after the 31 October deadline to pay and file. To qualify for the extension you must:

- File your return through ROS.
- Pay preliminary tax for the current year.
- Pay income tax balance due for previous year.
- Pay capital gains tax on gains arising from 1 January to 30 September in the current year.

To register for ROS go to www.ros.ie.

MONEY DOCTORS WEALTH WARNING

Don't get on the wrong side of the Revenue

If you are self-employed or a company director, the last thing you want is an investigation or audit by the Revenue Commissioners. You'll be pleased to discover, therefore, that it is possible to dramatically reduce your chances of being bothered by Revenue. All you have to do is follow a few very basic rules:

• If your return is late, this increases the Revenue's interest in you. By the same token, make sure you pay the tax you owe on time.

• Given that the Revenue Commissioners deal with every business in the country, they have a good idea about the sort of profits that you ought to be making. If you consistently appear to be making less than the industry average, they may decide to take a closer look.

• A low salary or low drawings may make them suspicious as well. They'll be wondering if you're earning cash and not declaring it.

• Incomplete returns. If your tax return has not been completed correctly, you are simply asking for trouble.

• Discrepancies. The Revenue Commissioners are not idiots, and if there is a discrepancy between, say, your VAT return and your annual tax return, eyebrows will be raised and questions will be asked.

• Erratic turnover figures. If your company or business seems to do well one year, and not the next, your inspector may decide to look a little closer.

• Ownership by an offshore entity. If the Revenue Commissioners notice that your shareholders are located in a tax haven – or if they see that you are doing a lot of business with a tax haven – this is bound to set off alarm bells.

The basic rules are: Stay on top of your paperwork, and pay your tax on time. Then you are much, much less likely to suffer the bother and expense of a Revenue investigation.

DO YOU NEED TO REGISTER FOR VAT?

You only have to register for value added tax (VAT) if your sales are in excess of:
- €37,500 per year if you provide services; or
- €75,000 per year if you provide goods.

Once you're registered for VAT you must charge it on all your invoices but – looking on the bright side – you can reclaim any VAT you pay out on business expenses (other than those for entertainment or motoring). Once registered, you will need to keep proper VAT records and complete a return every two months.

Don't forget your PRSI and USC

If you are self-employed you have to pay PRSI contributions of 4% of your gross income. For more information about PRSI see Chapter 5. USC rates are outlined in Chapter 20.

AND ANOTHER THING

If you are self-employed and operating your business from home, remember that this is now also a business premises, and you should advise your insurance company of this. In most cases, this is unlikely to affect your insurance premium – but it is important that you are covered if equipment is stolen or damaged, or if a business visitor has an accident while on your premises.

Incidentally, if you do use your home as a business premises, you can claim some of the running costs as expenses against your annual tax bill. Bear in mind, however, that if you pay yourself 'rent', this may have capital gains tax implications when you come to sell your home. This is because although there is no capital gains tax on a principal residence, there could well be a liability on a business premises.

Self-employment comes in many forms

The term 'self-employed' refers specifically to people who are:

- in business as a 'sole trader'; or
- in a partnership with one or more other people.

Many people who work for themselves actually do so as a 'contractor', working on a regular basis for someone else. You should be aware that if you work for an employer for more than eight hours a week you are entitled to a contract of employment. Such a contract would give you all sorts of benefits, such as the right to holidays, the right not to be dismissed unfairly, minimum notice and so forth. On the other hand, as a contractor, you aren't protected under employment legislation, and you must – of course – make your own tax arrangements.

Many self-employed people find it is worth their while to form a limited company and to trade in this way. The advantages of running a limited company include:

- limited financial risk;
- the ability to make more generous pension contributions to your retirement fund; and
- possible tax benefits.

However, don't rush into forming a company without taking legal and accounting advice.

WORKING OUT YOUR PROFITS

When you are self-employed you pay income tax on what the Revenue Commissioners refer to as **taxable profits**. Your taxable profits are your gross income (the total amount you make) less any expenses which are allowed for income tax purposes. So, if you earn a total of €20,000 a year and have expenses of €5,000, your taxable profits will be €15,000 a year.

EXPENSES

So, what expenses are allowable against your profits? In some ways it is actually easier to consider what expenses the Revenue Commissioners will definitely *not* allow:

- any money you spend which is not '**wholly and exclusively**' for the purpose of your business. For example, if you buy a suit for work, the Revenue Commissioners would say that it isn't 'wholly and exclusively' for business purposes. If you're considering any sort of major expenditure as part of your business, and you're not sure if it will be allowable, it's well worth checking with either the Revenue Commissioners or your accountant first.
- **entertainment**. With the exception of entertaining your staff, the provision of accommodation, meals or drink for your customers is not allowable. Indeed, if you take a client out to dinner not only will the expense be disallowed but you may also incur benefit in kind tax yourself.
- any sort of **personal expenses.**
- money spent on **improving your business premises**. This said, money spent renewing or repairing your business premises is allowable.

So what *can* you claim? Let me give you an example. Imagine that you are a chef who has opened his or her own restaurant. Here are some of the expenses that you could legitimately claim against your profits:

- rent
- wages paid to employees
- interest paid on business loans
- other property expenses, including electricity, gas, water, rubbish disposal, insurance, etc.
- furniture
- equipment for the kitchen
- linen, tableware, glasses and related items
- travel, stationery, telecommunications, postage and advertising

- cookery books
- trips overseas to source produce – not only for your restaurant but, perhaps, because you plan to go into the import and wholesale business
- ingredients
- uniforms for yourself and staff
- wine
- other beverages

You might also argue that you needed to eat in your competitors' restaurants for research purposes. The real point is: if you can show you had to spend the money to run your business, then it is almost certainly an allowable expense.

A WORD ABOUT CAPITAL EXPENDITURE

Many businesses require special plant, machinery or equipment. Buying such items is referred to as capital expenditure. Such expenditure is allowed as a business expense, but not all at once. Since December 2002, 12.5% of the cost is allowed as an expense each year. So if you spend, say, €1,000 on a photocopier, you can claim €125 a year as a cost against your income for the following eight years. This is one of the reasons why many people who are self-employed opt to lease rather than purchase certain items.

OTHER TAX-SAVING POSSIBILITIES

There are a number of ways in which someone who is self-employed can reap a tax advantage. These include:
- claiming for business expenses that would be disallowed for someone who was an employee;
- taking advantage of the special rules regarding pension plans; and
- using the self-assessment system to delay the payment of tax.

24

TAX AND PROPERTY

PROPERTY INVESTOR? HOW TO ENSURE YOU KEEP YOUR TAX BILL TO A MINIMUM

From a tax perspective, property is just about the most complicated investment you can make, which is why I have devoted this short chapter to the subject. The complications include:
- If you make a profit on the rent, you have to pay income tax on it.
- If you make a profit when you sell the property, you have to pay capital gains tax on it.
- There are all sorts of expenses you can claim against your profits – it is important to make sure you claim all of them.

The benefits of investing in property are huge, especially if you have been a property investor since the early 1980s or you are starting afresh in 2018.

THE TAX ADVANTAGES OF PROPERTY INVESTMENT

There are several generous tax advantages to property investment, including:
- In the current climate of relatively low capital gains tax, should you sell the property at a profit you will only have to pay tax at a rate of 33%.
- You can currently earn up to €14,000 a year in rent tax-free from the letting of a room in your own principal private residence.
- All the normal personal allowances are available to you, if you haven't already used them against other income.
- The Revenue Commissioners will allow you to set a surprisingly wide range of expenses against your rental income, thus helping to keep your income tax bill to a minimum.

A WORD OF WARNING

It is worth bearing in mind that rental income is treated in the same way as self-employed income. As a result, it may have the effect of pushing you into the higher tax bracket (in other words, 40% tax plus 4% PRSI and USC). Many people wrongly believe that they will reduce their tax liability by holding property through a limited company. This is not the case, because:

- The rate of **corporation tax** on rental income is 25%.
- Undistributed investment and rental income in a **close company** is liable to a further tax charge of 20%. (A 'close' company is one that is controlled by five or fewer shareholders or is controlled by any number of shareholders who are directors.)
- The effective corporation tax rate can be as high as 40%.

TAX INCENTIVES

There have been two property tax incentives you could have availed of recently:

- Capital allowances in relation to **industrial buildings**. The term 'industrial buildings' includes not just factories but nursing homes, crèche facilities, and even – in certain cases – holiday cottages.
- Tax incentives to **designated areas**. These designated areas are in rundown parts of Cork, Dublin, Galway, Limerick and Waterford. The idea was to encourage urban renewal. The best known of these tax incentives was the 'Section 23' relief in respect of expenditure on the construction, conversion or refurbishment of residential property in certain inner-city areas.

'GENEROUS' EXPENSES

Below is a list of the expenses that can normally be deducted from your rental income for tax purposes:

- any rates you have to pay on the property
- any rent (such as ground rent) that you have to pay on the property
- interest paid on money borrowed to acquire or improve the premises. Note that this is restricted to 80% of the interest paid on loans relating to residential investment property. This restriction does not apply to non-residential property.
- the cost of anything you supply to your tenant that isn't covered by their rent. For instance, if you pay for the electric light in the hallways, or for the lawns to be mown, it is an allowable expense.
- any maintenance, repairs, insurance or management/RTB fees

- a capital allowance of 12.5% a year on the value of any fixtures, fittings or furniture you have purchased specifically for the property. In plain English, this means that if you buy furniture for the flat you can write it off over an eight-year period.

Note that where your costs exceed the income from your rental property, the loss you incur may only be offset against future rental income. In other words, you can't use a loss from property investment to reduce, say, the tax you pay on your monthly salary.

25

TAX, BENEFIT IN KIND AND THE COMPANY CAR

HOW WORKING MOTORISTS CAN DRIVE DOWN THEIR TAX BILL

There was a time, in the distant past, when being provided with
a company car was a genuine perk. Not only were there major tax
advantages, but you did not have to purchase, maintain or run a vehicle
oneself. However, as the table below shows, it may not in fact be to your
advantage any more to have a company car.

BENEFIT IN KIND (BIK)

An employee is taxed on expense allowances (s 117 – Taxes Consolidation
Act 1997), benefit in kind (s 118), share options (s 128) and preferential
loans (s 122) obtained from the employer. A loan is regarded as
preferential if the interest rate is less than 4% in the case of a mortgage
loan, or 13.5% in the case of any other loan.

BIK treatment does not apply to:
* an annual or monthly bus or train pass (s 118(5A));
* a bicycle and associated safety equipment (costing up to €1,000)
  for travel to work;
* a qualifying shopping voucher worth not more than €500 (s 112B);
  or
* shares worth up to €12,700 received through an approved profit
  sharing scheme (s 510). This is increased to €38,100 for shares held
  in an employee share ownership trust for a minimum of 10 years.

Company cars

The employee is taxed on 'notional pay' based on the cash equivalent of
the benefit of use of a company car (s 121). This is calculated at 30% of
the original market value (OMV) of the car, up to 24,000km. For business
mileage exceeding 24,000km, the rates are:
* 24,000–32,000km – 24%
* 32,000–40,000km – 18%

- 40,000–48,000km – 12%
- 48,000km and upwards – 6%

A new set of rates, due to come into effect by ministerial order, are calculated as a percentage of the car's OMV, inclusive of duty and VAT, depending on your annual business travel and the car's CO_2 emissions category:

Category A: 0g/km up to and including 120g/km
Category B: More than 120g/km up to and including 140g/km
Category C: More than 140g/km up to and including 155g/km
Category D: More than 155g/km up to and including 170g/km
Category E: More than 170g/km up to and including 190g/km
Category F: More than 190g/km up to and including 225g/km
Category G: More than 225g/km

Where the annual business travel is:

- 0–24,000km, the BIK is:
    (i) 40% for categories F and G;
    (ii) 35% for categories D and E; and
    (iii) 30% for categories A, B and C.
- 24,001–32,000km, the BIK is:
    (i) 32% for categories F and G;
    (ii) 28% for categories D and E; and
    (iii) 24% for categories A, B and C.
- 32,001–40,000km, the BIK is:
    (i) 24% for categories F and G;
    (ii) 21% for categories D and E; and
    (iii) 18% for categories A, B and C.
- 40,001–48,000 km, the BIK is:
    (i) 16% for categories F and G;
    (ii) 14% for categories D and E; and
    (iii) 12% for categories A, B and C.
- 48,001km or more, the BIK is:
    (i) 8% for categories F and G;
    (ii) 7% for categories D and E; and
    (iii) 6% for categories A, B and C.

The BIK figure can be further reduced by the amount required to be made good, and actually made good, directly to the employer in respect of the car's running costs.

Civil service travel and subsistence rates

Compensation paid to an employee for the use of his private car is not taxed provided it complies with the following civil service travel rates:

Where the annual business travel is:
- up to 6,437km, the rate per km is:
    - (i) 39.12c where the engine size is up to 1200cc;
    - (ii) 46.25c where the engine size is 1201 to 1500cc;
    - (iii) 59.07c where the engine size is 1501 to 2000cc; and
    - (iv) 70.89c where the engine size is over 2000cc.
- over 6,438km, the rate per km is:
    - (i) 21.22c where the engine size is up to 1200cc;
    - (ii) 23.62c where the engine size is 1201 to 1500cc;
    - (iii) 28.46c where the engine size is over 1501cc; and
    - (iv) 34.15c where the engine size is over 2000cc.

A lunch or overnight allowance paid to an employee is not taxed provided it complies with the following civil service subsistence rates:
- €14.01 in respect of an absence of 5 to 10 hours;
- €33.61 in respect of an absence of 10 hours or more; and
- €125.00 (normal rate), €112.50 (reduced rate for extended stays), and €62.50 (detention rate).

As of 1 July 2015, class of allowances for Civil Service subsistence rates has been discontinued, meaning all employees, regardless of grade, are subject to the same rates.

MOTOR AND TRAVELLING EXPENSES

If you make a journey in your own car for business purposes, the money paid to you by your employer will not be taxable as a benefit in kind providing it does not exceed the **civil service mileage rate**. If you are going to claim motoring expenses from your employer, you should keep a track of the journeys you make and the mileage actually incurred.

Sadly, you cannot claim for journeys between your home and work.

The amount you can claim under the civil service mileage rate rules varies according to whether or not you use your car in the normal course of your duties, or only occasionally. The current rates are set out in the table below:

Civil service kilometre rates from 1 April 2017

Engine size		0–1200cc	1200–1500cc	1500cc and over
Band	Km Range	Cents per km	Cents per km	Cents per km
1	0 to 1,500	37.95	39.86	44.79
2	1,501 to 5,500	70.00	73.21	83.53
3	5,501 to 25,000	27.55	29.03	32.21
4	Over 25,000	21.36	22.23	25.85

A chance to claim more

Some trade unions and professional bodies have negotiated special, higher, flat-rate motoring allowances for their members. For instance, teachers, nurses, journalists and building workers may all claim their special flat rate allowance tax-free – without the Revenue Commissioners questioning it. It's worth checking with your own trade union or professional body to see if such an arrangement is in place.

OTHER TAX-FREE AND TAX-EFFICIENT PERKS

Below is a list of tax-free or tax-efficient benefits that it's possible for an employee to receive.

Daily and overnight allowances

If you're working away from home your employer can pay you a daily and/or an overnight allowance to cover the cost of any expenses you may incur, such as lunch, an evening meal, accommodation, and so forth. The amount you can receive tax free depends on your salary level. The more you earn, the more you can receive tax-free. However, the longer you stay away the less you can receive. The Civil Service subsistence allowances were last reviewed in 2016, and the current rates are set out in the chart below.

Civil service domestic subsistence rates from 1 April 2017

Overnight allowances			Day allowances	
Normal rate	Reduced rate	Detention rate	10 hours or more	5–10 hours
€133.73	€120.36	€66.87	€33.61	€14.01

Free or inexpensive accommodation

If your job necessitates it, your employer can offer you rent-free or subsidised accommodation without any tax being incurred. Naturally, your residence has to be in part of your employer's business premises and there has to be a clear work-related reason for your needing to live there.

Staff entertainment

Your employer is allowed to entertain you at a reasonable cost without you incurring any benefit in kind.

Communal transport to your place of work

If, for instance, your employer provides a company bus or shared taxi to bring you to or from your place of employment, this is tax-free.

Presents!

Your employer can give you **non-cash personal gifts** providing it isn't for some reason connected with your work. This is called the small-gift exemption and cannot exceed **€500** in value.

Meals

Meals, whether free or subsidised, are entirely tax-free if they're provided in a staff canteen. However, the facility has to be open to all the employees.

Lump sum payments

Lump sum payments for special reasons – such as redundancy, on account of an injury or disability, or relating to your pension scheme – may be totally exempt from tax depending on the amount and circumstances. Details relating to redundancy payments may be found in Chapter 31.

Educational fees

Any scholarship income or bursaries paid by your employer will be completely free of tax provided that the course is relevant to your employment.

Injury or disability payments

Payment made on account of an injury or disability will also usually be 100% tax-free.

Work tools

Equipment, tools, working clothes or anything else required to fulfil your employment will not be taxed.

Pension scheme payments

If your employer contributes to an approved or statutory pension scheme, those contributions are also tax-free. For more details on this, see Chapter 18.

Health insurance

If your employer pays the cost of permanent health insurance for you, this is tax-free.

Season tickets

Bus, train and Luas passes are tax-free. The only condition is that they are monthly or annual transport passes, so these don't have to be used exclusively for work purposes.

Childcare

Crèche and childcare facilities, provided by your employer on a free or subsidised basis, will not be taxed provided that they are not privately owned.

Relocation expenses

All your home relocation expenses will be tax-free provided you are being forced to move as a requirement of your job.

Sports and recreational facilities

Sports and recreational facilities, so long as they are located on an employer's own premises, can be enjoyed tax-free by workers. This includes a company gym or health spa.

Mobile telephones

Your company-provided mobile telephone is tax-free provided it can be justified on the basis of business use. This rule also applies to the provision of computers, and even broadband access at home.

Car parking

A free car-parking space will not be taxed either – potentially a very valuable benefit indeed if you happen to work in a city centre.

Exam payments

A cash award given to you in recognition of obtaining a qualification of relevance to your job will also be treated as tax-free provided it is roughly equivalent to the expenses incurred in studying for the exam.

Membership fees

If you need to join any professional body by reason of your employment, your subscription will be tax-free.

Health screening

If your employer insists on you having a medical check-up, it will be tax-free.

Long-service presents

If you work for your company for at least 20 years, they can buy you a present costing no more than €50 for each year of service, and it will be completely tax-free, a potentially €1,000 tax-free gift.

HAS YOUR EMPLOYER OFFERED YOU AN OPPORTUNITY TO BUY SHARES?

An increasing number of employees are being offered an opportunity to buy shares, directly or indirectly, in their employer's company. The tax treatment of different types of share schemes varies. Some offer an opportunity to save tax and others don't. You should also note that some employee share schemes won't cost you anything to participate in, whereas others will require you to make an investment. As this is a complicated area, I would always suggest taking professional advice before participating. However, to give you a general idea of how the different types of scheme work, I have outlined the seven (!) main options below, together with a few guidance notes.

Approved profit-share scheme: This is probably the most advantageous scheme from an employee's point of view, as it allows you to receive shares tax-free up to an annual limit of €12,700 provided certain conditions are met. Basically, provided you hold the shares granted to you for at least three years, they will be entirely tax-free.

Employee share ownership trusts (ESOTs): Employee share ownership trusts were created to run alongside company profit-sharing schemes and they work pretty much in the same way so far as the employee is concerned. One additional benefit, however, is that after ten years, a one-off additional payment of €38,100 can be made.

Stock options: A stock option allows you the opportunity to purchase shares in your employer's company at a pre-set price, normally within a certain timeframe. The benefit arises if the price at which you can buy the shares is less than their market value. This does, of course, constitute a gain from your point of view, and such a gain would be taxable. Stock options are rarely tax efficient.

Share subscription schemes: If you purchase new shares in your employer's company and hold them for at least three years, then you will achieve a tax benefit. However, there is an upper limit on the amount of tax you can save and you will, of course, incur a risk, since the value of the shares you buy may fall during the period you hold them.

Save as you earn (SAYE) scheme: This allows you to purchase shares in your employer's company over a period of time, with the cost of those shares being deducted from your salary as it's paid. There is the potential for some tax savings here, though they are not enormous.

Share incentive schemes: Share incentive schemes and employee share purchase plans offer you an opportunity to buy shares in your employer's company, but do not normally attract much of a tax benefit.

The free gift of shares: If your employer gives shares to you, without charge, you will be liable to tax on the benefit of receiving them but you should escape PRSI.

All the schemes outlined above have stringent conditions attached to them by the Revenue Commissioners, and I cannot over-emphasise the need to take professional advice.

REVENUE ONLINE SERVICE (ROS)

Revenue have extended the Revenue Online Service (ROS) to be available to PAYE taxpayers. Once you have registered you can avail of a full suite of services, including viewing information on your Revenue record and submitting tax credit claims and incomes information. You can also carry out a range of transactions without the need to fully register for the service. To access the site and register go to www.ros.ie.

MONEY DOCTORS WEALTH CHECK

You should find out if you are eligible for any refund of tax already paid, such as dental and medical expenses, etc., even going back as far as four years. This is particularly relevant to PAYE workers, who sometimes overlook their entitlements. There are two main companies in Ireland offering tax refunds on a 'no refund – no fee' basis:
- www.taxback.com is an award-winning company that specialises in this area. To start the ball rolling, text MONEYDOCTORS to 53135 (normal SMS rates apply) and they will be in touch with you to assess your situation within 48 hours.
- www.redoaktaxrefunds.ie also specialise in tax refunds.
Better in your pocket than theirs!

Nowadays, however, company cars are liable for PAYE, USC and PRSI. The amount of tax you have to pay is linked to the value of the car and the amount of mileage you do. For instance, if you do less than 24,000km a year, you will be taxed as if you had received a cash amount equivalent to 30% of the 'original market value' of the car supplied. This calculation does not change even if the car you drive is secondhand. Keep in mind, though, that if you do a very high annual business mileage, the amount of tax drops substantially. For instance, if you do more than 48,000km a year, you only have to pay the cash equivalent of 6% of the 'original market value'. Let's look at a real-life example:

> Your company provides you with a car worth €30,000 and your business travel is less than 24,000km a year. You will be taxed as if you had received 30% of €30,000 – in other words, €9,000 of extra salary a year. Assuming that you're paid monthly, you will be taxed on an extra €750 per month – one-twelfth of the €9,000 benefit you are considered to have received.

The cost of this can be brought down if you contribute towards the cost of the car and also pay for your own private fuel.

HOW TO SLASH THE COST OF YOUR BENEFIT IN KIND

It is possible to reduce your benefit in kind charge to a flat 20% providing the following conditions are met:
- You spend 70% or more of your time away from your place of work.
- Your annual business travel is between 9,600km and 24,000km.
- Your average working week is more than 20 hours.

To have any hope of reducing your benefit in kind tax bill, you must maintain a logbook detailing all your business trips, and make it available, if required, to your Inspector of Taxes.

Another clever way to cut your benefit in kind

If, for some reason, the car is not available to you for a period, the amount of tax will be reduced. For instance, supposing you gave the car back to your employer for one month a year, you would reduce your tax liability by one-twelfth.

SHOULD YOU HAVE A COMPANY CAR AT ALL?

For many people, the benefit in kind tax is so high that it makes better sense to use their personal car for business and take a mileage allowance instead of a company car. If you only receive the civil service kilometre rates (see table above), any money paid to you by your employer will be completely free of tax.

If you're entitled to a company car, and forgo it, you may also find yourself better off. As the tables below show, this will be particularly true if you do a relatively low business mileage each year.

Cost of car	Kilometric thresholds	BIK %	BIK
€20,000	24,135 or less	30	€6,000
€20,000	24,136 to 32,180	24	€4,800
€20,000	32,181 to 40,225	18	€3,600
€20,000	40,226 to 48,270	12	€2,400
€20,000	48,271 and over	6	€1,200

Car costing €20,000 and over 1500 cc

Kilometres per year	40,000	30,000	20,000	10,000	5,000
Depreciation	€6,500	€5,500	€4,000	€3,000	€3,000
Petrol	€8,000	€6,000	€4,000	€2,000	€1,000
Insurance	€1,000	€1,000	€1,000	€1,000	€1,000
Road tax	€350	€350	€350	€350	€350
Service/repairs	€2,000	€1,200	€750	€300	€300
Total running costs	€17,850	€14,050	€10,100	€6,650	€5,650
Mileage claims at civil service rates*	€13,384	€10,508	€7,662	€4,816	€2,953
Net running costs	€4,496	€3,542	€2,438	€1,834	€2,697
Benefit in kind	€1,200	€2,400	€4,800	€6,000	€6,000

* First 6,437km at 59.07 cent per km and balance at 28.46 cent per km.

Note: USC is payable on the benefit in kind.

100% TAX-FREE MOTORING!

There is one way to enjoy a company car with absolutely no tax liability whatsoever. Any car included in a **car pool** will be tax-free provided all of the following conditions are met:
- The car is available for use (and is actually used) by more than one employee, and isn't ordinarily used by any one such employee to the exclusion of the others.
- Private use by any employee is incidental to business use.
- The car is not normally kept overnight at, or in the vicinity of, any of the employees' homes.

Finally, if you work for your own company or are self-employed, the cost of purchasing a 'business' car will be reduced by capital allowances. As with other capital expenditure, you're allowed to write off the cost for tax purposes over a period of eight years. So if you purchased the car for €10,000, you can set an allowance of €1,250 per year against your tax bill.

26

CAPITAL GAINS TAX

DON'T PAY A PENNY MORE CAPITAL GAINS TAX THAN YOU HAVE TO

Just because capital gains tax – at a flat rate of 33% – is much cheaper than it used to be (at its peak it was 40%) it doesn't follow that you want to pay any more of it than you have to.

Capital gains tax planning is not easy, even though the rules relating to it have been much simplified. However, there are still some useful allowances and exemptions that do make it possible to reduce, delay and, in some instances, completely avoid this tax. As you'll discover in this chapter.

HOW THE TAX WORKS

If you buy something for one price and then sell it at a higher price or, for that matter, give it away when it is worth more than you paid for it, then the Revenue Commissioners consider that you have made a 'capital gain' and may, therefore, be liable for tax.

> **MONEY DOCTORS WEALTH CHECK**
>
> *Indexation relief*
>> If you owned whatever you have sold prior to 31 December 2002, there is good news – before 1 January 2003, something called indexation relief was applied to all possible gains, which has the effect of reducing tax liability. Indexation relief was, essentially, an allowance designed to take account of inflation, so that only gains above the rate of inflation were liable for tax. You can still apply indexation relief to assets held prior to 31 December 2002.

BASIC CAPITAL GAINS TAX PLANNING

Below is a list of the main ways in which capital gains tax can be reduced or avoided:

- It may seem a bit dramatic, but if you **move abroad** prior to making a disposal of assets (in other words selling them), you will not be liable for any Irish capital gains tax. The only exception to this is if you're selling Irish property or mineral/exploration rights. Obviously, you would want to be selling a fairly major asset to make it worth becoming non-resident. For further information about becoming non-resident see Chapter 29.
- The first €1,270 made as a capital gain in each tax year is tax-free.
- You do not have to pay capital gains tax from the **sale of your principal residence**, including up to one acre of land. However, if you sell your home for development, then you will be taxed on the profit attributed to the 'development value'.
- If you've bought a home for a **dependent relative** (this includes a relative who is unable to look after themselves, a widowed mother, and so forth), any gain you make on the sale of the property would be free of tax.
- If you give **a house site** to a child who then builds his or her private residence on it, providing that site is not worth more than €500,000, no tax is due.
- There is no capital gains tax on bonuses from **post office** or **state savings schemes**, or from the disposal of **government stocks**.
- You don't have to pay tax if you sell an asset with a **'predictable life'** of less than 50 years – for instance, if you sold a car or a horse at a profit.
- If you **hand your business** (including a farm) to a member of your family on retirement, there is no capital gains tax liability either. This is called 'retirement relief'.
- You can dispose of a **'moveable, tangible asset'** worth €2,540 or less without paying capital gains tax.
- Capital gains tax is not applicable to any **winnings** from gambling, the lottery, or competitions.
- Any benefits from **life assurance** policies or **deferred annuities** are tax-free.
- If you transfer something to your **spouse** there is no capital gains tax charge.

Incidentally, retirement relief not only applies when you pass an asset to a member of your family. Providing you're aged over 55, and have owned the farm or business for more than five years, if you sell that farm or business for a sum that is less than €750,000 you won't have to pay capital gains tax. (This €750,000 is a lifetime limit, which from 1 January

2014 was reduced to €500,000 for people aged 66 years or over.) If you sell the asset for more than €750,000 you will pay a reduced level of capital gains tax.

In Budget 2012, a new incentive relief from CGT was introduced for the first 7 years of ownership for properties, whether residential or non-residential, bought between budget night and the end of 2013, where the property is held for more than seven years. In order to free up stockpiled land banks of undeveloped property, the holding period was reduced from 7 to 4 years in Budget 2018.

ONE MORE USEFUL WAY TO REDUCE YOUR BILL

If you incur expenses relating to the item you are selling, or if you have improved it in some way, you may be able to claim them against your tax bill.

For instance, supposing you purchased an investment property and added an extra bedroom to the attic. The cost of doing this could be deducted from the sale price, thus reducing your tax liability.

27

CAPITAL ACQUISITION TAX

DON'T ALLOW YOUR GIFTS AND INHERITANCES TO BE TAXED UNNECESSARILY

Capital acquisition tax (CAT) is a tax on gifts and inheritances – and the purpose of this chapter is to ensure that your gifts and inheritances aren't taxed unnecessarily!

There are two key ways to lessen your exposure to capital acquisition tax (which operates at a flat rate of 33% on benefits taken on or after 6 December 2012 after reaching CAT thresholds):

- Make sure that the value of what you're leaving or giving falls below the tax-free threshold.
- Make sure that what you're leaving or giving is excluded completely from the tax. As there is a long list of excluded benefits, this is not as hard as it may seem.

TAKE FULL ADVANTAGE OF THE TAX-FREE THRESHOLDS

There are all sorts of gifts and inheritances that the government feel it would be unfair to tax. Or, to be more accurate, they feel it would be unfair to tax them unless the amount involved is fairly substantial. We are talking here about gifts and inheritance made to members of your immediate family and other people who are close to you. The allowances that apply are referred to as **tax-free thresholds**. The tax-free threshold system is not straightforward, but I'll do my best to summarise it.

Essentially, there are three different groups. The first is your **closest relatives**, the second is your slightly **more distant relatives**, and the third is **everyone else**. The thresholds are personal to the recipient, not to the donor (known legally as the **disponer**). For instance, for the current year the total amount a child can receive tax-free as gifts and/ or inheritances is €320,000 from a parent. So providing the amount a child inherits from either of his or her parents is beneath this figure, he or she will pay no tax on it. Where it gets complicated is in the case of, say, nieces and nephews, who may receive bequests from a number of uncles and aunts. Aggregates apply so if you receive your full threshold from one uncle, the next aunt or uncle inheritance received will attract CAT tax at 33%. Below are the current thresholds:

Group A – Children: €320,000 where the recipient is a child, or a minor grandchild of the benefactor if the parent is dead. In some cases, this threshold can also apply to a parent, niece or nephew who has worked in a family business for a period of time. This threshold also applies to a parent receiving an inheritance from a child. Foster children may also receive this amount providing they were maintained by and resided with the foster parent for a successive period of five years while under the age of 18.

Group B – Close relatives: €32,500 where the recipient is a brother, sister, niece, nephew, grandchild or linear ancestor/descendant of the benefactor, or where the gift is made by the child to the parent.

Group C – Everyone else: €16,250 is the threshold in all other cases.

In other words, as an individual you can receive €320,000 from a parent, as well as €32,500 from uncles and aunts and an additional €16,250 from friends or other more distant relatives, without incurring any tax.

These rates apply from 9 October 2018.

FIVE COMPLETELY TAX-FREE CATEGORIES

Five categories of gift or inheritance are excluded completely for purposes of capital acquisition tax. They are:
- Any gift or inheritance made **between spouses.**
- Any inheritance received from a **deceased child** that was originally given to that child by one or other of their parents.
- Up to **€3,000 worth of gifts or cash** in any single calendar year (so both parents can gift to their children).
- Irish government stock when given to a **non-Irish-domiciled beneficiary**. There are conditions attached to this – the main one being that the person receiving it must hold it for at least six years after receiving it. The legal definition of 'non-Irish domiciled' is complicated, but essentially it means someone who wasn't born in Ireland and who hasn't married someone born in Ireland.
- Your **family home**. Again, there are certain conditions. It should be your principal private residence (or the recipient's principal private

residence); the recipient should have been living in the home for the three years prior to the transfer; and the recipient should not have an interest in any other residential property. Furthermore, the recipient mustn't sell the home for at least six years.

As you can see from the list above, with a bit of careful planning it is possible to take the main family home and other assets out of one's estate for inheritance tax purposes.

TWO USEFUL WAYS TO AVOID CAPITAL ACQUISITION TAX

Because the government knows it would be unfair to include **farms** and **business assets** in the capital acquisitions tax net, both can be given away or bequeathed with only minimal tax liability.

The rules are written so that someone who wishes to reduce or avoid capital acquisition tax can, with a little foresight, transfer their assets into either a business or a farm and see them escape tax. As you can imagine, the rules governing these two tax loopholes are complex, so I will only summarise them below. It would be unwise, to say the least, to attempt to take advantage of these tax breaks without consulting a professional accountant and/or solicitor.

FARMS

With regard to farms, 'agricultural assets are valued at only 10% of their true market value when calculating a liability for capital acquisitions tax'. Farm assets, in this instance, include not just land but buildings, woodland, livestock, bloodstock and machinery. The recipient of the farm must be a 'farmer', meaning that at least 80% of his or her assets are farm assets. They must also hold on to the assets for at least ten years to avoid any claw-back of tax.

A farm may, of course, also be considered a family business, and the Revenue Commissioners very generously allow them to be taxed as such for capital acquisition tax purposes, if it means a lower tax bill in the hands of the recipient.

BUSINESSES

For business assets, once again, the primary condition is that the recipient must hold them for at least ten years after the transfer. The business itself must be Irish. Most businesses and business assets qualify, including property, unquoted shares, buildings, land and even machinery. However, businesses whose 'sole or main business is dealing in land, shares, or securities' are not covered by this loophole. The transfer of a business by way of gift or inheritance is not entirely tax-free under these circumstances, but the assets will be assessed at just 10% of their market value.

The person giving away or bequeathing either farm or business assets need not have owned them for very long. In the case of a gift it should be five years, but in the case of death it need be only two years.

28

LOVE, MARRIAGE AND LOWER TAXES

EXTRA TAX BENEFITS FOR THOSE WHO ARE MARRIED

Billy Connolly, one of my favourite comedians, famously said: 'Marriage is a wonderful invention, but, then again, so is a bicycle repair kit.' However, unlike a bicycle repair kit, marriage has some very tasty tax benefits attaching to it. And in this chapter I will explain how you can take advantage of them.

MARRIAGE BRINGS GREATER FLEXIBILITY

The first big benefit of being married is that you get to choose how you are taxed. The options open to you are:

Joint assessment: This means that you will be taxed as one unit. Some tax concessions not used by one spouse can be transferred to the other.

Separate assessment: This is very like joint assessment, except that all the available allowances are split evenly between you and your spouse.

Single assessment: This is where you and your spouse decide to be treated as if you were two single people for tax purposes.

Why this flexibility of benefit? Basically, you can choose to be taxed in the way that will produce the greatest possible tax advantage given your personal circumstances.

Under joint assessment and separate assessment, some unused allowances can be passed between husband and wife. This is particularly beneficial in the case of a two-income couple where one spouse earns more than another. Under normal circumstances, the Revenue Commissioners will assume that you wish to be taxed under joint assessment, and will calculate your tax liability accordingly. However, it is worth checking that you are taking full advantage of all the allowances and tax credits open to you, as the Revenue Commissioners may not be fully aware of your financial situation.

The only circumstances under which most married people might wish to be taxed under the single assessment system is where they are separated.

OTHER TAX CONCESSIONS MADE TO MARRIED COUPLES

A number of other generous tax concessions are made to married couples, including:

- Assets may be transferred between husband and wife without being subject to capital gains tax.
- Capital losses made by one spouse may be used by the other spouse to reduce a capital gains tax bill.
- Gifts or inheritances given by one spouse to the other are free of capital acquisition tax.
- Any money received by yourself or your spouse from a life assurance policy (providing you or your spouse were the original beneficial owners) will be completely tax-free.
- Married couples do not have to pay stamp duty when they transfer assets from one to another.

EVEN BETTER NEWS IF YOU'RE MARRIED AND SELF-EMPLOYED

If you are self-employed or run your own business, by employing your spouse, you may be able to save up to €5,000 a year in tax. To make this saving, the total amount of income you and your spouse earn each year must be at least €70,800. It doesn't, by the way, all have to come from your own business. Your spouse can earn up to €25,000 and you can still gain a tax benefit.

The reason why the tax saving can be made is the fact that a two-income family can take advantage of a €70,600 standard rate band as opposed to the €44,300 band available to a single-income family.

The best way to illustrate this is with a real example:

One income			Two incomes		
Income		€75,000	Income		€75,000
€44,300 @ 20%		€8,860	€70,600 @ 20%		€14,120
€30,700 @ 40%		€12,280	€4,400 @ 40%		€1,760
Total tax before		€21,140	Total tax before		€15,880
Tax credits			Tax credits		
Married person		€3,300	Married person		€3,300
PAYE	€1,650	€4,950	PAYE	€1,650	€4,950
Tax payable		€16,190	Tax payable		€10,930
Tax saving = €5,260					

MONEY DOCTORS WEALTH CHECK

Turn your children into a tax advantage

If you're self-employed and you have children, you may be able to avoid tax on up to €16,500 per child a year. This is because your children are entitled – like anybody else – to avail of tax credits. Of course, the child must actually be doing the work for which they are paid – and it may be necessary for you to register as an employer for PAYE and PRSI purposes – but given the tax saving this has to be worth it! However, the child may have to pay PRSI and USC of €789, and you as the employer will be liable for the employer's PRSI contribution.

29

TAX FOR THE EX-PAT

TAX PLANNING TIPS IF YOU'RE LIVING AND WORKING ABROAD

What happens to your tax position if you decide to live abroad? Much depends, of course, on where you go, what you do, and how long you're away. If, for instance, you move to a country with much lower rates of tax than we have here in Ireland, you could make a substantial saving. Since there are over 130 tax jurisdictions in the world, it's obviously beyond the scope of this book to look at all the possibilities. However, in this chapter I can, at least, explain how your Irish tax situation will be affected by a move overseas.

IT'S ALL ABOUT RESIDENCY AND DOMICILE

Each country across the world has its own rules about whom it taxes and under what circumstances. In some countries it's all about whether you **reside** there for legal purposes. This may have absolutely nothing to do with the amount of time you actually spend in the country. For instance, you can be tax-resident in Malta (thus taking advantage of a very liberal tax regime) but not set foot on the island from one end of the year to the other. Other countries have more complicated rules that are not only linked to your residence but also to your **domicile**, a rather complicated legal concept. Put simply, it is considered to be *the country that you call your natural home*. When you're born, you usually have the same domicile as your father. If you marry, or move abroad for a long time, your domicile may change.

Here in Ireland, your tax liability is determined by *both* your residence status and your domicile. Just to make things more complex, we have two types of residence: You may be **ordinarily resident** or simply **resident**.

You will be viewed as being resident here for tax purposes in the current tax year if:

- You spend 183 days or more in the state.
- The combined number of days you spend here in the current tax year and the the last tax year exceeds 280. In this case you are regarded as resident for year two.

Incidentally, the term 'day' really means whether you were in the state at any time during that day.

Once you've been in Ireland for three consecutive tax years, you are considered to have become ordinarily resident. You stop being ordinarily resident in Ireland once you've left the country for three consecutive tax years.

WHAT HAPPENS WHEN YOU MOVE ABROAD?

Assuming that you are resident, ordinarily resident and domiciled in Ireland, what happens when you decide to move abroad on a permanent, or at least long-term, basis?

The year you leave Ireland, you will still be considered resident. However, the year after your departure, you will not be considered resident. Since this could lead to an unfair situation, in which you're taxed in two countries simultaneously, the law says that:

> As soon as you depart Ireland you may apply to be granted **emigrant status**, which means that your earnings outside Ireland after that date will be ignored for Irish tax purposes.

If you move to a country that has a **double taxation agreement** with Ireland, then you won't be expected to pay tax on the same money twice.

A MONEY-BACK OFFER: TAX REBATES

If you leave a job in Ireland and move overseas to work, you may well be entitled to a tax rebate. In fact, you can claim a rebate going back up to four years. The reason you get this rebate is that under the PAYE system your various tax credits and allowances are spread out over an entire year. Under these circumstances, if you leave your job and move abroad halfway through the year, you'll only ever see the benefit of half your tax allowances and credits. You won't, however, be given this rebate automatically, though you may apply for it before you've even left the country.

WHAT IS YOUR TAX STATUS?

So, what is your tax status? There are four possibilities:
- If you are resident and domiciled in Ireland, you will pay Irish tax including income tax on your Irish income and on your worldwide income.

- If you are resident in Ireland but not domiciled here, and if you haven't lived here for at least three years (in other words you are not ordinarily resident in Ireland), you will pay Irish income tax on your Irish and UK income, and on any foreign income paid to you in Ireland. In other words, foreign income (unless it comes from the UK) that you don't deposit in an Irish bank or spend in Ireland escapes Irish tax.
- If you are ordinarily resident in Ireland, but not resident here for a particular tax year, then your tax status changes dramatically. In theory you're liable to Irish income tax on your whole worldwide income. However, employment or income that you earn wholly abroad (plus an extra €3,810) will be ignored for tax purposes. Furthermore, you may be able to take advantage of double taxation agreements to further reduce your tax bill.
- If you are not resident, or ordinarily resident – in other words, if you haven't lived in Ireland for at least three years – your only liability to Irish tax is on Irish income.

Budget 2010 introduced a **domicile levy**. From 1 January 2010, certain individuals who are Irish citizens and Irish domiciled in a tax year pay a levy of €200,000. Specifically the levy applies where the individual has:

- Irish-located property greater than €5 million;
- worldwide income in excess of €1 million; and
- an Irish income tax liability less than €200,000.

The Finance Bill clarified that Irish property is defined as all property located in Ireland but does not include shares in a trading company or a holding company that derive the greater part of their value from subsidiary trading companies.

The individual's Irish income tax liability for the year will be allowed as a credit in arriving at the amount of the domicile levy for that year. The levy will apply irrespective of where they live or where they are tax resident.

YOUR PERSONAL TAX CREDITS AND RELIEFS

What happens to your personal tax credits and allowances if you cease to be resident in Ireland? The answer will be determined by the source of your income, and your resident status.

GET PROFESSIONAL HELP!

In the excitement of moving abroad, many people omit to take professional advice on their tax position, and end up with an unexpected tax bill or – just as bad – a missed opportunity to claim back tax they've already paid. The Money Doctors' advice to anybody moving abroad is get professional tax help sooner rather than later.

THE MONEY DOCTOR SAYS ...

If you are living abroad, or lived abroad, you may be entitled to a tax refund. To start the process, simply text MONEY DOCTORS to 53135 and you will be contacted by tax refund specialists taxback. com.

30

SPECIAL TAX ADVICE FOR FARMERS

We city folk have an idyllic view of farming life – sun-drenched fields, wholesome food, a healthy lifestyle and happy people. There is all that, but there is an everyday issue the farming community face that we all face – tax. Tax is and has always been a thorny issue regarding farmers. Some city folk may think that farmers don't pay enough, and farmers might say that they deserve special status because of the importance of their role in Irish heritage – not to mention the produce they yield from Irish soil. Being married to a farmer's daughter, I tend to agree with the latter!

If you are a farmer, you need to consider a number of areas:
- Income tax
- Capital acquisitions tax
- Capital gains tax
- VAT
- Stock relief
- Compulsory disposal of livestock
- Capital allowances
- Stamp duty
- Farm consolidation relief
- Leasing of farm land

Let's look at these all in detail now.

INCOME TAX

A farmer needs to prepare accounts every year, showing all income earned during the year (from cattle sales, subsidies, etc.) and all related expenses. The net profit made during the year is subject to income tax.

Tax return

A farmer is obliged to submit an income tax return (**Form 11**) each year. For example, the income tax return for 2018 must be submitted before 31 October 2019. If it is submitted online via the Revenue Online Service (ROS), it doesn't have to be submitted until mid-November 2019.

Payment of tax

A farmer, like any other self-employed person, has to make a preliminary tax payment for a given year or on 31 October of that year. The amount to be paid is generally based on the farmer's tax liability for the prior year.

CAPITAL ACQUISITIONS TAX

A gift or inheritance of land, buildings and other agricultural property (e.g. machinery and livestock) may be reduced by 90% of its market value for capital acquisitions tax when received by a qualifying farmer as long as:
- the farmer is domiciled in Ireland; and
- 80% of the property's market value consists of agricultural property.

This relief is lost if the assets are disposed of within six-years, without being replaced within one year of sale, or within a period of six years in the case of a sale or compulsory acquisition made on or after 25 March 2002. Make any claims for agricultural relief on **Form IT41**.

Gifts or inheritances of agricultural property qualify for **business relief**, where the relevant criteria are met, in circumstances where it fails to qualify for agricultural relief. This similarly reduces the market value of the gift/inheritance by 90%. Again, business relief will be clawed back if the assets are disposed of within six years, without being replaced.

THE MONEY DOCTOR SAYS ...

Before you receive a gift of farm assets, make sure that 80% of your personal assets are agricultural assets after you have received the gift.

CAPITAL GAINS TAX

Retirement relief means that a **disponer** (the person giving the legacy, generally the mother or father) can hand over land to a child without capital gains tax liability for that child. However, the conditions are:
- The disponer must be over 55 years of age.
- She or he must have used the business assets for at least ten years prior to handing it over to the disponer's child.

You should note these points:
- Periods of ownership of a deceased spouse may also be included.
- 'Child' includes anyone who has worked substantially on a full-time basis for five years before the handover.
- Where proceeds do not exceed €750,000, relief on the disposal can be given to an unconnected person. There is marginal relief exceeding this amount.

Land that has been let for up to five years prior to a compulsory purchase order being made will qualify for retirement relief if it was used for farming for ten years prior to the letting.

Note that a farmer who participates in the EU 'Early retirement from farming scheme' by leasing the land qualifies for the relief. Therefore, while it is called 'retirement relief', you don't actually have to retire to qualify for this relief!

VAT

- A flat rate of 5.2% applies to supplies of agricultural goods or services.
- If you engage in any other services and your turnover exceeds €37,500 in a calendar year, normal VAT rates will apply – this includes the farming itself.
- Keep in mind that if you are a flat rate (5.2%) farmer, you can also reclaim this VAT on any expenditure incurred in the construction or improvement of farm buildings, farm structures, fencing, drainage and land reclamation.

STOCK RELIEF

Stock relief is a basic relief for first-time farmers (who meet certain criteria) whereby they can reduce their taxable trading profit by 100% of the increase in their farming stock at the end of their trading year over their farming stock at the beginning of that year. This relief has been extended to the end of 2018, as has the existing 25% general stock relief for farmers.

COMPULSORY DISPOSAL OF LIVESTOCK

There is a special relief for farmers (individuals and companies) in respect of profits resulting from the disposal of livestock due to statutory disease-eradication measures.

You can have tax on profits spread over four consecutive annual instalments *after* the year in which the profits arise or spread equally over the four years including the year in which the profits arise.

This relief extends to all animals and poultry.

CAPITAL ALLOWANCES

When a farmer spends money on capital expenditure, such as tractors, farm machinery, farm buildings and so on, they are *not* allowed to deduct all the cost against their profits in the one year. Instead, they have to spread the cost over a number of years in the form of capital allowances.

Below are the main types of capital allowances that a farmer can claim:

- **Plant and machinery:** If a farmer buys machinery, such as tractors, trailers, etc., for the farm, they can claim capital allowances over eight years at a rate of 12.5%.
- **Farm buildings:** If a farmer spends money on farm buildings, such as fences, roadways, drains, yards, land reclamation, etc., they can claim capital allowances over seven years (15% for the first 6 years and 10% for the seventh year).

STAMP DUTY

Essentially a tax on buying or transferring property or land, the duty payable is cut to half for related bequests (e.g. giving your son your farm), but to young, trained farmers this duty is nil. There are clawbacks when, within five years of receiving a stamp duty relief, the proceeds of that disposal of the property are not reinvested within one year in other land.

FARM CONSOLIDATION RELIEF

This is another type of stamp duty relief for exchanging farm land between two farmers to consolidate each other's holding. There are a number of conditions attached to this relief and you should consult your accountant for more advice on it.

LEASING OF FARM LAND

If you are over 40 and you lease your farm land, you are eligible for income tax exemption subject to certain thresholds – bear in mind the lease income of the husband and wife are treated separately for the purpose of the relief, whether jointly assessed or not.

In January 2007, a new exemption of €20,000 per annum was introduced for leases of 10 years or more duration. This measure was subjected to clearance with the European Commission under state-aid rules.

PART 9

WHEN THE LAST THING YOU WANT TO THINK ABOUT IS MONEY

This section of the book offers advice and information relating to five highly sensitive subjects:

- *redundancy*
- *separation*
- *divorce*
- *the death of a loved one*
- *personal insolvency and bankruptcy*

In each of these situations, of course, the last thing you'll want to think about is money. And yet, unfortunately, each of these difficult experiences has important financial implications.

31
REDUNDANCY

Whether you have opted for redundancy because of the financial benefits it offers you, or whether it was thrust upon you, it is vital that you know your rights in order to come out of it in as strong a financial position as possible. In this chapter I will explain your rights and offer general advice on making the most – from a money perspective – of the situation.

BACKGROUND BRIEFING ON 'REDUNDANCY'

The term 'redundancy' applies to a very specific situation, so the first thing you must do is find out whether or not you are covered by the relevant legislation. Essentially, in order to be eligible for a redundancy payment, you must:

- be aged 16 or over;
- have been working for at least eight hours a week for your employer; and
- have at least 104 weeks (in other words, two years) of continuous service for the same employer since the age of 16.

Redundancy can only exist when an employee is dismissed because:

- the employer is no longer undertaking the business activity which necessitated employing you;
- the employer is moving the location of the business; or
- the employer has decided to carry on business with fewer employees, or to carry out work in some different manner.

Voluntary redundancy – also known as 'voluntary parting' – is where an employer wants to reduce numbers of staff and asks for volunteers for redundancy. If you do volunteer, you will automatically be entitled to a **statutory lump sum payment.** Note that employers must give you at least two weeks' notice before making you redundant, and notice must be given using **Form RP1** at that time.

How much are you entitled to?

The law is very precise about the amount of money an employer must pay you if you are to be made redundant. It is calculated as follows:
- You should receive two weeks' pay for each year of employment continuous since the age of 16.
- You should also receive an equivalent of one week's normal pay.

However, there *is* an upper limit. No matter what your salary, one week's pay will never be more than €600.

What happens if the employer doesn't pay up?

There are situations where employers don't – or can't – make the lump sum redundancy payment. For instance, the employer may be inefficient, insolvent, or even dead. Under these circumstances, it may be possible to receive a payment from the government. To pursue this, contact:

Workplace Relations Commission
O'Brien Road, Carlow
Lo-call: 1890 80 80 90

What's the tax situation?

Depending on your circumstances, and the amount of money being paid, your redundancy lump sum may or may not be liable to tax. It will be totally exempt from tax if the payment was made:
- under the Redundancy Payments Acts of 1987–91;
- as a result of injury or disability; or
- from an approved pension scheme.

Even if your lump sum isn't entirely tax-free, you may be able to claim an extra tax-free amount. How much you can claim will be the highest of the three different exemptions outlined below. Where you are receiving a larger sum, it is likely to become taxable. Under these circumstances, you can either treat it as income in the year in which you receive it, and have it taxed as such, or else you can take advantage of something called **top slicing relief**, which works by calculating your average rate of tax for the five years prior to the tax year in which you received a lump sum.

It is often also possible to reduce your tax bill on a redundancy lump sum by using it to make an additional voluntary contribution to a pension scheme (see Chapter 18).

CLAIMING TAX RELIEF ON A REDUNDANCY PAYMENT

You can claim tax relief under one of these three exemptions:

Basic exemption: You can receive up to €10,160 as a lump sum, together with an additional €765 for each complete year of service, without paying a cent of tax. (This does not include statutory redundancy, which is tax-free.)

Increased exemption: The tax-free sum you are entitled to receive may be increased by €10,000 to a maximum of €20,160 (plus the additional €765 for each complete year of service) if you haven't made a claim for an increased exemption amount in the previous ten years, nor received a tax-free lump sum under an approved pension scheme.

Standard capital superannuation benefit (SCSB): This is a way for those with a long service record to receive a higher tax-free sum. The SCSB formula involves taking your average salary over the past three years, multiplying it by the number of years of service, dividing it by 15, and deducting any tax-free lump sum paid, or due, from a pension scheme.

Let me give you an example:

Peter, aged 65, has given 44 years' service to his company. His average salary over the last three years was €47,500. If you multiply this by 44 (the number of years service), you would get a total of €2,090,000. Then divide it by 15, giving you a total of €139,333.33 tax-free.

THE MONEY DOCTOR SAYS ...

If you have been working for an employer for a sufficiently long period of time to entitle you to a redundancy payment, there is no doubt in my mind that it's worth seeking professional help to ensure that you not only optimise that payment, but that you pay the least possible amount of tax on the benefit. There may also be an opportunity to claim top slicing relief on any taxed element of a redundancy payment.

32

SEPARATION

THE FINANCIAL CONSEQUENCES OF SEPARATION

Sadly, no book dealing with personal finances is complete without chapters covering separation and divorce. First of all, it's worth pointing out that from a legal perspective the breakdown of a marriage actually has three separate stages:

1. When a couple make the decision to **live apart**.
2. When a couple seek a **legal separation**.
3. When a couple seek a **judicial separation**.

In this chapter I will explain the consequences and issues surrounding a separation, and in the next chapter I will explain what happens as a result of a divorce.

THE IMPLICATIONS OF LIVING APART

Living separately from your husband or wife does not in any way alter the legal status of your marriage. For example, you don't automatically lose your Succession Act entitlements (see below) if you are separated from your spouse. However, do note that if a spouse is found guilty of **desertion** or **bad conduct**, they might well be deemed by a court to have forfeited these rights.

WHAT HAPPENS WHEN YOU LIVE APART?

The financial effects of living apart can be summarised as follows:

- In the case of a **temporary** or **short-term** separation, there will be no alteration in the income tax situation and you can still elect for joint, separate or single assessment.
- If the separation is considered to be **permanent**, the husband and wife will be assessed for income tax under the single assessment system. This only really changes if there are legally enforceable maintenance payments being made. In some circumstances, these will be tax deductible to the payer, and taxable in the hands of the recipient; in other circumstances, they will be ignored for income tax purposes.

- With regard to **capital gains tax**, a temporary separation will make no change in either spouse's tax status. In the event of a permanent separation, any transfer of assets that are connected with the separation itself will remain capital gains tax-free. However, other transfers will become taxable and unused capital gains tax losses will no longer be permitted.
- Couples who live apart continue to be exempt from **capital acquisitions tax** on the transfer of assets between each other.
- **Life assurance proceeds** continue to be tax-free, providing the beneficiary was originally named in the policy as such.

Couples who are separated continue to enjoy exemption from stamp duty when transferring property between each other.

LEGAL SEPARATION

A legal separation (often referred to as a 'Deed of Separation') is a voluntary agreement made between a married couple who have decided to live apart on a permanent basis. It does not change the legal status of a marriage. Its purpose is really to resolve the key financial and, where relevant, child-custody arrangements. Under normal circumstances, a legal separation makes provision regarding two key financial matters:

- any maintenance payments to be made by one spouse for the benefit of the other spouse and/or their children; and
- any desired change regarding rights under the Succession Act 1965.

With regard to Succession Act rights, these only change if altered legally by the Deed of Separation. However, on becoming legally separated, many people alter their wills to account for the new circumstances.

From an income tax perspective, a legal separation is no different from a married couple simply deciding to live apart. Thus, if the separation is likely to be permanent, and legally enforceable maintenance payments have been agreed, most couples decide to opt for separate assessment. In this case, maintenance payments are ignored for income tax purposes.

While the income tax situation may be relatively straightforward in the first year of separation, in subsequent years it may become slightly trickier. A number of different factors now come into play, including:

- voluntary maintenance payments, whether made to a spouse or for the benefit of a child;
- legally enforceable maintenance payments, whether made to a spouse and/or child;
- interest relief on mortgage repayments; and
- single-parent credits.

PRSI and **USC** may be payable on maintenance payments, depending on whether the separated couple have opted for single or separate assessment.

In most circumstances, there is a **tax benefit** to legally enforceable maintenance payments. This is because they are tax deductible for the spouse paying them, but will not necessarily be large enough for the recipient to have to pay tax on them.

Liability to capital gains tax, capital acquisition tax and stamp duty do not alter if you become legally separated as opposed to simply living apart.

WHAT IS A JUDICIAL SEPARATION?

If a couple cannot agree to a legal separation, one of them may apply to the courts for a judicial separation. In this case, instead of a voluntary arrangement regarding the marital assets, maintenance and so on, the court will make a number of **Ancillary Orders**, which are legally enforceable.

From a financial perspective, there is little difference between a legal separation and a judicial separation. There is one area, however, where a judicial separation is more like a divorce, and this is with regard to **pension benefits** (e.g. Pension Adjustment Orders). Under the Family Law Act of 1995, if a judicial separation takes place, a spouse's pension benefits will be treated in one of three different ways:

- **Earmarking** may occur. This means that when a pension becomes payable, a share of it is earmarked for the other spouse.
- **Pension-splitting** results in the pension benefits being split on a pre-set formula between the two spouses.
- **Offsetting,** whereby the spouse with pension rights may be entitled to keep them in exchange for something else. For instance, the spouse with pension rights might give up all entitlement to a family home.

A decree of judicial separation does *not* affect the legal status of a marriage – it merely means that a husband and wife no longer have to live together. The key difference between a judicial separation and a divorce is that a judicial separation will not allow either party to re-marry.

THE MONEY DOCTOR SAYS ...

Sadly, many separating couples take legal but not financial advice. I strongly recommend a thorough review of your finances both before and after separation.

You should consider every aspect of your finances – life cover, income protection, critical illness cover, borrowings, savings, investments and (especially) pension plans.

Given that after a separation both parties are likely to be managing on a lower income, it is also important to work out a new monthly budget. Contact consultation@moneydoctor.ie.

33

DIVORCE

THE FINANCIAL CONSEQUENCES OF DIVORCE

Although a great deal has been written about the legal, emotional, religious, moral and logistical aspects of divorce, there are very few sources of reference relating to the *financial* consequences of ending a marriage.

The financial consequences will, of course, vary considerably depending on a variety of factors, including:

- each partner's age;
- the income of each partner;
- whether or not there are any children;
- whether or not there is a family home;
- other joint and individually held assets;
- the pension entitlements of each partner;
- the health of each partner;
- whether or not any life assurance is in place for one or other partner; and
- whether or not they both live in Ireland.

Decisions over whether or not the family home should be sold, or concerning maintenance payments, are legal rather than financial and, therefore, outside the scope of this book.

If you are divorced, whatever settlement was reached – whether voluntary or decided by the courts – you now need to review your financial planning.

In this chapter, I will look at the key issues facing a newly divorced person, and I will make a number of specific suggestions relating to your personal finances.

THE IMPORTANCE OF BUDGETING

There is no doubt that divorce is expensive. Leaving aside the legal costs, both husband and wife are likely to find themselves now having to fund two homes where, previously, they only had to pay for one. By the same token, other assets are likely to be depleted:

- Extra life cover may become necessary.

- All sorts of living expenses will increase.
- You may be required to start or increase retirement savings.

In addition, the emotional strain of divorce is often such that people become somewhat reckless about their spending and borrowing habits. If you do find yourself in this unfortunate position, my advice is that – at the earliest possible moment – you sit down and work out a **new budget**.

If you would like assistance with this, I would refer you to my website (www.moneydoctors.ie), where you will find a free, online monthly budget planner.

HOW YOUR SITUATION WILL HAVE CHANGED

Once you are legally divorced, your financial position in relation to succession, tax, pensions, insurance and social welfare will all have changed:

- Your **succession rights** will automatically be lost. However, if you have made specific bequests in your will to your former spouse, they will stand unless you change your will or make a new one.
- In terms of **income tax** your position is broadly the same as if you were simply legally separated (see Chapter 32). If there are legally enforceable maintenance payments, you can usually opt to be taxed either under the single assessment or separate assessment systems. Under the single assessment system, maintenance payments are tax deductible for the person paying them, and taxable for the person receiving them. If you decide to be taxed under the separate assessment system, then maintenance payments will be ignored for income tax purposes.
- Any transfer of assets made because of the divorce will be capital gains tax-free. However, after that point, transfers will no longer be exempt from capital gains tax.
- Any transfer of assets or gifts made as a result of the divorce settlement are exempt from capital acquisition tax. As with capital gains tax, once you are divorced, the spousal exemption for capital acquisitions tax no longer applies.

MAKING PROPER PENSION PROVISION

Pension rights can be a very important part of the financial arrangements resulting from a divorce. Indeed, for many married couples, their pension rights can be as valuable, if not more valuable, than the family home. For this reason, I strongly advise you to take expert advice when you separate.

In fact, the law recognises the vital importance and value of pension rights – as a result, spouses are *not allowed* to arrange a **pension adjustment order** between themselves. Only a court of law has the right to decide what happens to pension rights after a couple separates or divorces.

Deciding on the value of the pension is not easy. It will depend on the beneficiary's salary, type of pension scheme, level of contributions, prescribed benefits, years of service and scheme performance.

A court will not necessarily make any decision regarding pensions if it believes that the rest of the agreed settlement is fair to both parties. However, there are three things concerning pension benefits that divorcing couples should be aware of:

- A court can make orders about the pension benefits of either spouse.
- Normally any decisions about pensions will be made at the time of the divorce, but if this doesn't happen, either spouse can go back to court for a **pension adjustment order** at any time during the lifetime of the pension scheme member.
- A court can order that part of a pension is paid either to a spouse or to a dependent child.

THE MONEY DOCTOR SAYS ...

If you are getting divorced, do not rely solely on the services of a solicitor – call in one or more financial professionals to help with financial planning, tax planning and pension planning. It is vital to do this at the earliest possible opportunity. Email consultation@ moneydoctors.ie.

34

COPING WITH BEREAVEMENT

WHAT TO DO ABOUT THE MONEY SIDE OF THINGS WHEN SOMEONE CLOSE DIES

When somebody close to you dies, tax and other financial matters are obviously the last thing on your mind. If there are dependants involved, however, it may be necessary to tackle such matters with a degree of urgency. Even if dependants aren't involved, there is a legal obligation on the personal representative to carry out certain responsibilities within a reasonable period of time.

Making and executing a will, especially after purchasing a property, is probably the most important legal task a person should perform. Despite that fact, very few people during their lifetime actually execute a will. Many of us have a psychological or emotional difficulty addressing thoughts of a will, or meeting a solicitor or other persons to instruct the drafting of a will and then executing it. This aversion is understandable – there is little as stressful or as morbid as planning for one's own death. However, as anybody who has been touched by bereavement knows, creating a will during one's lifetime will in fact minimise the grief and distress felt by surviving relatives.

A will also guarantees that the affairs of a deceased person will be dispensed with and distributed far more urgently than someone who dies either without having made a will (intestate) or with an invalid will. A will thereby minimises stress for surviving loved ones.

A SHORT LIST OF DEFINITIONS

Below are plain English definitions of the various legal terms used when sorting out the affairs of someone who has died.

Deceased: The 'deceased' is the person who has died.

Administrator: Where the deceased hasn't appointed a personal representative (in his or her will), the person looking after the financial situation is known as the administrator.

Beneficiary: A beneficiary is someone who inherits either part or the whole of the deceased's estate.

Estate: The estate is all of the assets that the deceased person owned. This includes bank accounts, property, jewellery, stocks and shares, furniture and so on.

Personal representative: This is the person ultimately responsible for sorting out and finalising the deceased's affairs.

Executor: If the deceased has written a will, he or she will have appointed an executor to ensure that his or her wishes are carried out. Many people appoint several executors, and it is normal for the personal representative to be one of them.

Intestate: If the deceased did not write a will, they are said to have died 'intestate'. 'Intestacy' is the situation where no will exists. What happens to the assets where there is no will is set out in the 1965 Succession Act.

Succession Act: This piece of legislation sets down the requirements for a valid will. Under Irish law, a spouse and children are legally entitled to a certain share in the property of a deceased parent or spouse – whether a will has been made or not. As it currently stands, if there are children then the spouse's share, by legal right, is at least one third of the estate. Where there are no children, the spouse is entitled to at least one half of the estate.

Trustee: If there is some reason why some or all of the deceased's assets cannot be distributed immediately to the beneficiaries, then the will may provide for certain assets or property to be held 'in trust'. This situation might arise, for example, if the deceased was leaving something to someone who was under the age of 18. The person whose responsibility it is to look after such property or assets is called the trustee. Many people appoint more than one trustee in their will.

Will: This is the legal document in which the deceased set out his or her wishes regarding his or her assets.

When there is a will

If there is a valid will, the following rules apply:
- On the death of a **married person with no children**, their surviving spouse is entitled to one-half of the deceased's estate.
- On the death of a **married person with children**, their surviving spouse is entitled to a one-third of the deceased's estate.
- The spouse is legally entitled to the appropriate share regardless of the actual terms of the will. The fact that the parties may have lived

apart for many years does not of itself affect their entitlements under the Act.

WHEN THERE IS NO WILL OR NO VALID WILL

If there is no valid will, the following rules apply:

- On the death of a **married person with no children**, the surviving spouse is entitled to the entirety of the deceased's estate.
- On the death of a **married person with children**, their surviving spouse is entitled to two-thirds of the deceased's estate and their children are entitled to the remaining one-third.
- If a **single person** or **widowed person** passes away without having made a valid will, their next of kin inherits their estate.

THE RIGHT OF THE SPOUSE TO INHERIT

A spouse, i.e. somebody who is legally married to another person, is entitled to share in the estate of that person on their death regardless of any will.

If a person has made a will and passes away, regardless of what is mentioned in that will (e.g. entire estate left to a third party), the spouse is entitled to one-half of the deceased's estate if there are no children.

If a person has died having made a will with a spouse and children, the spouse is entitled to one-third of the deceased's estate.

The spouse is also entitled to a portion of the family home, namely the place where the husband and wife normally resided prior to the death.

However, note that the right to a portion of the family home does not exceed the legal right share (i.e. one half if there are no children; one third if there are children). For example:

Mr and Mrs Murphy are legally married. Mr Murphy makes a will. They have no children and live in a house that is registered in Mr Murphy's sole name.

Mr Murphy dies, and when his will is read it appears that he has left everything to charity.

The value of Mr Murphy's estate is €2 million. Regardless of Mr Murphy's will, his spouse is entitled to:

- the family home; *and*

- one half of Mr Murphy's estate (including the family home).

If in this example, Mr and Mrs Murphy had children, Mrs Murphy would be entitled to only one third of the value of the estate (including the family home).

STATUS OF CHILDREN UNDER A WILL

If a party dies leaving children and no surviving spouse, these children will be deemed to be the next of kin of the deceased and entitled to share in the estate of the deceased.

However, they are only entitled to share in the estate of the deceased because they are the next of kin of the deceased for legal purposes.

It is a common misconception that an individual has an obligation to their children to leave a portion of their estate to them. Unlike a wife or husband (spouse), children over the age of 18 have no right to share in the estate of their parents and rank as beneficiaries of the estate of a parent purely in their position as next of kin.

A child over the age of 18 of a deceased person who has been disinherited in a will may challenge this will in the courts only on the grounds that the parent failed during their lifetime to make proper provision for the child.

A child has a right to challenge the will of a parent, but this does not mean that a parent has an obligation under law to leave anything to a child in their will. Irish children beware!

In other words, a party may make a will wherein they endeavour to disinherit their spouse and children, but the spouse has an automatic right to share in the estate regardless of what is in the will. The children do not have such automatic right. However, if a party dies without making a will, the children may share in the estate of the deceased person by virtue of the fact that they are the next of kin.

NON-MARITAL CHILDREN

The status of children born to an individual outside marriage is exactly the same as children born inside marriage.

For example, a couple may have never married but have three children. If one of them does not make a will and passes away, the partner will not be entitled to any share in the estate of the deceased, but rather the children as next of kin will be entitled to a share. If, however, the deceased has made a will leaving everything to the surviving partner, and the children are over the age of 18, the children have no automatic right to share in the estate of the parent who has passed away.

The matter becomes even more complicated in the following example:

> A married couple have three children. One party to the marriage has
> a fourth child outside of the marriage with another party. This parent
> passes away without making a will: all four children as next of kin are
> entitled to a proportionate share in the estate of the deceased parent.

NON-MARITAL RELATIONSHIPS

Non-marital partners have no right to share in the estate of a deceased
partner. For example:

> A man and woman may have lived together all their lives as husband and
> wife (often referred to as a common-law husband or wife) and the male
> partner passes away without having made a will. The surviving partner
> has no right to share in the estate of the deceased, and the estate will be
> inherited by the next of kin of the deceased person, e.g. parents, siblings
> or perhaps even children.

THE ROLE OF THE PERSONAL REPRESENTATIVE

When someone dies, it usually becomes clear fairly quickly whether they
have left a will. If they have, this will list one or more executors, one of
whom will be appointed as the personal representative of the deceased.

If a personal representative has not been appointed in the will, or no
valid will is in existence, the courts will appoint an administrator to act as
a personal representative (usually the next of kin).

The personal representative should, within a reasonable period of time,
collect the deceased's assets, pay any debts and distribute the remaining
assets to the beneficiaries.

OBTAINING THE GRANT OF REPRESENTATION

The Grant of Representation (i.e., Grant of Probate or Letters of
Administration) is an Order from the High Court allowing the party to
whom the grant is issued to deal with the affairs of a deceased person. It
is effectively an authority from the Court for this person to step into the
shoes of the deceased person and carry out the wishes of the deceased
person if there is a will or, alternatively, deal with the estate as per the
law of the land if there is no will.

A Grant of Representation allows the personal representative to execute documents for the sale, lease or remortgage of property, for the transfer of property to other members of the family who may inherit under the will or the law, to close bank accounts, transfer money and discharge debts.

In order to obtain the Grant, clearance must be sought from the Revenue Commissioners.

THE IMPORTANCE OF NOTIFYING THE TAX OFFICE

Prior to obtaining the Grant of Representation from the Probate Office, the Personal Representative must settle the deceased's **tax affairs**. Before financial institutions can release money, the personal representative must apply to the Capital Taxes Office of the Revenue Commissioners for something called a **Letter of Clearance** – effectively stating that all taxes have been paid to date, or are in the process of being paid. Without this document, banks, building societies, credit unions, insurance companies and other financial institutions are prohibited by law from releasing any monies, other than those held in the joint names of the deceased and his or her surviving spouse.

The application to the Revenue Commissioners will also contain details of the beneficiaries to the estate of the deceased person.

The Probate Office will not release a Grant until such time as the **Tax Clearance Certificate** or
Letter of Clearance from the Revenue Commissioners has been delivered, not just addressing the tax affairs of the deceased but also the tax affairs of the beneficiaries to the estate.

What the personal representative could be liable for

If the personal representative makes payments or passes assets to the beneficiaries of the estate without paying any outstanding tax liabilities, he or she will be liable to pay the tax out of his or her own pocket. By the same token if, as personal representative, you fail to claim a tax rebate due to the deceased, then the beneficiaries will be entitled to come after you for this money.

If the deceased was an employee, there may be a PAYE tax rebate due. This can be arranged by asking the deceased's employer to send a **Form P45** to the tax office. If, on the other hand, the deceased was self-employed, you will need to file an outstanding income tax return and business accounts to the deceased's tax office. You may also need to deal with outstanding VAT and PRSI matters.

Before the Probate Office can process the application for the Grant of Representation, they will require a certified **Revenue Affidavit** from the Capital Taxes Office. It is the responsibility of the personal representative to provide the Revenue Commissioners with a Revenue Affidavit. The Revenue Affidavit requires the personal representative to supply:

- full details of the deceased's assets and liabilities;
- information about assets passing outside of the will; and
- details of the beneficiaries and the value of the benefits taken.

THE BENEFITS OF JOINT OWNERSHIP

Regardless of the law in relationship to intestacy or the will drafted by an individual, the **Rule of Joint Ownership** is extremely important. Joint Ownership effectively takes precedence over either the law or the will.

Under law, two parties or more can own property in two ways. They can own it as **Tenants in Common** or by **Joint Tenancy**. When two parties or more are said to own property as Tenants in Common, they are said to own shares in that property. For example:

> Mr Murphy and Mr Smith buy a house as **Tenants in Common**. They own a half share each. On the death of either person, their share is passed on to that person's devisees or heirs, either by will or by intestate succession.

If, in our example above, Mr Murphy and Mr Smith buy a property and own the same as **Joint Tenants**, they do not own shares in the property, but rather they own the property jointly. If Mr Smith were to die, Mr Murphy would be the surviving/remaining owner of the property, and would be deemed to automatically inherit the property.

> If, for example, Mr Murphy, Mr Smith and Mr Jones were to purchase a property as **Joint Tenants** and Mr Smith were to pass away, Mr Murphy and Mr Jones would be the surviving joint owners. If Mr Jones were then to pass away Mr Murphy would be the remaining owner of the property.

Joint Ownership is important in relation to family financial planning. If a husband and wife have bank accounts in joint names, they do not own shares in this bank account but rather they own the bank account jointly. If the husband or wife pass away, the surviving spouse is said to be the surviving or remaining owner of the property, i.e. the bank account.

The same concept applies to all property, including the family home. If a family home is held in joint names, neither the husband nor wife own a share of the property, but rather they own the property jointly. If one party passes away the other is deemed to be the surviving owner of the property.

Regardless of any will made, if property is held jointly it cannot be severed.

HOW IS IT THAT ASSETS CAN PASS OUTSIDE OF THE WILL OR INTESTACY?

This is best explained by an example. The deceased may have taken out a life insurance policy or pension scheme in which the beneficiaries have been named. Under these circumstances, the insurance or pension company would pay the beneficiaries directly without any reference to a will or estate.

THE MONEY DOCTOR SAYS ...

- Sorting out the financial dealings of someone who has passed on is an emotional business. Help whoever will be looking after your affairs by making a proper will and keeping a file somewhere containing all your financial documents.

- Many parties believe that there is no necessity to make a will as they are happy to allow their spouse or their next of kin inherit as per the Succession Act rules. However, a will should *always* be made – this means that the estate is distributed more quickly, and also distributed in accordance with your wishes. There may be relatives or others you may want to acknowledge. Remember it really is a simple process – you will need two independent witnesses (who cannot gain from the will) and a nominated person to execute your wishes (executor/executrix), then date the will and sign it.

- It is extremely important if you are involved in a non-marital relationship that you ensure you have proper wills drafted to ensure inheritance for your surviving partner and your or their children.

- It is also important to take professional and perhaps legal advice in relation to the drafting and execution of a will, especially where there are complications. Many homemade wills can be ineffective and can often lead to further confusion after death. Remember: the bulk of wealth in Ireland is in property – a solicitor will be required to effect the transfer of ownership.

- Another reason to make a will – you can specify who your personal representative is, the person charged with the responsibility of dealing with your affairs after your death. This way, you will avoid any application to the courts to appoint somebody who is inappropriate for that purpose.

• Many people apply to the Revenue Commissioners and the Probate Office to be appointed as the personal representative of the deceased themselves. Both the Revenue Commissioners and the Probate Office are extremely co-operative when dealing with members of the public. Again, depending on the complexity of the estate, legal accounting and financial advice should be sought prior to contact with these offices.

• Ensure that all family and marital property is held jointly, including the family home – it is better for all concerned.

If involved in a non-marital relationship, both partners should ensure that all property is held *jointly*, so that the death of one partner will ensure the other partner inherits.

35

MARP, PERSONAL INSOLVENCY AND BANKRUPTCY

In September 2013, the Insolvency Service of Ireland came into being, along with Personal Insolvency Arrangements (PIAs) and Personal Insolvency Practitioners (PIPs). While the flow of resolved debts since then has not been as plentiful as expected from the banks and the PIPs points of view, at least the mechanism is now in place. Dignity and hope can be restored to lives brought crashing down to Earth, primarily from the property collapse.

Until recent years, declaring bankruptcy in Ireland was not only regarded as a slight on your character, but you were also banned for 12 years from running a business or borrowing, at least in your own name. In the UK, there are 50,000 bankruptcies every year, while in the US, it is over one million annually!

Very simply, when you do not have sufficient income to service a debt, and you have no assets to sell to repay that debt, the creditor can bring you to court and have a 'judgment' served against you. This effectively means:

- It stays there against your credit record on Irish Credit Bureau (www.icb.ie – for €6 you can order the credit report on yourself).
- If you repay what is owed, a 'satisfaction' is registered.
- But the judgment is recorded and remains there on your credit history for life.
- Borrowing again from a financial institution or creditor with a judgment against you is extremely unlikely.
- The final procedure, when you are unable or unwilling to repay, is bankruptcy.

In the UK, the Insolvency Act 1986 brought into effect a real workable alternative to bankruptcy proceedings, known as the Individual Voluntary Arrangement (IVA). This process, which has limited court involvement, ensures a cheaper, more expeditious distribution of the debtor's assets to his creditors than under bankruptcy. It also provides greater flexibility to both debtor and creditor alike, and offers a possibility of reviving a previously unsuccessful business. It offers the debtor an opportunity to come to some arrangement with his creditors and to continue in business, which is not possible under bankruptcy. The arrangement must be implemented by a supervisor, who is usually a licensed insolvency practitioner, accountant or solicitor, and who is usually empowered to realise the debtor's assets and distribute the proceeds amongst the creditors in the priority set down by law.

Bankruptcy is defined as 'a law for the benefit and relief of creditors and their debtors in cases where the latter are unable or unwilling to pay their debts'. The procedure is instigated either by the debtor himself filing for bankruptcy or by an aggrieved creditor petitioning the courts.

Recent Irish legislative changes saw a reduction of the period for automatic discharge from bankruptcy from 12 years to 3 years, and then to the current 1 year, through the Personal Insolvency Bill published in June 2012. However, as then Minister for Justice Alan Shatter stated on the launch, 'This Bill does not relieve solvent debtors of their responsibility to meet their contractual obligations.'

The reform of Ireland's bankruptcy laws was a condition of the EU/IMF bailout agreement, and the 1 year discharge period is in line with recommendations made by the Law Reform Commission (LRC) in 2010.

The last 10 savage years have changed all government thinking on debt. First of all, the lenders and the Central Bank recognised the need to help borrowers, especially with their home loans. As Taoiseach Enda Kenny said, 'It's not your fault.' House prices dropped by up to 70% while unemployment rose to 14.8%. Even if properties could be sold, householders were staring at massive deficits they were unable to repay, plus they still had to live somewhere.

THE FIRST STEPS IN THE PROCESS

The first initiative was the **Mortgage Arrears Resolution Process** (MARP), a system for helping mortgage holders with their arrears, introduced in December 2010. This was updated on 1 July 2013, giving lenders greater power in dealing with struggling borrowers. Changes included the abolition of the limit of three successful unsolicited communications per month – it is now limitless 'within reason' – and also, more alarmingly, the ability of the lender to remove customers' valuable tracker rates and apply standard variable rates.

The Central Bank's Code of Conduct on Mortgage Arrears (CCMA) sets out the framework that lenders **must** use when dealing with borrowers in mortgage arrears or in pre-arrears. It requires lenders to handle all such cases sympathetically and positively, with the objective at all times being to help people meet their mortgage obligations.

Under the CCMA, lenders must operate a Mortgage Arrears Resolution Process when dealing with customers in arrears or pre-arrears.

The 5 steps of the MARP are:

1. Communication
2. Financial information
3. Assessment
4. Resolution
5. Appeals

The process requires lenders to wait 8 months before taking legal action on arrears. However, this requirement does not apply if a borrower is not cooperating with the lender.

Regardless of how long it takes your lender to assess your case, and provided that you are cooperating, you must be given 3 months' notice before they can commence legal proceedings where either:

- your lender does not offer you an alternative repayment arrangement; or
- you do not accept an alternative repayment arrangement offered to you.

This gives you time to consider other options, such as voluntary surrender, voluntary sale or a Personal Insolvency Arrangement.

If you are classified as not cooperating, your lender may commence legal proceedings immediately. Before you can be classified as not cooperating, your lender must first write to you and warn you that this might happen, and tell you what steps you need to take to avoid this.

1. Communication

A mortgage arrears problem arises as soon as you fail to make a mortgage repayment, or only make a partial mortgage repayment, on the date it is due.

If the arrears remain outstanding 31 days from this date, the lender must inform you in writing of the status of the mortgage account. This letter must include full details of the payment(s) missed and the total amount now in arrears. It must also explain that your arrears are now being dealt with under the MARP; the importance of cooperating with the lender; the consequences of non-cooperation; and the impact of missed repayments/repossession on your credit rating. You should also receive an information booklet on MARP and contact details for MABS.

For as long as you are in arrears, the lender must give you a written update on the status of your account every 3 months.

If no alternative payment scheme is arranged and your arrears continue to a third consecutive month, you should be warned of the possibility of legal action that could lead to repossession, and the likely costs involved.

2. Financial information

Lenders must provide a standard financial statement (SFS) to obtain financial information from a borrower in arrears or in pre-arrears, so that they can assess your financial position and identify the best course of action. The Central Bank has developed a standard format for this and, since 1 July 2011, all lenders must use this SFS, together with a guide to its completion. When providing the financial statement, the lender must ensure that you understand the MARP process. They must tell you about the availability of independent advice (from MABS, for example) to help in completing the SFS.

The lender must pass the completed SFS to its Arrears Support Unit (ASU) for assessment.

You may be required to provide supporting documentation to verify the information in the SFS.

3. Assessment

The lender's ASU must assess the completed SFS and examine your case on its individual merits. The ASU must base its assessment of your case on your full circumstances. These include your personal circumstances; overall indebtedness; information provided in the standard financial statement; current repayment capacity; and previous payment history.

4. Resolution

The lender must explore all options for alternative repayment arrangements. These options must include:
- an interest-only arrangement for a specified period;
- an arrangement to pay interest and part of the normal capital element for a specified period;
- deferring payment of all or part of the usual repayment for a period;
- extending the term of the mortgage;
- changing the type of the mortgage, except in the case of tracker mortgages;
- capitalising the arrears and interest; and

- any voluntary scheme to which the lender has signed up, e.g. a Deferred Interest Scheme.

Lenders must not require a borrower to change from an existing tracker mortgage to another mortgage type as part of an alternative arrangement offered to the borrower in arrears or pre-arrears, unless none of the options that would allow the borrower to retain the tracker interest rate are sustainable for the borrower's individual circumstances.

If this is the case, the lender may offer the borrower an alternative repayment arrangement that requires the borrower to change from an existing tracker mortgage to another mortgage type, provided that:

- an alternative repayment arrangement is affordable for the borrower; and
- it is a long-term sustainable solution, consistent with the Central Bank of Ireland policy on sustainability.

When the lender offers an alternative repayment arrangement, they must give you a clear written explanation of the arrangement. As well as the basic details of the new repayment amount and the term of the arrangement, the lender must explain its impact on the mortgage term, the balance outstanding and the existing arrears, if any.

The lender must give details of: how interest will be applied to your mortgage loan account as a result of the arrangement; how the arrangement will be reported to the Irish Credit Bureau and the impact of this on your credit rating; and your right to appeal the lender's decision, including how to submit an appeal.

The lender must also advise you to take appropriate independent legal and/or financial advice. The lender must monitor the arrangement on an ongoing basis and formally review its appropriateness for you at least every 6 months. This review must include checking with you whether your circumstances have changed since the start of the arrangement or since the last review.

If an alternative arrangement is not agreed

It may not be possible for you and your lender to agree on an alternative repayment. If the lender is not willing to offer you an alternative repayment arrangement, they must give the reasons in writing. If they do offer an arrangement, you may choose not to accept it. In both of these cases, the lender must inform you in writing about other options, including voluntary surrender, trading down or voluntary sale, and the implications for you of each option. They must also inform you of your right to make an appeal to their Appeals Board about the ASU's decision, the lender's treatment of your case under the MARP, and their compliance with the requirements of the CCMA.

If you breach an alternative arrangement

If you cease to adhere to the terms of an alternative repayment arrangement, the lender's Arrears Support Unit must formally review your case, including the standard financial statement, immediately.

5. Appeals

The lender's Appeals Board will consider any appeals that you submit and will independently review the ASU's decision, the lender's treatment of your case under the MARP and the lender's compliance with the requirements of the CCMA.

The lender must allow you a reasonable period to consider submitting an appeal. This must be at least 20 business days from the date you receive notification of the ASU's decision.

The Appeals Board will be made up of three of the lender's senior personnel who have not yet been involved in your case. At least one member of the Appeals Board must be independent of the management team and must not be involved in lending matters.

There must be a written procedure for handling appeals, to include points of contact, timescale, etc.

Repossession proceedings

The lender must not apply to the courts to commence legal action for repossession of your property until every reasonable effort has been made to agree an alternative arrangement. If you are cooperating with the lender, they must wait at least 8 months from the date your arrears were classified as a MARP case (31 days after the first missed repayment) before applying to the courts.

When a lender is calculating the 8-month period, it must exclude any period during which you are complying with the terms of an alternative repayment arrangement, appealing to the Appeals Board or complaining to the Financial Services Ombudsman under the CCMA. It must also exclude the period during which you can consider making an appeal.

For pre-arrears cases, the 8-month period must exclude the period between your first contact about the pre-arrears situation and the setting up of an alternative repayment arrangement.

The 8-month period does not apply if you do not cooperate with the lender; or if you perpetrate a fraud on the lender; or if there is a breach of contract by you other than the existence of arrears.

Regardless of how long it takes your lender to assess your case, and provided that you are co-operating, you must be given three months' notice before they can commence legal proceedings where your lender does not offer you an alternative repayment arrangement or you do not accept an alternative repayment arrangement offered to you.

The lender or its legal advisers must notify you in writing before it applies to the Courts to start any legal action on repossession.

Your property may be repossessed either by voluntary agreement or by court order. Even if court proceedings are started, the lender must still try to maintain contact with you to seek an agreement on repayments, and must put legal proceedings on hold if agreement is reached.

The lender must explain to you that, if the property is sold and the sale price does not cover the amount you owe, you are still liable for the rest of the amount you owe.

If your property is repossessed and sold, the lender must write to you promptly with the following information:

- The balance outstanding on your mortgage loan account
- Details and amounts of any costs arising from the disposal that have been added to the account
- Interest rate to be charged on the remaining balance

Having gone through the above process, and perhaps through no fault of your own, you may be one of the many who simply have not the wherewithal to maintain your commitments. The old saying 'you can't get blood from a stone' rings true for many who would be happy to divest themselves of assets if this would repay their debts. Unfortunately, these assets, even if sold, may not repay the debts.

PERSONAL INSOLVENCY BILL 2012

In January 2012, the government announced plans to launch the Personal Insolvency Bill later in the year. This would address the outdated bankruptcy laws and allow dignity back into debtors' lives by creating closure on debts they are unable to repay via a non-judicial process.

Under the proposals unveiled by Justice Minister Alan Shatter and published on 29 June 2012, the new Personal Insolvency Service was established to process three separate types of non-judicial arrangement. But how do they work in practice?

Debt Relief Notice (DRN)

This provides for the forgiveness of **unsecured debt** (such as an overdraft or credit card debt) **now under** €35,000 for debtors with little or no capacity to pay off debts – no assets, no income. The debtor applies to the Insolvency Service, who then examine the income and outgoings of the applicant and decide whether a DRN is appropriate. If granted, a 3-year moratorium period applies, during which creditors cannot pursue action against the debtor for the debts covered by the DRN. At the end of the moratorium period, the applicant is discharged from the debts. Applications for a DRN must be submitted on behalf of the debtor by an authorised Approved Intermediary (AI) body, e.g. the Money Advice and Budgeting Service (MABS).

This Approved Intermediary would:

- advise the debtor as to their options and the qualifying requirements;
- assist in the preparation of the necessary Prescribed or Standard Financial Statement (SFS), which must be verified by means of a statutory declaration – plus include any other required documentation; and
- transmit the debtor's application to the Insolvency Service to have a DRN approved if the qualifying criteria are met.

General conditions for application for a DRN:

- Debtors would have qualifying debts of €35,000 or less.
- Debtors would not be eligible where 25 percent or more of the qualifying debts were incurred in the 6 months preceding the application.
- Debts qualifying for inclusion in a DRN are most likely to be unsecured debts: e.g. credit card, personal loan, catalogue payments, etc.
- Debtors will have a net monthly disposable income of €60 or less after provision for 'reasonable' living expenses and payments in respect of excluded debts (if any).
- Debtors would hold assets (separately or jointly) to the value of €400 or less. There is an exemption from the asset test for essential household appliances, tools and equipment required for employment or business and one motor vehicle up to the value of €1,200.
- Debtors must act in good faith and co-operate fully.
- Debts excluded from a DRN include taxes, court fines, family maintenance payments and service charges arrears.

After the Insolvency Service has received the application, and is satisfied with same, they issue a certificate to that effect to the court. The court then consider the application and, if satisfied, issue the DRN and notify the Insolvency Service.

During the DRN period, creditors may not initiate or prosecute legal proceedings, seek to recover payment for a debt, recover goods or contact the debtor.

A DRN lasts 3 years from its date of issue. At the end of this period (and subject to no other action), the DRN terminates, the qualifying debts are discharged and the debtor is removed from the Register of Debt Relief Notices.

Only one DRN per lifetime is permitted, and not within 5 years of completion of a Debt Settlement Arrangement (DSA) or Personal Insolvency Arrangement (PIA). There is a restriction on the debtor from applying for credit over €650 during the DRN supervision period without informing the creditor of his/her status.

The debtor must inform the authorised intermediary and the Insolvency Service of any material change in their financial circumstances. So as not to reduce the incentive to seek employment following approval of a DRN, there is provision for the debtor to repay a portion of the debts in circumstances where his or her financial situation improves. These circumstances include the receipt of gifts or windfalls over €500 (e.g. the Lotto) or where the debtor's income has increased by over €250 per month. The debtor will transmit funds to the Insolvency Service to be paid on an equal basis to the listed creditors.

If a debtor makes repayments totalling 50 per cent of the original debt, they will be deemed to have satisfied the debt in full. The DRN will then cease to have effect, the debtor will be removed from the Register and all of the debts will be discharged.

2. Debt Settlement Arrangement (DSA)

This provision also covers **unsecured debt**, but is concerned with debts above €35,000. In this arrangement, the Insolvency Service design a plan by which the debtor pays a specified amount to creditors over a five-year period – with a possible agreed extension to 6 years – after which the debts are considered discharged. The creditors are required to approve the DSA.

The application for a DSA must be made through a personal insolvency practitioner (PIP) appointed by the debtor. The PIP must:

- advise the debtor as to their options in regard to insolvency processes.
- assist in the preparation of the necessary Prescribed or Standard Financial Statement (SFS), which must be verified by means of a statutory declaration, plus any other required documentation.
- Apply to the Insolvency Service for a **Protective Certificate** in respect of the preparation of a DSA if the qualifying criteria are met. A joint application is permitted where the particular circumstances warrant such an approach. The debtor must normally be resident in the State or have a close connection. Only one application for a DSA in a lifetime is permitted.

Certain debts are excluded from the DSA, including Court fines in respect of a criminal offence. In addition, certain other debts are also excluded, such as family maintenance payments, taxes, local authority charges and service charges, unless the relevant creditor agrees otherwise. In addition, any debt that would have a preferential status in bankruptcy will also have a preferential status in a DSA.

The Insolvency Service, if satisfied as to the application, issues a certificate to that effect and furnishes the certificate and supporting documentation to the court. The court considers the application and, subject to the creditors' right to appeal, if satisfied, issues the Protective Certificate and notifies the Insolvency Service. Once approval is granted, the Protective Certificate is registered in the Register of Protective Certificates and a 'stand-still' period of 70 days applies to permit the PIP to propose a DSA to the listed creditors. That period may, on application to the court, be extended, for no more than a further 40 days. The PIP informs the creditors of the issue of the Protective Certificate.

Following the issue of the Protective Certificate, the creditors may not initiate or prosecute legal proceedings, seek to recover payment for a debt, recover goods or contact the debtor. The rights of secured creditors are unaffected.

A DSA proposal does not require the debtor to dispose of or cease to occupy their principal private residence – their home – where this is involved. If the DSA proposal is accepted by 65% in value of the creditors present and voting, it is binding on all creditors. The PIP informs the Insolvency Service who then transmit the agreement to the relevant court for approval. If satisfied and if no objection is received by it within 10 days, the court approves the DSA and notifies the Insolvency Service, which then registers it in the Register of Debt Settlement Agreements, whereupon it comes into effect. The PIP then administers the DSA for its duration.

The Insolvency Service has no role in the negotiation and agreement of a DSA.

Unless otherwise agreed, the default position is that creditors are paid on an equal or proportionate basis. Conditions attach to the conduct of the debtor during the DSA. There is provision for an annual review of the financial circumstances of the debtor, and the agreement can if necessary be altered or terminated. On the termination or failure of the DSA, a debtor could risk an application for adjudication in bankruptcy.

At the satisfactory conclusion of the DSA, all debts covered by it are discharged.

3. Personal Insolvency Arrangement (PIA)

This arrangement is designed to cover both secured and unsecured debt, and will be appropriate if the Insolvency Service conclude that a five-year DSA would not be sufficient to make the debtor solvent. Under this provision, a portion of the unsecured debt is written off and the remainder repaid over a 6-year period, possibly extended to 7 years. The secured debt, a mortgage for example, is also written down and its repayment period extended, reducing the repayments further. The creditors are required to approve the PIA. Should the debtors' financial circumstances improve over the course of the PIA, they are obliged to notify the Insolvency Service, now under interim Chief Executive Chris Lehane.

The application for a PIA or a DSA must be made through a personal insolvency practitioner (PIP), appointed by the debtor.

- The PIP must advise the debtor as to their options in regard to insolvency processes. A debtor may only propose a PIA if he or she is cash flow **insolvent** (i.e. unable to pay his or her debts in full as they fall due), and there is no likelihood that within a period of 5 years the debtor will become solvent.
- The PIP must assist in the preparation of the necessary Prescribed or Standard Financial Statement (SFS), which must be verified by means of a statutory declaration, along with any other required documentation.
- The PIP may apply to the Insolvency Service for a **Protective Certificate** in respect of the preparation of a PIA, if the qualifying criteria are met (which include cooperation with the secured creditor in respect of the debtor's principal private residence, under a mortgage arrears process approved or required by the Central

Bank). A joint application or an interlocking PIA can be permitted where particular circumstances warrant it. The debtor must normally be resident in the State or have a close connection. Only one application for a PIA in a lifetime is permitted.

Certain debts are excluded from the PIA, including court fines, family maintenance payments, taxes, local authority charges and service charges, unless the relevant creditor agrees otherwise. In addition, any debt that would have a preferential status in bankruptcy will also have a preferential status in a PIA.

If the Insolvency Service is satisfied with the application, they issue a certificate to that effect and furnish the certificate and supporting documentation to the court. The court considers the application and, if satisfied and subject to the creditors' right to appeal, issues the Protective Certificate and notifies the Insolvency Service.

Once approval is granted, the Protective Certificate is registered in the Register of Protective Certificates and a 'stand-still' period of 70 days applies to permit the PIP to propose a PIA to the listed creditors. That period may, on application to the court, be extended, for no more than a further 40 days. The PIP will inform the creditors of the issue of the Protective Certificate.

Under the Protective Certificate, creditors may not initiate or prosecute legal proceedings, seek to recover payment for a debt, recover goods, enforce security or contact the debtor.

A PIA proposal does not require the debtor to dispose of or cease to occupy their principal private residence where this is involved. There are certain specific protections for secured creditors, including a 'claw back' in the event of a subsequent sale of a mortgaged property where the mortgage has been written down.

If the PIA proposal is accepted, it is binding on all creditors. A PIA must be supported by at least 65% (it was 75% originally) of all creditors voting at the creditors' meeting – based on the value of the total of both secured and unsecured debt owed to those voting creditors – and more than 50% of secured creditors voting (based on the lesser of value of the security underpinning the secured debt or the amount of that debt) and 50% of unsecured creditors (based on the amount of the debt).

The PIP informs the Insolvency Service of the agreement, and the Service then transmits the agreement to the relevant court for approval. If satisfied and if no objection is received by it within 10 days, the court approves the PIA and notifies the Insolvency Service. It is registered in the Register of Personal Insolvency Arrangements and it comes into effect. The PIP then administers the PIA for its duration.

Conditions attach to the conduct of the debtor during the PIA. There is provision for an annual review of the financial circumstances of the debtor, and the agreement can if necessary be altered or terminated. On the termination or failure of the PIA, a debtor could risk an application for adjudication in bankruptcy.

The Insolvency Service has no role in the negotiation or agreement of a PIA.

At the satisfactory conclusion of the PIA, all unsecured debts covered by it are discharged. Secured debts are only discharged at the conclusion of the PIA, and only to the extent specified in the PIA. To the extent that they are not provided for in the PIA, all other debt obligations remain.

BANKRUPTCY

The Personal Insolvency Bill 2012 made a number of amendments to the law, introducing a more enlightened, less punitive and less costly approach to bankruptcy. These amendments continue the reform of bankruptcy law begun in the Civil Law (Miscellaneous Provisions) Act 2011. The main new provisions are as follows:

- A creditor bankruptcy summons:
    - The new minimum amount for a creditor or combined non-partner creditors petition for bankruptcy is €20,000. (The limits were €1,900 for a creditor and €1,300 for combined non-partner creditors.)
    - Fourteen days' notice must be provided to ensure that a bankruptcy summons is not brought prematurely by a creditor, so as to allow the debtor to consider other options such as a Debt Settlement Arrangement (DSA) or a Personal Insolvency Arrangement (PIA).
- Presenting a petition for bankruptcy: the creditor must show evidence of a debt of more than €20,000 (the limit was €1,900). Where a debtor presents a petition, they must:
    - swear an affidavit that they have made reasonable efforts to make use of alternatives to bankruptcy, such as a Debt Settlement Arrangement or Personal Insolvency Arrangement; and
    - present a statement of affairs, which must disclose that their debts exceed their assets by more than €20,000.
- Adjudication of a creditor's petition for bankruptcy: the court will be required to consider the assets and liabilities of the debtor

and assess whether it may be appropriate to adjourn proceedings to allow the debtor to attempt to enter into a Debt Settlement Arrangement or Personal Insolvency Arrangement.

- Excepted articles: the maximum value of household furniture or tools or equipment required by a bankrupt for a trade or occupation is increased from €3,100 to €6,000.
- Avoidance of fraudulent preferences and certain transactions made before adjudication in bankruptcy: the period of 1 year has been extended to 3 years.
- Avoidance of certain settlements: the time periods in regard to certain voluntary settlements of property made before adjudication in bankruptcy is extended from 2 years to 3 years.
- Discharge from bankruptcy: the following new provisions apply:
  - The automatic discharge from bankruptcy after 1 year from the date of adjudication (reduced from 3 years).
  - Bankruptcies existing for 1 year or more at the time of commencement of the Act will be automatically discharged after a further six months have elapsed, this further time to allow for any creditor objection.
  - The bankrupt's unrealised property will remain vested in the Official Assignee in Bankruptcy after discharge from bankruptcy and the discharged bankrupt will be under a duty to co-operate with the Official Assignee in the realisation and distribution of such of his or her property as is vested in the Official Assignee.
  - The Official Assignee or a creditor may apply to the court to object to the discharge of a person from bankruptcy. The grounds for such an objection are that the debtor has failed to co-operate with the Official Assignee or has hidden or failed to disclose income or assets. The court may suspend the discharge pending further investigation or extend the period before discharge of the bankrupt up to a maximum of 8 years from the date of adjudication.
  - The court may order a bankrupt to make payments from his or her income or other assets to the Official Assignee for the benefit of his or her creditors. In making such an order, the court must have regard to the reasonable living expenses of the bankrupt and his or her family. The court may vary a bankruptcy payment order where there has been a material change in the circumstances of the discharged bankrupt. Such an order must be applied for before the discharge from bankruptcy and may operate for no more than 5 years.

There are no prohibitions in the Bankruptcy Act 1988 regarding restrictions on the nature of employment or profession of a person adjudicated bankrupt. Such prohibitions, where they exist, are contained in sectoral legislation – e.g. in the electoral acts regarding to membership of Dáil Éireann or in contracts of employment, e.g. in the legal profession.

With effect from 3 December 2013, the Official Assignee in Bankruptcy is now based within the Insolvency Service of Ireland.

Limits on usage within the Personal Insolvency Act 2012

You can be involved in only one of the 3 mechanisms (DRN, DSA or PIA) or in the bankruptcy process at any one time. If you use one of these 4 processes, you will generally have to wait some years before applying to use another.

You may use each of the 3 mechanisms only once in your lifetime. (There is no such limit on bankruptcy, but it would be rare for anyone to go bankrupt twice.)

Running up debts

You must not deliberately stop paying (or underpay) your creditors while these procedures are being set up, and this may make your application ineligible.

Provision of information

You will have to complete a Prescribed Financial Statement, giving full and honest information about your financial circumstances. The required information is specified in the regulations. You will have to sign a Statutory Declaration to this effect. You must act in good faith and co-operate fully with the process.

You will have to give your written consent to the accessing of certain personal data held by banks and other financial institutions so that your financial situation can be verified. Government departments and agencies will have the power to release certain information about you.

Public registers

If you use any of these 3 mechanisms, your name and details will be published on a register that is accessible to the public. The success or failure of the process will also be recorded.

REGULATION OF PIPS

PIPs are authorised and supervised by the Insolvency Service of Ireland (ISI). An individual may make an application to practice as a PIP if that individual:

- is a solicitor in respect of whom a practising certificate (within the meaning of the Solicitors Acts 1954 to 2011) is in force; or
- is a barrister at law called to the Bar of Ireland; or
- is a qualified accountant and a member of a prescribed accountancy body (within the meaning of section 4 of the Companies (Auditing and Accounting) Act 2003; or
- is a qualified financial advisor who holds a current qualification from the Life Insurance Association of Ireland (LIA), the Insurance Institute or the Institute of Bankers School of Professional Finance; or
- holds a qualification in law, business, finance or other appropriate similar qualification to the satisfaction of the Insolvency Service recognised to at least level 7 of the National Qualifications Framework by Quality and Qualifications Ireland (or equivalent).

They must also demonstrate to the satisfaction of the Insolvency Service that they have relevant knowledge and experience of, and have completed a course of study and passed an examination on, the law and practice generally as it applies in the State relating to the insolvency of individuals; and the Act.

Other stringent conditions are also imposed, such as a high level of professional indemnity insurance, operating systems capable of handling the book-keeping elements of the transactions, proven tax compliance, etc.

In May 2014, I was appointed a PIP by the Insolvency Service of Ireland. You can see my name and all the other PIP appointees through this link: http://www.isi.gov.ie/en/ISI/Pages/PIPs

HERE'S WHAT TO DO

For a **Debt Relief Notice** (DRN), your application must be made through an Approved Intermediary (AI). You can choose an AI from the Register of Approved Intermediaries published by the ISI. Several Money Advice and Budgeting Services offices (MABS) have been authorised as AIs. MABS operates a screening process to check if you satisfy the eligibility criteria for a DRN.

Before contacting MABS to be screened, you will need to assemble all the relevant information about your debts, assets, income and circumstances. Go to www.mabs.ie for advice and help on how to do this.

For a **Debt Settlement Arrangement** (DSA) or a **Personal Insolvency Arrangement** (PIA), you must apply through a Personal Insolvency Practitioner (PIP). See the link above for PIPs.

Further information is available from the ISI's helpline: 0761 06 4200, and from its website: www.isi.gov.ie.

36

NON-NATIONALS – A GUIDE TO LIVING IN IRELAND

Welcome, O life! I go to encounter for the millionth time the reality of experience and to forge in the smithy of my soul the uncreated conscience of my race ...

James Joyce, *A Portrait of the Artist as a Young Man* (1902)

As a young man of 22, I celebrated my first year as a banker – a cool term then – by being promoted to cashier status. The number 1 cashier in my bank branch. There were queues all the time during opening hours (then 10am to 12.30pm and 1.30pm to 3pm), so you had to have your wits about you.

One of the customers in my queue was a young woman whom I knew worked as a receptionist for a local company. I was looking forward to serving her for the first time. She gave me a sum of money to lodge into an account on behalf of the company she worked for and noticing her foreign accent, I asked her where she was from. She said, 'Russia.' 'How long have you been here?' I asked. 'Three years,' was her reply. I then said, if she didn't mind, what did she do before she came to Ireland? Her answer startled me: 'I was a rocket scientist.'

That was the moment when I realised that non-national working Europeans, Asians, Africans and South Americans arriving in our country have difficult hurdles to overcome despite their talents, intellect and qualifications held in their own country.

A non-national is a person who has decided to work or live in Ireland but was not born in Ireland or does not hold an Irish passport. To all non-nationals arriving in Ireland, welcome and thank you for choosing Ireland. This chapter is a guide to help and support you in all facets of living in this country.

In April 2016, there were 535,475 non-Irish nationals living in Ireland, a 1.6% decrease on the 2011 figure (544,357). The top six nationalities are Polish (122,515), British (103,113), Lithuanian (36,552), Romanian (29,106), Latvian (19,993) and Brazilian (13,640).

The proportion of the population who are non-Irish nationals has fallen from 12.2% in 2011 to 11.6% in 2016. This fall can in part be explained by the rise in the number of those with dual Irish nationality, who are classified as Irish in the census. Persons with dual-Irish nationality increased by 87.4% to 104,784 persons in 2016. The largest proportion was Irish-American, followed by Irish-UK and Irish-Polish.

There are many reasons why people come to Ireland apart from a holiday visit. They come to work, to set up businesses, to study, to join family members or to retire. Some non-EEA immigrants like the Irish education system or the fresh air. They invest their money into obtaining visas so they can migrate here to work or set up businesses.

Citizens of the following countries do not need a visa to live or work in Ireland:

All countries of the EU, plus Andorra, Antigua & Barbuda, Argentina, Australia, Bahamas, Barbados, Belize, Bolivia, Botswana, Brazil, Brunei, Canada, Chile, Costa Rica, Dominica, El Salvador, Fiji, Grenada, Guatemala, Guyana, Honduras, Hong Kong, Iceland, Israel, Japan, Kiribati, Lesotho, Liechtenstein, Macau (Special Admin. Region), Malaysia, Maldives, Mexico, Monaco, Nauru, New Zealand, Nicaragua, Norway, Panama, Paraguay, Saint Kitts & Nevis, Saint Lucia, Saint Vincent & the Grenadines, Samoa, San Marino, Seychelles, Singapore, Solomon Islands, South Africa, South Korea, Swaziland, Switzerland, Taiwan, Tonga, Trinidad & Tobago, Tuvalu, United Arab Emirates, United States of America, Uruguay, Vanuatu and Vatican City.

PERMISSION, STAMPS AND CONDITIONS

If your application for permission to stay in Ireland is successful, an immigration officer will put a stamp in your passport. This usually happens during a visit to a registration office. There are several types of stamp, and each indicates a type of permission, including what you can, and cannot, do in Ireland and the period you are allowed to stay.

If you break the conditions of your stamp, you may have to leave the country. The time you accumulate on certain stamps may be used to calculate your 'reckonable residence' (subject to conditions) if you apply for citizenship by naturalisation. For more information, go to www.inis.gov.ie/en/INIS/Pages/registration-stamps

Stamp 1: Issued to a non-EEA national who has received either an employment permit or a business permission.

Stamp 2: Issued to a non-EEA national student who is permitted to work for up to 20 hours a week during term and up to 40 hours a week during holidays. (The student must be attending a full-time course of at least a year which is recognised by the Department of Education and Science).

Stamp 2A: Issued to a non-EEA national student who is not permitted to work.

Stamp 3: Issued to a non-EEA national who is not permitted to work, (for example, a visitor, a tourist, a retired person).

Stamp 4: Issued to the following categories of people, all of whom are permitted to work without needing an employment permit or business permission:

- Spouses and dependents of Irish and EEA nationals
- People who have permission to remain on the basis of parentage of an Irish child
- Convention and Programme refugees
- Former asylum-seekers granted leave to remain
- Non-EEA nationals on intra-company transfer
- Temporary registered doctors
- Non-EEA nationals who have working visas or work authorisations.

Stamp 4 (EU FAM): Issued to non-EEA national family members of EU citizens who have exercised their right to move to and live in Ireland under the European Communities (Free Movement of Persons) Regulations 2006. People holding this stamp are permitted to work without needing an employment permit or business permission, and they can apply for a residence card under the Regulations.

Stamp 5: Issued to non-EEA nationals who have lived in Ireland for at least 8 years and who have been permitted by the Minister for Justice, Equality and Law Reform to remain in Ireland without condition as to time. People holding this stamp are permitted to work without needing an employment permit or business permission.

Stamp 6: Can be placed on the foreign passport of an Irish citizen who has dual citizenship, and who wants their entitlement to remain in Ireland to be endorsed on their foreign passport. This stamp certifies that the holder of the passport is permitted to remain in Ireland without condition.

BUSINESS IMMIGRATION PROGRAMMES

Ireland currently offers two business immigration programmes. The first is the **Immigrant Investor Programme** (IIP), which essentially Ireland's investor visa. Requirements include:

- A minimum net worth of €2 million.
- Investors and their immediate family enter Ireland on multi-entry visas and remain here for up to five years, with the possibility of ongoing renewal.
- Successful applicants do not have to live in Ireland to avail of the programme, but they must visit Ireland at least once per year.

The investment must be one of the following:

- **Enterprise Investment:** A minimum €1 million investment in a new or existing Irish businesses for a minimum of three years. The enterprise can be a start-up registered by the investor. The investment can be in a single Irish enterprise or spread over a number of enterprises. The enterprise must be registered and headquartered in Ireland and must support the creation or maintenance of employment.
- **Investment Fund:** A minimum of €1 million investment in an investment fund for at least three years. Investment funds must invest in Irish businesses and projects.
- **Real Estate Investment Trust** (REIT): A minimum investment of €2 million in any Irish REIT listed on the Irish Stock Exchange. The investment may be spread across a number of Irish REITs.
- **Endowment:** €500,000 to a public project benefiting the arts, sports, health, culture or education. The endowment can be €400,000 per investor if it is pooled by at least five individuals.

The second programme is the **Start-up Entrepreneur Programme** (STEP), which requires an innovative business idea and a minimum investment of €50,000 to come and set up a business in Ireland. Where more than one principal is involved in establishing the business, the minimum investment for the second and subsequent entrepreneurs will be €30,000 per principal.

Eligible start-up ventures must:

- introduce a new or innovative product or service to international markets;
- be involved in manufacturing or internationally traded services;
- be capable of creating 10 jobs in Ireland and realising €1 million in sales within three to four years of starting up;
- be led by an experienced management team;

- be headquartered and controlled in Ireland; and
- be less than five years old.

A 12-month immigration permission is available for foreign entrepreneurs attending incubators or innovation bootcamps in Ireland. The 12-month permission allows these entrepreneurs to prepare an application to the STEP, and thus provides an identifiable route for migrant entrepreneurs to move from the start-up to the realisation phase of their projects. This 12-month period will also be made available to non-EEA students who graduate with advanced STEM (Science, Technology, Engineering and Mathematics) degrees in Ireland and who wish to work on preparing an application for the STEP.

Both visa programmes are open to citizens of non-EU/EEA countries only, as EU/EEA citizens already have the freedom to move to Ireland and pursue their legitimate business goals in the country

You may be looking for international protection and intend to apply for refugee status or subsidiary protection. Before you come to Ireland, you need to know first of all whether or not you are entitled to live here. Your right to live in Ireland depends mainly on your nationality and what you intend to do when you come here.

After you have established whether or not you are entitled to come and live in Ireland, you will need other information about the formalities of living here. This guide is an overview of the main things, financial and otherwise, you need to know if you are proposing to come to Ireland to live.

With the demographics in Ireland changing over the next 30 years to an aging one – there will be 3 times the current number of citizens over the age of 66 by 2050 – we will need non-nationals to help support the economy through their work and entrepreneurial abilities. I personally extend a welcome to them all.

SO YOU HAVE ARRIVED IN IRELAND

Congratulations and welcome! As a citizen of the European Economic Area (EEA) or Switzerland, you are allowed to live in Ireland. The EEA consists of the 28 EU member states plus Iceland, Norway and Liechtenstein.

European Union (EU) citizens thinking of moving to Ireland, either temporarily or permanently, can enjoy the famous 'four freedoms' set out in the Treaty of Rome, namely the free movement of persons, goods, services and capital within the EU. The rights of EU citizens in Ireland are established and guaranteed.

If outside the EEA or Switzerland, there are various forms of residence rights that will allow you to remain in Ireland. Permission to remain in Ireland is granted by the Department of Justice and Equality and takes the form either of a special residence stamp on your passport or possession of a residence card. The various types of stamp and their meanings are explained in the web page www.citizensinformation.ie/en/moving_country/moving_to_ireland/

10 THINGS YOU MAY WANT TO CONSIDER WHEN YOU FIRST ARRIVE IN IRELAND

1. Personal Public Service (PPS) number

In order to work or open a bank account here, you will need a PPS number. This also allows you to access social welfare benefits, public services and information in Ireland. You can obtain a PPS number (or ask for your old number, if any, to be traced) at your local social welfare office or Intreo centre. You can find your local social welfare office at www.welfare.ie

If you are a non-national, you will need your passport or your Garda National Immigration Bureau (GNIB) certificate of registration and supporting documentation such as household bills. You will need this number to register with the Revenue Commissioners if you are taking up employment.

Employers are obliged to register new employments, in all circumstances except where it is the employee's first employment in the State. You can register the employment with Revenue by submitting a new RPN (Revenue Payroll Notification) request for that employee. RPNs are available in real time for new employees. This removes the need for emergency tax in most cases. Find details at www.revenue.ie

2. Bank or An Post Money accounts

To open an account with a bank or An Post, you will need to bring with you:
- your passport or GNIB certificate of registration;
- a household utility bill linking your name to your home address in Ireland;
- your PPS number; and,
- if you are a student, a school letter.

3. Housing and finding a job

These are probably going to be the top of your priorities. Food, accommodation and clothing – they all cost money. It is a good idea, though not a requirement, if you can arrange employment and accommodation before you arrive.

Rent and mortgage supplements

Housing Assistance Payment (HAP)

HAP was introduced in 2017 with the long-term goal of replacing Rent Supplement for those in need of ongoing housing assistance. Help is provided in the form of finance only – those in receipt of the supplement must find their own property. Although local authorities pay HAP directly to landlords, they do not source property for tenants.

If you are asked to switch from Rent Supplement to HAP and have received a letter from the Department of Employment Affairs and Social Protection to this effect, you must apply to do so within six weeks. In cases where a household applying for HAP in Dublin is homeless, there are processes in place to increase the rent limits.

Unlike Rent Supplement, you may be entitled to HAP if you are in full-time employment. In order to qualify, you must be on your local authority's housing list. You can find out how to pay your landlord, the rent limits per county and per household size and everything else you need to know by visiting the HAP website: www.hap.ie

Rent Supplement

This means-tested supplement exists to assist those on low incomes who are struggling to afford the rental market. Although those in receipt of long-term Rent Supplement may be switched to HAP (as outlined above), there are instances where people still qualify for Rent Supplement.

In order to qualify for this supplement, you must:

- have been in receipt of Rent Supplement in the year prior to your application;
- have been living in private rental accommodation for at least six months of that year, but your circumstances changed so drastically after the onset of your tenancy that you are no longer able to pay the rent to which you agreed at the beginning of your lease;
- have been living in homeless accommodation for a minimum of six months of the previous year;
- not work more than 30 hours per week, or be self-employed; and
- not be in full-time education.

For more information, contact your local Social Welfare Office at www.welfare.ie

Rent to buy

Similar to a hire-purchase model for buying a car, a rent-to-buy scheme is an option afforded by some sellers through which buyers may rent a property for a defined period of time before being offered the chance to purchase it. As with a car, or a traditional home purchase, it is not unusual for an upfront payment to be part of the deal; this, along with the rental payments, may be deducted off the final price, should the dweller eventually opt to purchase the property.

Social housing

For those unable to afford to own or rent their own home, or those with specific needs (such as members of the Traveller community, homeless people or people with disabilities), reliance on social housing through local housing authorities is the main course of action. Property is either owned and managed by the local authority or by an approved housing body (such as a housing cooperative); leased by the local authority and rented out to tenants; or acquired through a Rental Accommodation Scheme, where properties are rented from private landlords.

To see if you are eligible, for more information, or to apply for local housing, find your local authority at www.housing.gov.ie

Mortgage to Rent Scheme

For homeowners at serious risk of losing their homes to foreclosure, the government Mortgage to Rent Scheme is a realistic option. While handing over the reins to someone else might sound like a last resort when you have worked hard to own your own home, there is an option to buy back after five years should your situation improve.

Homes being considered for this scheme must be worth no more than €365,000 if a house or €310,000 if an apartment or townhouse in Dublin, Kildare, Meath, Wicklow, Louth, Cork or Galway; or €280,000 if a house or €215,000 if an apartment or townhouse anywhere else in the country.

In order to qualify for this scheme, you must:
- qualify for social housing;
- not own another property or have more than €20,000 in assets;
- live in a property suitable to your needs, i.e. not be a couple living alone in a five-bedroom house;
- have completed a Mortgage Arrears Resolution Process with your lender; and
- have a yearly income of less than €25,000–€35,000, depending on where you are in the country (view the bands at www.bit.ly/IncomeCaps).

European Employment Services (EURES)

EURES is a network of employment services throughout the EEA, working with the European Commission. It aims to provide:

- a European job placement service for jobseekers;
- advice and guidance on how to look for a job in the EEA;
- a recruitment service to employers who wish to recruit in EEA member states; and
- information on living and working conditions in EEA member states

The EURES website (www.ec.europa.eu/eures) also provides information on jobs and living/working conditions in the EEA.

You should also check there are no restrictions that could stop you from working here.

If you have a professional career qualification, you should check with the Irish branch of your professional body about whether your qualifications are accepted in Ireland.

Recruitment offices throughout the country display job vacancies – there is no charge to talk to recruiters. They are paid by employers for placing employees with them so are well compensated.

4. Borrowing

All lending is based on your ability to repay. If you do not have a job, you probably have no capacity to repay and any application for borrowings will be turned down. Credit unions and An Post Money are generally more flexible than the high street banks (AIB, Bank of Ireland, Ulster Bank, Permanent TSB and KBC). Avoid moneylenders, especially the unauthorised ones. The Central Bank of Ireland's website (www.centralbank.ie) lists the 38 active authorised moneylenders on their website, but even the authorised ones can charge up to 200% per annum.

You need at least Stamp 4 to apply for a home loan.

5. Transport

Full driving licences from all other EU member states, and some other countries, are recognised for use in Ireland.

Buses, trains and Dublin's **DART** (Dublin Area Rapid Transport), **Luas** (light rail) and **Dublin bikes** (for €25 per annum you can take and return bicycles around the city centre) are good transport options.

Leap card is a good way of saving money, as it can save up to 32% of the cost of a single fare. A student leap card is cheaper again – for €20 per week you can travel anywhere by Dublin Bus.

Tax saver is also good for employees – you can save up to 52% of travel costs as a result of Income Tax, PRSI and USC savings. There is also the saving on time - employees no longer need to queue for bus or rail tickets.

6. Language

English is one of the most widely spoken languages in the world. It is important, if you are not a native speaker, that you master the language as soon as possible. There are free lessons online, including at www.perfectlyspoken.com, www.fluentin3months.com and www.talkenglish.com

7. Healthcare

If you are a national of the European Economic Area (EEA) or Switzerland, or if you are normally resident in Ireland (i.e. you have been living in Ireland for at least a year or you intend to live here for at least one year), you are entitled to receive the same level of health care as Irish citizens. Depending on your income, you may be eligible for a medical card, which entitles you to the full range of medical services at no cost.

If you are not from an EEA member state or Switzerland, you will be entitled to certain services free of charge and you will have to pay for the remainder.

Entitlement to health services is primarily based on residency and means, rather than on your payment of tax.

There are two types of eligibility for people who are ordinarily resident:

- Full eligibility for medical card holders
- Limited eligibility for people who don't have a medical card

Medical card holders

Everyone aged 70 years or older is automatically entitled to a full medical card, irrespective of income. For most other people, eligibility for a full medical card or a GP visit card is means-tested, based on disposable income (gross income less tax and PRSI). If you do have a **medical card**, you are entitled to:

- *free GP services;*
- *prescribed drugs and medicines, subject to a charge for each item prescribed;*
- *public hospital services;*
- *dental, optical and aural services;*
- *maternity and infant care services; and*
- *community care and personal social services.*

Non-medical card holders

If you do not have a medical card, you are entitled to free public hospital services but you may have to pay in-patient and out-patient hospital charges. You are also entitled to subsidised prescribed drugs and medicines and maternity and infant care services.

Unless you hold a GP visit card, you are not entitled to free GP services. You may be entitled to some community care and personal social services (ask your GP about community care services in your area, or contact your local Health Office).

8. Saving

We all need to save. Whether it is for the holiday to go back home, your very own car or that deposit for your new home, it is important to start saving.

Mortgage lenders will also want to see you have the ability to save – a saving track record.

Christmas, holidays, family birthdays and anniversaries, Valentine's Day, Mother's Day, Father's Day ... they all cost money, so why not adopt a saving strategy in your monthly expenditure? Most importantly, start. You should ideally have between 3 and 6 months' net monthly income as a rainy day fund.

One way to do it is to put, say, 20% of your net monthly pay away in a separate account, preferably in a different institution than your regular bank account (and it is always harder to access funds when you are either allowed only one withdrawal a year or you have to personally go to that deposit-taker to access your money).

Regular saver accounts are special deposit accounts that all the banks offer, in which you save between €100 and €1,000 per month and receive the best interest rates on offer. The best rate at time of going to press is in EBS (now an AIB company) at 1.25% gross, an account that only allows one withdrawal per annum.

You can also save regularly with your local post office or credit union – they are more personal and have generally better opening hours.

You could email me for a fact sheet on the best interest rates currently at jlowe@moneydoctors.ie or telephone (+353 1) 278 5555.

9. Insurance

As a non-national it will be important to distinguish between all the various insurances and assurances you can take out. Some are necessary and some are not.

Life insurance is life protection for the term of the insurance cover. If you die during the term of the policy, the insurance company will pay a tax-free sum to your beneficiaries. But, if you outlive the term of the policy, your beneficiaries or estate will not receive any payment.

Life assurance typically means that a payment is made when the policyholder dies.

I am reminded of the famous quip from US comedian Woody Allen when he said, 'My worst nightmare is being stuck in a lift with an insurance salesman.' While all insurance has to be sold, there are times when it is compulsory:

Mortgage protection – if you are under 50 years of age and applying for a home loan, it is a legal obligation to take out life cover on the mortgage in case of death of any mortgage-holder. There are differing policies:

Decreasing life cover: As you pay back the loan on a monthly basis, part of that payment will be to repay the capital. This in turn will decrease the original amount you borrowed (so by the end of the loan, all the capital is repaid). If you die at any time during the term, the balance of the capital is paid by this policy. This is the cheapest type of life cover.

Level term cover: This covers the policy holder(s) for the full amount borrowed right up to the last day of the mortgage, irrespective of what the balance is. Any surplus after the mortgage is repaid goes to the estate of the deceased.

Whole of life cover: This is the most expensive, as it covers a certain sum of money and pays out when you die. The older you become, the more expensive this type of assurance can be. Once you have dependents – younger or older – you may need to take out this cover in case anything happens to you. With children, it is usually until they complete third-level education, about age 22 to 23.

You can also take out insurance to protect your income (called **Permanent Health Insurance** or **income protection**) that pays up to 75% of your monthly income less any social welfare benefits until you resume work or you reach pension age. Benefit starts after 13, 26 or 52 weeks – of course, the longer you wait for the benefit, the cheaper the premiums.

Serious Illness Cover protects you against contracting a serious illness and pays a lump sum to you while you cope with the illness – usually up to 2 years' income cover.

Private Health insurance: There are 3 health insurance companies (VHI, Laya HealthCare and Irish Life Health) insuring up to 2 million people in Ireland for their medical costs. It can be expensive, and the price goes up by 2% once you are aged over 34 years. You can compare the 3 health insurers' plans at www.hia.ie, the Health Insurance Authority website.

10. Retirement planning

If you intend to stay here in Ireland, planning for an income when you retire is both necessary and cost-effective. You may qualify for the State pension (currently €243.30 per week), but it may not be enough to keep you in the luxury you want to become accustomed to.

Depending on your age, the Irish government allows a certain percentage of your income to be invested into a pension, locking it away for the future. For example, if you are between 30 and 40 years old, you can invest up to 20% of your annual income and receive up to 20% or 40% of this back in tax relief. See Chapter 18, 'Pensions made easy'.

SUPPORT GROUPS

In no particular order, the following are support groups that can help those arriving in Ireland.

Garda Racial, Intercultural and Diversity Office (GRIDO)

GRIDO is responsible for advising, monitoring and co-ordinating police activity around racial, ethnic, religious and cultural diversity. A recording mechanism captures data concerning racially motivated incidents. This data is made available to all Garda stations in the State, so that reports and complaints can be tracked. Ethnic Liaison Officers (ELOs) monitor racist incidents. They also liaise with representatives of the various minority communities and with victims of racist incidents to ensure that they are afforded adequate protection. GRIDO runs initiatives to promote mutual awareness and understanding, and provides links with services providing support to victims of crime concerning racial issues.

c/o Garda Community Relations Bureau
Garda Headquarters
Harcourt Square, Dublin 2
Tel: (01) 666 3150
www.garda.ie

Irish Tourist Assistance Service (ITAS)

Taking basic precautions can help you avoid being a victim of crime. However, if you have experienced crime, ITAS is a free, nationwide service offering support and assistance. It liaises with embassies or consulates, helps with language difficulties, deals with medical needs, arranges accommodation or meals if needed and helps to replace stolen travel tickets. ITAS does not, however, provide financial assistance, replace lost or stolen items or offer legal or insurance advice.

c/o 6-7 Hanover Street East, Dublin 2
Tel: (+353 1) 661 0562
Locall: 1890 365 700
www.itas.ie
info@itas.ie

Foreign embassies and consulates

A number of foreign embassies and consulates in Ireland provide consular services to nationals of their countries, including advice and practical help with travel documentation. If you lose your passport or travel documentation when you are in Ireland, your country's embassy or consulate can issue you with temporary travel documents. They can also assist you in the case of a medical emergency. They can advise relatives or friends about an accident or illness, act as a liaison with hospitals and doctors and arrange for interpretative services, if necessary.

If you are the victim of a crime while in Ireland, your embassy or consulate can liaise with local police and let your friends and family know of your situation. Likewise, if you have been arrested or imprisoned, your embassy or consulate can contact legal representation, ensure that your rights are respected and advise you of your entitlements. If a member of your family dies while abroad, your embassy or consulate can assist you in dealing with the formalities, such as death certificates and police reports.

Immigrant Council of Ireland (ICI)

The ICI is an independent, national organisation that supports migrants coming to Ireland for work, study, family reunification, self-employment or simply to visit. The ICI provides an information service and a limited legal service, as well as running a training service and organising public events. It produces publications on immigrant issues such as citizenship and residence rights, visas, employment permits, family reunification and voluntary return. The ICI works with immigrant groups to influence government policy on issues relating to immigrants and to campaign for immigrants' rights.

It has produced a directory of migrant-led organisations, which is a useful resource for people seeking contacts within migrant communities, with the media, service providers or businesses. The ICI runs regular clinics for migrant workers, offering free and confidential employment law advice.

2 St Andrew Street, Dublin 2
Tel: (+353 1) 674 0200
www.immigrantcouncil.ie

Migrant Rights Centre Ireland (MRCI)

The MRCI is a national organisation providing support to migrant workers and their families. It targets families in vulnerable circumstances and tries to improve their social and economic conditions. The MRCI's drop-in centre provides information, advice and assistance. The MRCI also encourages migrants to get involved in their community.

13 Lower Dorset Street, Dublin 1
Tel: (+353 1) 889 7570
www.mrci.ie
info@mrci.ie

Crosscare Migrant Project

Crosscare Migrant Project provides information, support and advocacy to migrants. Its information and referral service is available to immigrants and members of new communities living in Ireland, as well as to intending, existing and returning Irish emigrants. Its website is a guide to all aspects of living in Ireland and is available in English, Portuguese, Arabic, Russian and Chinese.

1a Cathedral Street, Dublin 1
Tel: (+353 1) 873 2844
www.migrantproject.ie and livinginireland.ie
migrantproject@crosscare.ie

Reception and Integration Agency (RIA)

The RIA is responsible for co-ordinating the provision of services both to asylum seekers and to people granted international protection (refugee status or subsidiary protection) in Ireland. It arranges accommodation and works with statutory and non-statutory agencies to co-ordinate the delivery of other services, such as healthcare, social services, welfare and education. The RIA is also responsible for responding to crisis situations that result in large numbers of refugees arriving in Ireland within short periods.

If you are applying for refugee status, you can obtain rent-free accommodation at a regional centre. Each adult is entitled to a personal allowance of €21.60 per week and €21.60 for each child. More information can be obtained from:

PO Box 11487, Dublin 2
Tel: (+353 1) 418 3200

Scheme of repatriation
The Reception and Integration Agency works with the Department of Employment Affairs and Social Protection (DEASP) to support the repatriation of nationals of newer EU member states. The scheme applies to people who have failed the habitual residence condition attaching to social assistance payments. Any citizen of a former EU accession state, and certain other 'special-case' EU nationals, who find themselves destitute during their time in Ireland can apply for repatriation. If you wish to apply for this scheme you should contact the DEASP's representative (formerly known as the Community Welfare Officer).

International Organisation for Migration
If you are an asylum seeker or an irregular migrant from a non-EEA state, and you wish to return voluntarily to your country of origin but do not have the means to do so, the IOM may be able to assist you. An independent international organisation, the IOM's Voluntary Assisted Return and Reintegration Scheme can help with travel documentation and arrange for transit and arrival assistance if needed. When you travel with the IOM, you travel independently and without an escort. The reasons for your stay in Ireland remain confidential and are not shared with anybody outside the voluntary return process. If you return voluntarily and you have no outstanding criminal court proceedings, you may apply to re-enter Ireland legally.

116 Lower Baggot Street, Dublin 2
Tel: +353 (0)1 676 0655
Locall: 800 406 406
www.iom.int/countries/ireland
iomdublin@iom.int

Citizens Information
Citizens Information is a comprehensive source of information on public services and rights in Ireland, including issues such as residence rights, employment rights, health services, housing, social security entitlements

and general information about moving to Ireland. Citizens Information is available by telephone through the Citizens Information Phone Service or in person by calling to a Citizens Information Centre (CIC) near you.
Tel: 0761 07 4000

Homelessness

If you are homeless, you should contact your local authority for information about accommodation. Threshold, a voluntary organisation, provides advice and support to people who are homeless or at risk of becoming homeless. You can also get advice about your situation from your nearest Citizens Information Centre.

Migrant workers and unemployment

If you have come to work in Ireland and you lose your job, it can be a very difficult situation. If you are not an Irish citizen you need to find out your rights and entitlements in relation to redundancy, looking for work, social welfare and getting a tax refund.

If you are an EEA or Swiss national, you can stay in Ireland if you are unemployed and looking for work.

Employment permits

If you are a non-EEA national with an employment permit, and you have been made redundant within the last 6 months, there are special conditions that apply. You should notify the Department of Business, Enterprise and Innovation within 28 days of your dismissal.

If you have been made redundant after working on a work permit for 5 consecutive years, you no longer need a permit to work in Ireland.

If you entered the State on a valid employment permit but you fell out of the system through no fault of your own, or you have been badly treated or exploited in the workplace, you may be eligible for a Reactivation Employment Permit.

Redundancy

If you are dismissed by your employer, you should check if it is a redundancy situation – for example, the closure of a business. If it is not a genuine redundancy or if you think you have been unfairly selected for redundancy, you may qualify to bring a claim for unfair dismissal. Your employer must prove that it was a genuine redundancy situation and that fair procedures were followed.

If it is a genuine redundancy situation, you may be entitled to a redundancy payment if you have been working for your employer for 2 or more years. You may have other entitlements such as notice and holiday pay in lieu.

Social welfare payments

Jobseeker's Benefit (JB): To get JB you must be unemployed and looking for work and you must have paid a certain number of social insurance (PRSI) contributions. EEA migrant workers may combine social insurance contributions paid in another EU country to help them qualify for JB. Non-EEA migrant workers who qualify for JB can get it as long as they are legally resident in Ireland.

Jobseeker's Allowance (JA): If you are not entitled to JB, you can apply for JA, which is a means-tested payment. To qualify, you must be unemployed, looking for work and habitually resident. You must also pass a means test.

EEA migrant workers who do not qualify for JB will meet the habitual residence requirement for **Supplementary Welfare Allowance** (SWA) if they are actively looking for work. If you have been working in Ireland for less than 12 months, you are entitled to get SWA for 6 months from the date your employment ended. If you have been employed for more than 12 months you are entitled get SWA as long as you are actively looking for work.

Rent Supplement: If you are getting Jobseeker's Benefit, Jobseeker's Allowance or Supplementary Welfare Allowance and paying rent to a private landlord, you may be entitled to Rent Supplement. However, to qualify you must pass a means test and be habitually resident in Ireland.

Non-EEA students are not entitled to social welfare payments in Ireland.

Tax

You may be entitled to a tax refund, if you have paid tax and you are now unemployed. If you have not paid any tax, you will not be due a refund.

If you are getting another income which is taxable, for example Jobseeker's Benefit, you should wait for 8 weeks from the date you became unemployed before applying for a refund.

If you are not getting Jobseeker's Benefit and have no other taxable income, you should wait 4 weeks from the date you become unemployed before applying for a refund.

If emergency tax was being deducted by your former employer, you should apply immediately.

Department of Business, Enterprise and Innovation
Employment Permits Section
Earlsfort Centre, Lower Hatch Street, Dublin 2
Tel: (+353 1) 417 5333
Locall: 1890 201 616
www.dbei.ie
employmentpermits@dbei.gov.ie

Naturalisation
To learn about becoming an Irish citizen by naturalization, go to www.inis.gov.ie/en/INIS/Pages/WP16000022#eligibility

37

JIM POWER'S 2020 ECONOMIC GLOBAL UPDATE

THE WORLD IN 2019

It is now just over 12 years since the global economy was plunged
into the most significant economic and financial crisis since the 1930s.
Economic activity in the developed world collapsed, unemployment soared
and government finances almost everywhere deteriorated sharply. Policy
makers worldwide were forced to pursue very dramatic responses, including
introducing historically low official interest rates and massive central bank
purchases of government bonds (i.e. quantitative easing).

These aggressive policy responses eventually proved effective, and
over the past five years the global economic backdrop has improved
quite markedly. However, there is still a significant economic and
political legacy of the crash. The economic legacy includes high levels
of government debt, poorly functioning banks and high levels of
unemployment in some countries. The political legacy includes the rise of
more extreme political forces in response to the fiscal austerity imposed
on some countries in the aftermath of the crash.

2017 was a particularly good year for the global economy, with a strong
and synchronised economic recovery almost everywhere. This strong
momentum carried over into 2018, but as the year progressed, there
was a considerable weakening of activity levels and confidence in many
countries. This carried over into 2019, and the global economic outlook is
currently more uncertain than we have seen for some time.

Growth in the euro area has slowed sharply over the past year.
The annual rate of growth has slowed from a high of 3% in the final
quarter of 2017 to just 1.2% in the second quarter of 2019. Italy and
Germany are of particular concern, with both economies hovering on
the brink of recession.

The labour market in the eurozone continues to improve, with the
unemployment rate down at 7.5% of the labour force in July.

Growth in the US was given a considerable boost in 2018 from the tax cutting package implemented by President Trump. However, growth has eased from 3.5% in the second quarter of 2018 to 2% in the second quarter of 2019.

In the UK, the impact of Brexit has become very pronounced over the past year. It is no surprise that reduced business investment has led the slowdown, because no sensible business would commit to significant investment in the absence of clarity about the nature of the future relationship between the UK and the EU. Consumer spending has also slowed sharply and house prices are now in decline.

Elsewhere in the world, the Chinese economy has slowed markedly, largely due to trade tensions with the US and past policy tightening; a number of emerging economies, such as Brazil, South Africa, Turkey and Argentina, are struggling; and global geo-political tensions are intensifying.

Global Indicators

REGION	GDP (Q2 2019 % YEAR-ON-YEAR)	UNEMPLOYMENT RATE
EU-28	1.4%	6.3%
Euro area	1.2%	7.5%
Belgium	1.2%	5.7%
Germany	0.4%	3.0%
Ireland	6.3% (Q1)	5.2%
Greece	1.9%	17.2%
Spain	2.3%	13.9%
France	1.4%	8.5%
Italy	-0.1%	9.9%
Netherlands	1.8%	3.4%
United Kingdom	1.2%	3.8%
United States	2.0%	3.7%
Japan	1.3%	2.3%
China	6.2%	3.6%

Source: Eurostat & Bloomberg

THE WORLD IN 2020

As we move into the final quarter of 2019 and towards 2020, there are considerable uncertainties surrounding the global economic outlook:

- There is a growing trend towards isolationism, protectionism and nationalism. This is manifesting itself in the rise of the right in Europe, the US and the UK.

- The ongoing trade dispute between China and the United States has already damaged growth in the US and China and is undermining global economic and business confidence. If this trade dispute is allowed to escalate it could seriously damage free trade and growth and do considerable damage to global economic activity. The next risk is that President Trump starts to direct his anti-free trade tendencies towards the EU.
- At the time of writing, it is not clear how Brexit will unfold. Nobody knows with certainty how the process might evolve and, as we approach the Brexit deadline of 31 October, there is still no clarity on whether a deal will be done between the UK and the EU; or if the UK will crash out without a deal; or if there will be a further delay to the exit date. Any of these eventualities remains distinctly possible, and others besides. Any type of Brexit represents bad news for Ireland and the UK, but a UK exit without agreeing a deal with the EU would represent a serious economic threat to Ireland and the UK.
- Global equity markets have been trending upwards since the first quarter of 2009. This is a very long equity cycle by historical standards, but is being kept going by the artificial liquidity conditions emanating from quantitative easing and the very low level of short- and long-term interest rates.
- Disinflationary pressures are building again, meaning that interest rates will remain at very low levels for a protracted period of time, causing further imbalances in financial markets and real-debt burdens to increase.
- The lack of growth momentum in the EU is a cause of deep concern. Demand across the EU needs to be stimulated, but there is very limited scope on the monetary policy front. Countries such as Germany have a responsibility to utilise looser fiscal policy, but the political appetite and willingness to do this is non-existent.
- Climate change is the biggest challenge facing the human race. Failure to address it will cause extreme weather events to intensify over the coming years. However, a meaningful effort to address it will necessitate massive changes in industrial, agricultural and personal behaviour. Politically this will be very difficult to manage.

All in all, it is likely that 2020 will be another challenging year for the global economy and a tricky one for investors, given the persistence of historically low short- and long-term interest rates. Global growth is likely to slow further and some countries will struggle to avoid or emerge from recession.

INTEREST RATES

One of the biggest changes to occur over the past year has been the dramatic adjustment in interest rate expectations. Between December 2015 and December 2018, the US Federal Reserve increased official interest rates from zero to 2.5%. The expectation in the middle of 2018 was that rates would rise to 3.5% in 2019. In the event, the Federal Reserve cut official rates by 0.25% in July 2019, and further cuts may be seen over the coming months.

Back in the first half of 2018, growth momentum in the eurozone economy suggested that the European Central Bank might consider the possibility of moving to normalise official interest rates towards the end of 2019. However, the opposite has happened. Economic growth has slowed and inflation remains very subdued at 1%, and it appears likely that further monetary easing will be seen through cuts to various interest rates and a possible return to quantitative easing. There appears to be no possibility of any increase in official interest rates for the next couple of years at least.

Long-term interest rates have also fallen back again in dramatic fashion, reflecting poor growth, the lack of any inflationary pressures and continued artificial liquidity in markets.

10-Year Bond Yields

COUNTRY	%
Unites States	1.63%
United Kingdom	0.59%
Germany	-0.59%
France	-0.29%
Italy	0.94%
Ireland	0.00%
Greece	1.61%

Source: Bloomberg

THE IRISH HOUSING MARKET

The latest house price data from the Central Statistics Office (CSO) show that the process of moderation in house price inflation that commenced in April 2018 continues. In the 12-month period to June 2019, national average house price inflation declined to 2%, the lowest annual rate of price increase since June 2013. The annual rate of increase outside Dublin decelerated to 3.9%, the lowest rate since February 2014; and the annual rate in Dublin has decelerated to just 0.1%, effectively the lowest annual rate since October 2012 (it was flat in May).

It is important to point out that in the context of what prices have done since 2013, what we are experiencing is a price stabilisation, rather than a significant price correction. Between October 2018 and June 2019, national average prices declined by just 0.4%. Within this national average, prices outside Dublin have increased by 1.8%, while average Dublin prices have declined by 2.6%. In Dún Laoghaire-Rathdown, which boasts some of the highest house prices in the country, prices declined by 4% on a year-on-year basis to June.

The key drivers of this moderation in house prices are high prices and the prudent mortgage lending restrictions imposed by the Central Bank of Ireland. These factors are combining to reduce affordability, which is causing the housing market to moderate. Supply is also increasing, and Brexit is undermining confidence. This is all positive movement, as house prices need to moderate, but greater supply will be necessary to satisfy unmet demand in the market.

THE CONTEXT FOR THE IRISH ECONOMY

For the small, open Irish economy, the health of the global economy is of the utmost importance. Indeed, the strong recovery in the Irish economy over recent years has been helped by the reasonably benign global economic backdrop.

The momentum in the Irish economy so far in 2019 has been positive and looks likely to be sustained over the remainder of the year, though the more uncertain external backdrop and Brexit represent two significant threats.

Domestically, the challenges are quite clear:

- Although house price inflation is moderating and is likely to continue to do so, housing costs are soaking up household disposable income and are undermining the competitiveness of the economy. Housing supply needs to remain the focus.
- The pressure to increase expenditure on public services, particularly health, remains strong and will pressurise the public finances. Public sector pay pressures will be a particular challenge. Ireland still has a dangerously high level of Government debt that needs to be brought under control. At the end of 2018, Ireland had gross Government debt of €206.2 billion.

- As the economy steadily moves towards full employment, wage pressures are likely to intensify and the recruitment and retention of workers will become an increasingly significant challenge for all employers. This will act as a constraint on economic growth.
- The personal sector will remain pressurised due to a combination of the high personal tax burden; subdued wage growth for the past decade, although wages will rise more strongly in 2019 and 2020; rising house prices and rents continuing to soak up household disposable income; and Brexit, which remains a source of deep concern and uncertainty.

The external risk factors and challenges are also very clear:

- Brexit.
- The global economic outlook is under some pressure as global momentum is waning. The protectionist stance of President Trump poses a significant threat to the well-being of the global economy.
- Pressure to reform global corporation tax structures is intensifying and change looks inevitable in the longer term. This will pressurise Ireland's very successful FDI model.

In the face of these challenges, it seems inevitable that Irish growth will be slower in 2020. It is very difficult to model for Brexit, but a disorderly Brexit would have a significant impact on consumer and business confidence and real economic activity.

There is not a lot Ireland can do to influence our global threats and challenges, but it is imperative that a prudent approach is maintained to the management of the public finances; that competitiveness, particularly in the costs of doing business, is managed very carefully; that housing supply is increased; and that the current historically low long-term interest rate environment is exploited to deliver effective and efficient capital investment.

ECONOMIC BACKGROUND TO BUDGET 2020

The economic background against which Budget 2020 was presented is generally positive, but there are some obvious signs of easing in economic activity and numerous external threats. The Department of Finance has upped its growth forecast for 2019 to 5.5%, but growth of just 0.7% per cent is forecast for 2020. This forecast is predicated on a hard Brexit, and if this can be avoided, growth next year should comfortably exceed 3%. The hard-Brexit growth scenario would translate into a budget turnaround of around €6.5 billion in 2020, compared to a soft-Brexit situation.

The preparation of Budget 2020 was complicated due to the possibility, but not certainty, of a hard Brexit; the fact that it is most likely the last budget before a general election; the uncertain external economic and political background, with the escalation of barriers to trade a serious threat to the well-being of the global economy; and the domestic economic background, which is undoubtedly becoming more uncertain. In addition, outstanding government debt in Ireland stood at €205.9 billion at the end of 2018, which is equivalent to 63.5% of gross domestic product. When measured as a percentage of real economic activity (modified growth measure GNI*), this debt stands at a still very high 104%.

THE ECONOMIC ASSUMPTIONS

The framing of Budget 2020 was seriously complicated by Brexit. The budget had to be based on a hard Brexit scenario, meaning that the Minister for Finance was very limited in what he was able to do. In the Summer Economic Statement published in June, the Minister committed to a budget package of €2.8 billion regardless of the Brexit situation. Of this, €2.1 billion was already pre-committed to items such as public sector pay and pensions, the National Children's Hospital and the National Broadband Plan, leaving just €700 million to be assigned on budget day. In the event, he raised €300 million in extra taxes and was able to deliver a net package of €2.9 billion.

Economic forecasts accompanying the budget indicate that the Department of Finance believes that 2020 would see the worst impact of a hard Brexit, with growth forecast at just 0.7% in 2020, but recovering to 2.5% in 2021.

The medium-term economic assumptions underlying Budget 2020 are:

(% Year On Year)	2019	2020	2021	2022	2023	2024
GDP	5.5%	0.7%	2.5%	2.8%	2.7%	2.6%
GNP	4.3%	-0.1%	2.4%	2.5%	2.4%	2.3%
Personal Consumption	2.7%	1.4%	1.9%	2.1%	2.3%	2.4%
Gov. Consumption	4.5%	3.5%	2.0%	2.0%	2.0%	2.0%
Investment	50.4%	-24.0%	-3.6%	3.9%	3.9%	3.9%
Exports	10.2%	0.9%	4.2%	4.1%	4.0%	3.9%
Imports	22.6%	-6.5%	2.9%	4.4%	4.6%	4.5%
Inflation (HICP)	0.9%	1.1%	1.4%	1.8%	2.0%	2.1%
Employment	2.4%	0.8%	1.1%	1.5%	1.7%	1.9%
Unemployment Rate	5.2%	5.7%	5.9%	5.9%	5.7%	5.5%
Wages	3.5%	3.0%	3.2%	3.4%	3.7%	3.9%

Source: Department of Finance

THE FISCAL ASSUMPTIONS

The White Paper on Receipts and Expenditure published ahead of Budget 2020 contained the estimates on receipts and expenditure for 2019 and 2020 before any budget day changes to taxation or expenditure were announced.

Prior to the budget changes, the Department of Finance was forecasting a General Government Surplus equivalent to 0.2% of GDP in 2019 and a balanced budget in 2020. Following the changes announced in the budget, a deficit equivalent to 0.6% of GDP is now anticipated. The Minister stressed the extent to which this forecast is very uncertain due to the deep uncertainty around Brexit.

The debt-to-GDP ratio is projected to decline to 53% by 2024. However, the real burden of debt remains very high and will constrain fiscal management for some years to come.

The following are the projected key fiscal parameters following Budget 2020:

	2019	2020	2021	2022	2023	2024
General Gov. Balance (% GDP)	0.2%	-0.6%	-0.2%	0.1%	0.4%	0.7%
General Gov. Debt (% GDP)	59.3%	56.5%	56.4%	54.4%	53.8%	53%

Source: Department of Finance

Following the budget changes, total tax revenues are projected to expand by 4.3% or €2.5 billion. Customs Duties are projected to grow by almost 240% in 2020, an increase of €875 million. This reflects the impact of tariffs in the event of a no-deal Brexit. However, of the €1.24 billion projected, €995 million will be handed over to the EU. Another interesting aspect is that Corporation Tax receipts are projected at €10.5 billion in 2020 and €12.1 billion by 2024. This reflects an assumption that the current boom in Corporation Tax will be sustained. There are risks associated with this assumption, but the Department seems to be on top of this issue.

Estimates of tax receipts post-Budget 2020

Category	2019 (€m)	2020 (€m)	% change
Customs	365	1,240	+239.7%
Excise Duty	5,855	5,905	+0.9%
Corporation Tax	10,280	10,535	+2.5%

Capital Gains Tax	1,000	1,015	+1.5%
Capital Acquisitions Tax	495	495	-
Stamp Duties	1,610	1,645	+2.2%
Income Tax	22,910	23,900	+4.3%
VAT	15,140	15,465	+2.1%
Motor Tax	965	925	-4.1%
Total	58,625	61,125	+4.3%

Source: Department of Finance

THE KEY FEATURES OF BUDGET 2020

- The Minister of Finance has announced the setting up of an emergency fund of €1.2 billion to help the economy cope with a potential hard Brexit. €650 million will be directed at Enterprise, Agriculture and Tourism and to help stabilise the worst-affected regions. €410 million is being set aside to support those experiencing unemployment as a result of a hard Brexit. Of this, €365 million will be allocated through Social Protection and €45 million for labour market activation supports. An additional €160 million will be allocated to facilities and infrastructure at some ports and airports.
- For the motor industry, the 1% diesel surcharge has been replaced by a VRT Environmental Health (NOx) surcharge. This will hit diesel cars, and particularly older imported diesel cars, most.
- The VRT relief for hybrids and plug-in hybrid electric vehicles has been extended.
- The Help-to-Buy scheme has been extended for another two years.
- The electricity tax has been equalised for business with that of non-business.
- €6 per tonne increase in Carbon Tax, but funding will be provided for those experiencing fuel poverty and a €31 million fund is being set up to help the midlands deal with impact of Bord na Móna peat activities.
- There is a one-year extension to the reduced rate of USC for medical card holders.
- The Home Carers' Tax Credit has been increased by €100. Carers will also be allowed to work outside the home for an extra 3½ hours per week.
- The Inheritance Tax threshold has been lifted by €15,000 to €335,000.
- Excise Duty on cigarettes increased by 50 cent.

- Increase of €150 in Earned Income Credit for self-employed, which takes it up to €1,500.
- Dividend Withholding Tax has been increased from 20% to 25%.
- An increase of 1.5% in the Stamp Duty on commercial property from 6% to 7.5%.
- Changes have been made to the Key Employee Engagement Programme (KEEP).
- The Employee and Investment (EII) tax relief has been changed to allow full Income Tax relief (40%) in the year in which the investment is made.
- Spending on health is projected to increase by €1 billion in 2020 to €17.4 billion.
- Spending on social welfare is projected to increase by €690 million in 2020 to reach €2.1 billion.

OVERALL ASSESSMENT

Budget 2020 was justifiably and unavoidably cautious and was framed against a slower economic growth background as a result of an expected hard Brexit. In the event of a hard Brexit being avoided, economic growth will be significantly stronger and all of the budgetary parameters will then change. No changes have been made to Income Tax, and much of the focus has been on expenditure.

It is a budget that took a long time to deliver, but which contained a lot of small changes and not a lot of any real substance, other than the Brexit package. No risks were taken, but the pressure points in health and social protection are very obvious and very significant.

It is now a matter of waiting to see how Brexit will unfold.

Jim Power is one of Ireland's leading and best-known economic analysts. Jim has a wealth of experience in delivering insightful economic analysis, forecasts and commentary to both Irish and international audiences. He writes regularly for national newspapers and is a regular contributor to radio and TV debates and discussions.

Tel: (+353 1) 499 0097

jim@powereconomics.ie

APPENDIX 1

LEARN TO SPEAK THE LANGUAGE

A QUICK GUIDE TO IMPORTANT 'PERSONAL FINANCE' TERMINOLOGY

One of the first things about finance that puts people off is the language. The moment an expert starts to bandy around terms like 'dividend', 'yield', 'compound interest' and 'net present value' it can all start to sound intimidating.

Like every other area of life, finance has a specialised language and its own jargon. Jargon is actually very useful – we need precise terms that are clearly defined so that there is no confusion about what is being said. On the other hand, if you don't understand what the jargon means, you are at a disadvantage. I believe many financial institutions use this deliberately to confuse customers. After all, customers who don't understand something are hardly in a position to ask awkward questions – or to compare value for money.

In this appendix we will look at four important terms used in personal finance. Never again will you be dependent on someone else to explain the following to you:
- Percentages
- The difference between capital and income
- Compound interest
- Gearing

Other useful terminology is explained in the 'Jargon Buster' section of www.moneydoctors.ie.

PERCENTAGES MADE EASY

You are not alone

If you aren't entirely comfortable with percentages you are not alone. In a survey designed to test graduates on their knowledge of percentages, only 8% could calculate a percentage accurately, and only 19% actually understood what a percentage was. In other words, more than eight out of ten people with a third-level education were completely at sea when it came to one of the key mathematical concepts used in personal finance. Under these circumstances, is it any wonder that the majority of people struggle to sort out their money matters?

What is a percentage?

The word 'percentage' literally means 'parts per 100' – *cent* being the Latin word for a hundred. Because percentages always deal with parts per hundred, they allow you to compare things that would be difficult to compare otherwise. They are particularly useful when it comes to choosing a loan or deciding on the relative worth of investment opportunities.

How to work out percentages

You calculate a percentage by turning your numbers into a fraction, dividing it out and then multiplying by 100.

Imagine that you have three apple trees, and you want to know which one produces the highest proportion of good – as opposed to rotten – apples. When you harvest the apples from each tree, you keep a note of the total number of apples picked and the number of apples that have to be thrown away. Your note looks like this:

Tree	Apples on tree	Apples spoiled
A	750	150
B	550	88
C	670	101

From the above figures, it isn't easy to gauge which is your best tree. However, if you express the figures in percentage terms, it will immediately become obvious.

On Tree A, 150 out of the 750 were rotten. So your calculation would look like this:

$$\frac{150}{750} \times 100 = 20 \text{ per cent}$$

If you were using a calculator you would key it in like this:

$$150 \div 750 = 0.2 \times 100 = 20$$

On Tree B, 88 apples out of the 550 were rotten, so the calculation would be:

$$\frac{88}{550} \times 100 = 16 \text{ per cent}$$

On Tree C, 101 apples out of the 670 were rotten, so the calculation would be:

$$\frac{101}{670} \times 100 = 15 \text{ per cent}$$

Converting the numbers to percentages allows us to make a fair comparison between the 'performance' of the apple trees. So, 20% of the apples on Tree A were rotten; 16% of the apples on Tree B were rotten; but just 15% of the apples on Tree C were rotten – making it the best-performing apple tree in the orchard!

It is hard enough comparing apple trees with apple trees – but even harder to compare apple trees with – say – orange trees. This is where percentages are so useful. By giving everything a base of 100, we can compare things that aren't alike in other ways.

Now, let's put percentages into context – you are told the **yield** in a property you wish to buy is 6% while the **Internal Rate of Return** (IRR) is 11%. The first element, the yield, is the return or rental income in proportion to the cost of the property excluding stamp duty and costs.

For example, an investment property costing €300,000 with a rental income of €18,000 per annum will give you an initial rental yield of 6% per annum (18,000 is 6% of 300,000). Capital growth on the property is also expected over the next few years. Taking the first five years of ownership together with the yield, the combination is called the **Internal Rate of Return** (IRR), and is generally in excess of the initial yield. If in five years' time the property is worth €450,000, the returns would be:

Growth = 50% (five years)

Annual rental yield = 6%

IRR = 16% per annum (on an un-geared investment and before tax)

MONEY DOCTORS WEALTH WARNING

Don't trust your calculator!

Don't always believe the answer the calculator gives you. Why not? Because the tiniest slip of your finger can give you a completely wrong answer without your being aware of it. Here are five things you can do to avoid calculator error:

1. Estimate your answer before you begin a calculation.
2. Do every calculation twice.
3. Know your calculator.
4. Don't be overawed by your calculator.
5. Hang on to common sense and what you know.

THE VITAL DIFFERENCE BETWEEN CAPITAL AND INCOME

All money is not equal

One of the most important financial concepts to understand is the difference between capital and income. **Capital** is something – it could be money, a property, shares or some other investment – that generates an **income** for whoever owns it. A good way to remember the difference is to think of a fruit tree. The tree itself is the 'capital'. The fruit it produces is the 'income'. You continue to own the tree (capital) and it continues to bear fruit (income) every year. Your wage or salary is the income which comes from the capital of your labour – hence, the expression 'human capital'. Money is not just money – it is either capital or income.

And then there is 'interest'

When you own capital and it produces an income you have a number of choices:
- You can hold on to the capital and spend the income.
- You can hold on to the capital, add the income to it, and generate even more income.
- You can dispose of some or all of the capital and thus reduce the income you receive.

Let's use the example of chickens and eggs! You have some hens (capital) which lay eggs (income). You can do one of three things:
- You can hold on to the chickens (capital) and eat the eggs (income).
- You can hold on to the chickens (capital) and leave the eggs to hatch into more chickens (more capital) that in turn will produce even more eggs (income) for you.
- You can eat your chickens (thus eating into your capital) and thus reduce the total amount of eggs (income) you receive.

There are lots of different names for the income produced by capital. In the case of property, for instance, it is called 'rental income'. In the case of a cash deposit in a bank it is called 'interest'.

THE MIRACLE OF COMPOUND INTEREST

A financial concept that can make or break you

When you are earning it, it has the power to make you very rich. When you are paying it, it has the power to make you very poor. Albert Einstein described it as 'the greatest mathematical discovery of all time'. It is the reason why banks, building societies, credit card companies and other financial institutions make so much profit from lending money. And it is the reason why ordinary investors can make themselves rich simply by doing nothing.

Perhaps the easiest way to understand compound interest is to look at a hypothetical example. Imagine that you have €1,000, and that you invest it in a savings account that pays interest at a rate of 10% per year. At the end of one year, you will get €100 interest. If you withdraw this interest but leave your capital, at the end of the second year you will be entitled to another €100 interest. Supposing, however, that you don't withdraw the interest, but instead leave it to 'compound'. At the end of your first year, your €1,000 has become €1,100. At the end of your second year, you will have earned €110 interest, meaning that your original €1,000 is now €1,210. Put another way, your interest is earning you more interest.

You will sometimes see the initials CAR in relation to interest. This is the compound annual rate. This is the amount of interest you will receive if you keep adding your interest to your capital in the way I have just described.

Let's look at a real example:

> According to research, the Irish stock market has produced an annual average return of 14% since 1989. At this rate, if you invested €1,000 today and every year for the next 10 years, it would be worth €24,497 in 10 years' time.

Still not impressed? How much do you think your money would grow by if, at the age of 25, you had started saving €100 a month (that's €25 a week) for just 10 years at the same return? €15,000? €18,000? You are not close. At the age of 35 your money would be worth €25,000. Better still, at age 65 your money would be worth €1.5 million!

No wonder lenders love you

When you borrow money, compound interest is working against you. Supposing, for instance, you borrow €5,000 on a credit card at an interest rate of 15% – which isn't high by today's standards. The credit card company allows you to make a minimum payment of 1.5% each month. After two years, you will still owe approximately €4,700, having made repayments of €1,750, of which €1,450 has been swallowed up in interest. Work out for yourself how long it will take you to pay off the full debt!

Compound interest is your greatest enemy and your greatest ally. When you are in debt, it works against you. But when you have money to invest, you can make compound interest really work for you.

GEARING

Allowing other people to make you rich

Using borrowed money to buy an asset is called gearing. If you can make it work in your favour, gearing can dramatically boost your profits. For instance:

> Supposing you buy a €200,000 apartment using a €40,000 deposit and a €160,000 mortgage. After one year the apartment is worth €240,000. It isn't just that you have made a €40,000 profit – you've actually doubled the €40,000 you originally invested. In other words, you've achieved a 100% gain in just 12 months.

Even if you deduct the mortgage interest you've had to pay for the year you've owned your apartment – you have still done very well. However, what goes up can also come down. In the UK between 1987 and 1989, house prices fell by around one-third. If this happened to someone selling an apartment they bought for €100,000 using an €80,000 mortgage, they would not only have seen their €20,000 deposit wiped out – they would owe an additional €13,333 (the difference between the mortgage of €80,000 and the €66,666 you would get for the apartment). When this happens it is called being in '**negative equity**'.

Gearing is the easiest and most effective way of increasing the potential profit from any investment. It is also the most effective way of increasing the potential loss, something every investor contemplating gearing would be well advised to remember.

There is a commonly held view that owning property is a one-way bet. But in the recent history of many European countries there have been periods when residential property prices fell. In fact, over the long term the Irish stock market has outperformed Irish property. Remember, it is vitally important to diversify your investments, thus spreading your risk.

Many people re-mortgage their homes in order to have a deposit with which to buy a second investment property. This can be very sensible. However, if you have an existing mortgage on your home it might make more sense to pay that off first and then to invest in another area – such as the stock market. It very much depends on your circumstances.

Without gearing, most of us would never be able to own our own homes. It also allows us to make other, highly lucrative investments. Nevertheless, you should think carefully before you embark on any investment that requires you to borrow money. You want to make sure that the investment is going to earn you more than the loan is going to cost you.

THE MONEY DOCTOR SAYS ...

- It is well worth your while to practise calculating percentages, as these are the most common way of comparing both investment and lending products.
- If you are trying to remember the difference between capital and income, think of an apple tree. The tree is your capital and its annual crop of fruit is your income.
- Compound interest can make you rich, and it can make you poor too.
  In the case of an investment it is the process whereby the interest you earn from something is added to the capital to produce even more interest. In the case of a loan it is the process whereby the interest you owe is added to the capital you owe, making it harder to get out of debt.
- Gearing allows you to buy an asset with borrowed money. There is no better way to achieve dramatic investment returns but, remember, it can work the other way too.
- You'll find a full explanation of all the most commonly used financial expressions and terms in the Money Doctors' jargon buster at www.moneydoctors.ie.

APPENDIX 2

TAX RATES AND CREDITS

	Budget	
Tax credits @ 20%	2020	2019
Personal tax credits	€	€
Single person	1,650	1,650
Married (assessed jointly)	3,300	3,300
Widowed person in year of bereavement	3,300	3,300
Widowed person – no children	2,190	2,190
Additional allowances for widowed persons in the years after bereavement		
Year 1	3,600	3,600
Year 2	3,150	3,150
Year 3	2,700	2,700
Year 4	2,250	2,250
Year 5	1,800	1,800
One-parent family	1,650	1,650
Home carer's credit (max.)	1,500	1,200
PAYE tax credit	1,650	1,650
Age tax credit		
Single/widowed	245	245
Married	490	490
Incapacitated child tax credit	3,300	3,300
Blind person's tax credit		
One spouse blind	1,650	1,650
Both spouses blind	3,300	3,300
Tax allowances @ marginal rate		
Additional allowance for guide dog	825	825
Incapacitated person		
allowance for employing a carer (max.)	50,000	50,000

Exemption limits	2020	2019
(Being abolished over a 4 year period from 2011)	€	€
Single/widowed, 65 years of age or over	18,000	18,000
Married, 65 years of age or over	36,000	36,000
Additional for dependent children		
1st and 2nd child (each)	575	575
Each subsequent child	830	830
Marginal relief tax rate	40%	40%

Tax Rates and Tax Bands	2020	2019
Personal circumstances	€	€
Single/widowed without dependent children	€35,300 @ 20% Balance @ 40%	€35,300 @ 20% Balance @ 40%
Single/widowed qualifying for one-parent family tax credit	€39,300 @ 20% Balance @ 40%	€39,300 @ 20% Balance @ 40%
Married couple (one spouse with income)	€44,300 @ 20% Balance @ 40%	€44,300 @ 20% Balance @ 40%
Married couple (both spouses with income)	€44,300 @ 20% (with an increase of €26,300 max.) Balance @ 40%	€44,300 @ 20% (with an increase of €26,300 max.) Balance @ 40%

The tax band of €70,600 available to married couples with 2 incomes in 2019 is transferable between spouses up to a maximum of €44,300.

Universal Social Charge (USC)	2020	2019
On the first €12,012	0.5%	0.5%
On the next €7,862	2%	2%
On the next €50,107	4.5%	4.5%
On the balance	8%	8%

There is a surcharge of 3% on individuals who have non-PAYE income that exceeds €100,000 in a year.

APPENDIX 3

TAX COMPUTATION TEMPLATE

	Example		Enter your figures	
Taxable income	€	€	€	€
Gross income		40,000		
Add: Benefit in Kind		1,000		
		41,000		
Deduct: Pension contributions		(2,000)		
Total taxable income	A	39,000		
Tax payable				
34,550 (43,550 married) @ 20%		6,910		
39,000 - 34,550 = 4,450 @ 40%		1,780		
Tax before tax credits		8,690		
Deduct: Tax credits Personal credit (3,300 married)	1,650			
PAYE credit (each PAYE employee)	1,650	(3,300)		
Total tax after credits	B	5,390		
Income after tax	A–B	33,610		
Deduct: Universal Social Charge (see rates in Appendix 4)		(1,234)		
Deduct: PRSI 4% of gross income and BIK		(1,640)		
Net income after tax, USC and PRSI		30,736		

APPENDIX 4

THE MONEY DOCTORS' ANNUAL BUDGET ACCOUNT*

Description	Monthly/quarterly	Total
Electricity		€
Home heating (oil/gas)		€
Telecoms (land/mobile/broadband)		€
TV licence/cable TV		€
Household insurance (contents)		€
Car insurance/tax/service/fuel		€
Food/drink/eating out/cinema/concerts		€
School fees/uniform and sportswear		€
extracurricular school costs		€
Alarm/security		€
Repairs/cleaning/waste/garden		€
Health insurance/medical expenses (incl. dentistry)		€
Christmas and birthday expenses		€
Mini breaks/holidays		€
Clothes/footwear		€
Club subscriptions/donations		€
Other		€
Totals		€

* Does not include mortgage and loan repayments, life assurance or pension costs.

When you have totalled your expenditure and divided by 12, that is the amount you have to provide monthly from your net income to meet that expenditure. All other costs (e.g. capital expenditure, new washing machine, TV, etc.) must be found outside of this budget (the Rainy Day Fund).

THE MONEY DOCTORS' STUDENT MONTHLY BUDGET

Category	Totals	
	Weekly	Monthly
Rent		€
Home heating (oil/gas)		€
Mobile		€
Books		€
Course materials		€
Printing/photocopying		€
Commuter expenses (Bus/Train/DART/Luas)		€
Food		€
Household items/toiletries		€
Medical expenses/dentistry		€
Clothes		€
Gym/club subscriptions		€
Movies/theatre/concerts		€
Other (pubs, clubs & incidentals)		€
Loans		€
Total		€

When you have totalled your expenditure, multiply by 12 and that is the money you have to provide to pay for that expenditure. All other costs (e.g. holidays, buying hardware, etc.) must be found outside of this budget.

APPENDIX 5

MONEY DOCTORS SERVICES

Providence Finance Services Limited, trading as Money Doctors, was founded on 1 December 1999 with an intention to tell and not sell. The company is authorised and regulated by the Central Bank of Ireland and has built up an enviable reputation of executing professional, independent and transparent advice with no bias to any one financial supplier, delivered through a first-class service and administrative back up. We act for most of the financial product providers, from banks and insurance companies to investment houses, without bias. The client comes first.

This is the company mission statement:

As an independent financial advisory company for mortgages and debt management, insurance, savings, pensions and investments, Money Doctors aspire to give to clients the best financial advice, service and aftercare in the most transparent, honest and professional manner. We are always at your service.

Now you can avail of all the personal finance services from Money Doctors.

MONEY DOCTORS CONSULTATIONS

Avail of a 20-minute Money Doctors consultation face to face, telephonically or by email for the same price as a visit to your local GP.

- You pay €65 per 20 minutes (credit card or cheque or can be paid prior to the consultation if preferred).
- A Fact Find is emailed to you for completion and return to Money Doctors prior to the consultation (to set out your financial circumstances, for Central Bank compliance and also so that appropriate solutions, action plans, recommendations and strategies can be prepared and given to clients at the consultation).
- Book the appointment for specific issues and a complete financial makeover. First meetings generally take 40 minutes, covering:
  - Budget planning – how to set them and your goals.
  - Evaluation of your debt management.
  - Savings – are you getting the best rates and terms?
  - Investments – understanding and appraising them.

- Life and health cover – are you over-insured? Perhaps no insurance at all? Paying too much? Get all the facts.
- Income protection – is it worth it? Do you need it? Better than serious illness cover?
- Pensions and retirement planning – knowing the end game and what's in store for you on retirement. Are you saving enough for your retirement? Maximising your pension tax relief? Annuities and ARFs/ AMRFs – the complexities unraveled and explained.

Following the consultation, you receive a comprehensive email with relevant documents, fact sheets, templates and a plan to sort your finances and better manage your money

Each further visit or contact will entail a fee of €65 per 20 minutes for additional face to face or telephonic financial advice, similar to a GP... *we do for your wealth what a good doctor does for your health*

PAYING FOR ADVICE

When you seek independent and authorised financial advice and do not pay a fee, you should ask yourself: How is the adviser earning income? If the only way the adviser can earn an income is to sell you a product, the adviser therefore has a vested interest in that product, and their advice is not impartial.

The benefits of paying for financial advice

You receive unbiased, impartial information together with a wealth of financial experience – Money Doctors tell, *not* sell. Find out where the best/safest deposit and mortgage rates are, whether to fix interest rates or not, investment advice, how to deal with credit card debt, negative equity, personal debt, pensions and investments, redundancy, separation and divorce, life and health cover, general insurances, budgeting and tax credits and allowances.

We analyse the A to Z of your finances from head to toe and can then implement and execute any actions you may require arising from consultations, being fully authorised and regulated by the Central Bank of Ireland.

MONEY DOCTORS EMPLOYER–EMPLOYEE FINANCIAL WELL-BEING SEMINARS

'Financially Healthy For Life' financial well-being seminar

In 2018, Money Doctors relaunched an employer-sponsored financial well-being seminar for the benefit of hard-pressed employees, empowering them to structure and budget their own finances, slash living costs and reduce and manage debt, while also maximising their savings and investments.

How Money Doctors can help
John Lowe, author of the *Money Doctors* guides and one of Ireland's best-known personal finance gurus, is offering employers the opportunity to support and improve the financial education and well-being of their employees and, in so doing, contribute additionally to the bottom line of their own company with greater loyalty and productivity.

The employee financial well-being seminar package:
- One-off seminar or series of seminars covering all aspects of personal finance and planning – one-and-a-half-hour duration to include a Q&A session at any time to suit employer/employee.
- One-to-one financial counselling on-site also available if required.
- Fact sheets, templates and action guides emailed to all employees after the seminar.
- Latest *Money Doctors* finance annual offered to all employees at a discount price. 'A terrific book that you can dip in and out of – and written in a very user-friendly way.' – Gay Byrne
- Presented in person by John Lowe and his team.
- Complete turn-key package and very cost-effective.

Benefits to the employer
Research suggests that a well-executed workplace financial education programme is likely to reap great rewards. It is:
- a practical and inexpensive way to help staff with one of their greatest worries: their personal finances.
- a cost-effective way of boosting staff loyalty.
- highly topical and demonstrates employers' understanding of what is important to their employees.
- the cornerstone of family-friendly employment policy.
- a help in reducing absenteeism. (€793m lost per annum, 3.5% or 8 working days per year – that's 12 million days every year, according to the Small Firms Association. This study found that back pain/injury and stress were the principal reasons for being absent.)
- a help in reducing employee turnover rates (this can be calculated in monetary terms).
- increasing employee productivity and competitiveness.
- increasing contributions to the company pension scheme.

Benefits to the employees

With the recession beginning to show its teeth, helping staff to better manage their money and look to the future has to be a major driver to attend this presentation funded by an employer. This is what they will learn:

- How to plan, set budgets and financial goals.
- Coping with and managing debt quickly and easily.
- Cutting down banking bills.
- Savings and investments – where the best deals are and maximising the returns.
- Life and health cover – what they should have and what they should drop.
- Pensions – all you ever wanted to know but didn't have the time to ask.
- Insuring your possessions – the right way.
- Fact sheets on:
    - Top 100 money-saving tips.
    - Best rates for savings and loans.
    - Tax rates, tax credit entitlements and tax refund processes.
    - Budgeting, including templates.

There is a Q&A after each seminar, with the Money Doctors team on hand to answer any immediate queries employees may have.

These seminars will help change employee behaviour patterns that negatively affect job performance, while also building their assets and reducing their debt. They will also far better appreciate the employer-provided benefits, while it may even increase their ability to retire early or at least on time.

Everyone knows the real challenges that businesses are experiencing in the current economy, and most employees are willing to work with employers to ensure the survival of the business.

In every aspect of current workplace sentiment, whether job satisfaction, motivation, morale, perceived stress levels or job security, for employers in survival mode, it is important to recognise the value of a fully focused workforce.

'Reduced incomes, levies, increased living expenses, servicing immediate household debt and concerns about the future value of pensions and savings are causing sleepless nights for a large portion of the population,' says John Lowe of Money Doctors.

'We are experiencing a huge increase in enquires from stressed, anxious and worried people seeking help from the Money Doctors because they feel they have lost control of their lives as the economic recession grinds on, as unemployment numbers rise and as financial security appears to be evaporating. What employees need is sound, independent, impartial financial advice in plain English from someone they feel they can trust to bring financial stability and options to their lives.'

While most surveys have been carried out in America and the UK, it would be fair to say that Ireland's employees would be even more affected than our overseas brethren.

- Workers' financial stress may hurt productivity (*USA Today*).
- Poor personal financial planning behaviours breed productivity-inhibiting stress for roughly 15 percent of US workers (Dr E Thomas Garmen).
- Job stress leads to increased absenteeism, tardiness and desire to quit (*Journal of Occupational and Environmental Medicine*).
- One in four American workers are seriously financially distressed, causing negative impacts to individuals, families and employers (Dr E Thomas Garmen).
- Employee financial education is a critical component of employee-wellness programmes.

The cost of each seminar will depend on location and numbers both in terms of staff attending and the seminars themselves. For a seminar series, economies of scale will also apply but in the first instance, please contact seminars@moneydoctors.ie or call (01) 278 5555.

WANT TO JOIN THE WINNING TEAM ?

Finally, if you are:
- a Qualified Financial Adviser (QFA) or higher status;
- any age or gender;

and have:
- Central Bank authorisation and a tax clearance certificate;
- A curriculum vitae with a background in finance; and
- Good references;

... and you are interested in being one of the Money Doctors for your area, please contact Stephanie Cahill at scahill@moneydoctors.ie or (+353 1) 278 5555 to receive exciting news on our new Money Doctors territorial representatives opportunity.

Providence House
Lower Kilmacud Road
Stillorgan, County Dublin
A94 A2F7
Tel: (+353 1) 278 5555
Fax: (+353 1) 278 5556
Email: info@moneydoctors.ie
www.independentfinancialadvice.ie
www.moneydoctors.ie

APPENDIX 6

USEFUL ADDRESSES

REVENUE COMMISSIONERS

Check www.revenue.ie for contact details for your local Revenue office numbers, addresses and email addresses.

You can also avail of the Revenue Online Service at: www.ros.ie or at:
Revenue Online Service Helpdesk
Revenue Online Service
2nd Floor, Trident House
Blackrock, County Dublin
Tel: (1890) 20 11 06 or from outside the Republic of Ireland (+353 1) 7023021
Opening hours: Monday–Thursday, 8.30am–8.30pm; Friday, 8.30am–6.00pm

COMPANIES REGISTRATION OFFICE

CRO Public Office
Gloucester Place Lower
Mountjoy, Dublin 1
D01 C576
Email: info@cro.ie
Tel: (01) 8045200 Lo-call: (1890) 220 226
Fax: (01) 8045222
DX No. 145001

COMPETITION AND CONSUMER PROTECTION COMMISSION (CCPC)

Bloom House
Railway Street, Dublin 1
D01 C576
Tel: (01) 4025500
Lo-call: (1890) 43 24 32
www.consumerhelp.ie

INSTITUTE OF CHARTERED ACCOUNTANTS IN IRELAND

Chartered Accountants House
47–49 Pearse Street, Dublin 2
Tel: (01) 6377200
www.icai.ie

ASSOCIATION OF CHARTERED CERTIFIED ACCOUNTANTS

La Touche House
IFSC, Dublin 1
Tel: (01) 447 5678
www.accaglobal.com

INSTITUTE OF CERTIFIED PUBLIC ACCOUNTANTS IN IRELAND

17 Harcourt Street, Dublin 2
Tel: (01) 4251000
www.cpaireland.ie

CENTRAL CREDIT REGISTER

First Floor, Block E
Adelphi Plaza, George's Street Upper
Dún Laoghaire, County Dublin
Tel: (01) 2245500
Lo-call: (1890) 100050
Email: myrequest@centralcreditregister.ie
www.ccr.ie

IRISH CREDIT BUREAU

ICB House
Newstead
Clonskeagh Road, Dublin 14
Tel: (01) 2600388
Fax: (01) 2600390
www.icb.ie

Law Society of Ireland

Blackhall Place, Dublin 7
Tel: (01) 6724800
Fax: (01) 6724801
www.lawsociety.ie

Money Advice Budgeting Services (MABS)

Cork MABS
12 Penrose Wharf
Penrose Quay, Cork
Tel: (021) 4552080
Fax: (021) 4552078
Email: cork@mabs.ie

There are numerous MABS offices in Dublin, so to find the one closest to you go to www.mabs.ie/contact_mabs/.

Galway MABS
The Halls (3rd Floor)
Quay Street, Galway
Tel: (091) 569349
Fax: (091) 569478
Email: galway@mabs.ie
Limerick MABS
Unit 9, Tait Business Centre
Dominic Street, Limerick
Tel: (061) 310620
Freephone: (1800) 418088
Fax: (061) 404605
Email: limerick@mabs.ie

Waterford MABS
6b Wallace House, Maritana Gate
Canada Street, Waterford
Tel: (051) 857929
Fax: (051) 841264
Email: waterford@mabs.ie

St Vincent de Paul

SVP House
91–92 Sean McDermott Street, Dublin 1
Tel: (01) 8386990
Fax: (01) 8387355
www.svp.ie

The Samaritans

National Helpline: (1850) 609090
Dublin Branch: (01) 872 7700

APPENDIX 7

IMPORTANT TAX DATES

Form 12 is the short version for those whose main source of income is from an employment or pension (other than a company director for whom there is a separate Form 12) and is therefore taxed under PAYE.

Form 11 or **Form 11E** must be completed each year by self-employed persons or those with income not taxed at source. To download these forms, go to www.revenue.ie/forms

The initial instructions for Form 12 are: 'You are hereby required, under Section 879 Taxes Consolidation Act 1997, by the Inspector of Taxes named above to prepare and deliver, on or before 31 October 2019, a tax return on this prescribed form for the year 1 January 2018 to 31 December 2018.'

You must make a return of income on Form 11 if, in the year 2018, you:

- opened a foreign bank account;
- acquired a material interest in offshore funds in a member state of the EU, EEA or the OECD with which Ireland has a double taxation agreement; and/or
- invested in a foreign life policy issued from a member state of the EU, EEA or the OECD with which Ireland has a double taxation agreement.

To assist you in completing this return, each section of the form has been colour-coded into the different categories of income, tax credits, allowances and reliefs.

All Revenue forms and information leaflets are available from the Revenue Forms and Leaflets Service at LoCall: (1890) 30 67 06 (ROI only), from the Revenue's website: www.revenue.ie, or from any Revenue office.

PENALTIES

There are penalties for failure to make a return, or for making a false return or helping to make a false return, or for claiming tax credits, allowances or reliefs that are not due. These penalties include fines up to €126,970, up to double the tax in question and/or imprisonment.

IMPORTANT TAX DATE DEADLINES

October is an important month in the tax calendar, as 31 October is the last day by which an individual taxpayer must Pay and File for the tax year ended on the previous 31 December.

The table below shows what dates in October returns and payments become due. Some returns are required more than once a year (e.g. every month in the case of PAYE and PRSI), as indicated in Column 2.

Date	Frequency	Category	Description
14	Monthly	Income tax, PAYE/PRSI	Payment of PAYE/PRSI deductions to 30 September
14	When applicable	Dividend withholding tax	Due date for payment and filing of returns of withholding tax on dividends paid by companies in September 2020
14	Bi-monthly	VAT	Filing of VAT 3 return together with payment of any VAT due
14	Monthly	VAT	Filing of Intrastat return for September
15	Annually	Capital gains tax	Filing of return of capital gains tax for 2020. Payment of capital gains tax on disposals from 1 January to 30 November 2020 payable by 15 December and from 1 December to 31 December 2020 payable by 31 January 2021
14	Monthly	Income tax, PAYE/PRSI	Payment of PAYE/PRSI deductions to 30 September
14	When applicable	Dividend withholding tax	Payment and filing of returns of withholding tax on dividends paid by companies in September 2020
14	Bi-monthly	VAT	Filing of VAT 3 return together with payment of any VAT due
14	Monthly	VAT	Filing of Intrastat return for September
15	Annually	Capital gains tax	Filing of return of capital gains tax for 2020. Payment of capital gains tax on disposals from 1 January to 30 November 2020 payable by 15 December and from 1 December to 31 December 2020 payable by 31 January 2021
21	Annually	Corporation tax	Company year-end 30 November 2020: first instalment due, minimum 72% of total liability for the year

21	Annually	Corporation tax	Company year-end 30 April 2020: second instalment due, bringing cumulative payment to 90% of total liability for the year
21	Annually	Corporation tax	Company year-end 31 January 2020: payment of balance of corporation tax and filing of corporation tax return and Form 46G
28	Annually	Company secretarial	Filing of annual returns dated 30 September 2020
31	Annually	Corporation tax	Company year-end 30 April 2019: close companies with undistributed profits may have to make a distribution by this stage to avoid surcharge
31	Annually	Company secretarial	Company year-end 31 January 2020: final date for holding Annual General Meeting and latest possible annual return date for 2020
31	Annually	Income tax, PAYE/PRSI	Income tax and payment of preliminary PAYE/PRSI tax for 2020, payment of income tax balance for 2019, filing of 2019 tax return all due 31 October or ROS deadline date
31	Annually	Pensions	Payment of retirement annuity premiums, PRSA premiums and personal contributions to occupational pension schemes for tax year 2020 – you must also elect to have these treated as paid in the tax year 2020
31	Quarterly	VAT	Filing of VIES return for calendar quarter ending September

APPENDIX 8
100 WAYS TO SAVE CASH

Are you having trouble making ends meet? Do you run out of money before payday? Are you extravagant with your money? Do your current financial circumstances require you to do a complete overhaul on your lifestyle and spending? What are the areas that will allow economies in your spending?

Almost every item of expenditure should be queried – do you need it and if so, are there better or cheaper alternatives? Many of the following tips are practical and easily implementable. Some you will know or will have heard before, but they may give you the impetus to focus on your own finances and to start saving money now when it matters.

FINANCIAL

1. **Plan a yearly household budget** – add up all your yearly household bills and divide by twelve. That figure is the amount you need to put away each month to meet those bills just to run the home. Any capital or 'luxury' spending must be found outside of this annual budget. You could also adopt a monthly budget if preferred, but you should in any event put at least two hours every month into planning your finances to ensure you are on track with your spending. Remember, if your expenditure exceeds income, you have two choices – earn more or cut costs. You should in any event query *every* item of expenditure – ask yourself, do you need it and is there a better or cheaper alternative? If you are frittering money away, download the free Money Doctors app from Google Play or the AppStore to track and control your spending.
2. **Think smart with your surplus cash** – do not leave surplus money in your current account or low interest-bearing accounts. At least transfer it into your bank's best deposit account and when you need funds to meet commitments, transfer it over a couple of days before it's due. If that deposit account is sizeable, negotiate with your bank – if their rates are much less than, for example, KBC Bank (0.15% – the best rate on-demand up to €100,000 at the time of going to press along with Permanent TSB), they may have

the discretion to increase that deposit rate in order to hold on to your business. Beware, however, banks are now charging interest on credit union deposits!

3. **Check your bank charges on a regular basis and cut down your banking bills** – there are too many cases of overcharging from all the banks to accept that your bank is not one of them! Sometimes, these charges can be waived at the discretion of the manager – if you don't ask, there'll be no waiving. Try to avoid exceeding your overdraft permission if you have an overdraft. The surcharges and fees are punitive. You should also operate online bank accounts – better deals, easier to operate and no waiting in queues, plus savings on time and travel expenses. Check out An Post Money's new Smart Account, Billpay or www.mybills.ie. For current account comparisons, log on to www.ccpc.ie/currentaccounts or www.bonkers.ie.

4. **Check your mortgage and loan interest rates** – sometimes we go to great lengths at the initial stages of obtaining a mortgage or loan to get the most competitive interest rate at the time. Once taken out, there is a tendency to overlook the maintenance of that loan. You could very easily find out that your lender's original rate or current advertised interest rate bears no resemblance to your own. This is also a time to check if you are currently on a variable rate, and if you should go fixed. If your lender is uncompetitive, perhaps you should switch to another lender.

5. **Avail of your annual capital gains tax (CGT) exemptions** – the first €1270 of chargeable gains to an individual arising from the disposal of a capital asset (e.g. shares) is exempt. This is allowable for each tax year but is not transferable between spouses. The rate payable on CGT is 33% over the threshold. For Capital Acquisition Taxes (CAT), remember the threshold from parent to child (Group A of three groups) is currently €320,000 for each child. The tax rate for CAT is also 33% over the thresholds.

6. **Check your life and health cover** – you could be over-insured. Do a review on all your insurances. Are you getting the best value? What happens if you or your spouse die or become permanently incapacitated? If you took out life cover (with home mortgages it is mandatory) you may have been a smoker at the time. Once you are smoke free for 12 months, you could save yourself over 50% of the annual premiums. Worth checking out.

7. **Health insurance comparison** – with only three health insurers in Ireland (VHI, Laya and Irish Life Health – the latter bought out the remaining 51% of Glohealth, plus Aviva Health, and merged the two in the summer of 2016), it is really important that you continually update yourself on the best deal for you. The Health Insurance Authority does an excellent comparison of all three and updates it – check out www.hia.ie.

8. **Check your general insurance** – is your home buildings and contents cover competitive? If you have commercial or residential investment property insurance, is that competitive? Do you require any special risk insurance that you 'risked' being without to date – you may not be so 'lucky' next year? Public liability, professional indemnity, PC hacker, virus insurance, even insuring for that round of drinks after a hole in one on the golf course, etc.

9. **Avail of any exemptions on income tax liability plus claim any tax reliefs and allowance entitlements up to the last four years** – this includes medical expenses, dental, pension relief, etc. Text MONEYDOCTORS to 53131 to start the tax refund process (normal SMS rates apply). You may be unwittingly exempt from paying income tax (e.g. An Irish resident artist producing originals that have cultural and artistic merit, income from woodlands, etc.). You should also ensure, if self-employed and your partner is working in the business, that the full entitlement of income tax exemptions is taken up by the partner. In other words, pay her/him her/his dues tax-free!

10. **Private college fees** – tax relief at the standard rate is available for approved courses undertaken by a taxpayer or dependants in approved private colleges. The courses must be full-time undergraduate courses of at least two years' duration. Postgraduate courses of between one and four years' duration in public colleges and approved private colleges now attract similar tax relief.

11. **Help your parents or be helped by your children** – covenants are also still popular with tax relief available for the donor: you. To qualify for tax relief, the payments must be capable of lasting for at least six years, while the recipient has to have unused tax credits to make the covenant work. If a person is over 65, their son or daughter can pay them up to 5% of their income under a deed of covenant and the son or daughter will get tax relief on the amount paid. The covenant must be legally documented in order for the person making the payment to receive the tax benefits. Tax at

the standard rate (20%) must be deducted and only the net amount paid over. For example, if a daughter gives her mother €1,000 a year, she makes out a covenant and pays €800 to the parent. The mother then gets the other €200 by way of a tax rebate from Revenue, while the daughter also gets tax relief of €200. The net cost to the daughter is €600, while the mother gets the benefit of €1,000. The Revenue regards the €1,000 as the mother's. The daughter has already paid €400 in tax (40%) on the €1,000 and the tax is now being returned. Effectively, €200 goes back to the daughter and €200 to the mother. The person making the covenant should get tax form R185 from his or her local tax office and submit.

12. **Think pensions** – if you are self-employed, a 5% equity-holding director or perhaps in an occupational pension scheme (where pension holders can make further payments through an Additional Voluntary Contribution), you should review your pension requirements. Age thresholds still apply – e.g. At 50 years old, you can invest 30% of your net relevant earnings into a pension plan – while for every euro you invest in the fund, you will save tax at your marginal rate depending on the type of pension. Ask yourself, if you were retiring now you could live off the €248.30 per week from the State pension? Less than half the working population have provided for themselves outside of the State pension, while in 2018 there were five workers for every person retiring. In 2050, there will be just two. The incentives are still there to start. Apart from the tax relief on premiums, all growth in the fund is tax-free, plus 25% of the fund can be taken on retirement as a tax-free lump sum (now capped at €200,000 tax-free but any excess is taxed at only 20%). Still worth it.

13. **Approved Retirement Funds and Approved Minimum Retirement Funds** – recent changes in the pension laws now allow *you* to decide what you want to do with your retirement fund when you have reached the age of retirement. Up to 1999, the only choice you had was to take out an annuity (a fixed rate deposit account where you receive a monthly interest cheque until you die – a guaranteed income where the rate never changes) with a life insurance company. When you die, however, the capital or fund stays with that life insurance company, and your estate loses out. For PRSA and AVC pension holders, that has all changed now and that fund can eventually be passed on to your estate through an

Approved Retirement Fund (ARF), introduced in 1999. Three main conditions apply:

• You must either have minimum €12,700 pension before investing your fund in an ARF (today's State pension now exceeds this amount when you include the Christmas bonus, so those over the age of 66 (67 from next year) can invest **all** into their ARF); or

• If you do not have a pension, put €63,500 of your fund into an Approved Minimum Retirement Fund (AMRF) until age 75.

• You then must withdraw 4% (5% over 71 years of age but 6% over €2 million fund) of the ARF each year (this is called 'imputed distribution'). The annuity system is still available and has its merits too. It is important to have growth in this fund, otherwise you will run out of money. Contact your regulated adviser or your preferred pension provider for further details.

14. **Operate a charge card or a prepaid card as opposed to a credit card** – you are probably aware that credit card balances are normally charged between 9% and 24%+ depending on the credit card company. By switching to a charge card (e.g. American Express) you *must* pay it off when you receive your statement or it is debited to your bank current account. Another option is prepaid cards, where you can only spend what you lodge into the card – better discipline! Watch out for the debit card from An Post Money's Smart Account, launched in June 2017.

15. **Think about other forms of investment** – for instance, gold, rock'n'roll memorabilia, philately or forestry investment. Ireland is the least forested country in the EU, with forest cover of 9% as compared with the EU average of 31%. The mild, wet Irish climate is the most ideal in the Northern Hemisphere for tree growing – trees grow three times faster here than in some other parts of Europe. Timber products are also the second-largest import into the EU after oil. The EU and the Irish government promote forestry through grants and premia payments. They are keen to reduce agricultural output, of which there is a surplus in the EU, and substitute it with timber-producing forests, of which there is a growing internal EU shortage.

16. **Review your investments monthly** – products are launched every week and you should be wary of their performance on a regular basis. Rates change, some investments go out of favour – you have to be vigilant. If there is a better rate or greater potential, do not be afraid to move. Better in your pocket.

17. Claim all your tax reliefs on residential investment properties – these include:

- 100% of annual mortgage interest paid
- Maintenance and repair costs
- Services charges (including buildings/block insurance)
- Property Management Charges
- Residential Tenancies Board (RTB) fees
- 12.5% of furnishings costs for each of the first eight years after purchase (receipts must be maintained)
- Life insurance premiums if any on residential investment property loans
- Legals (buying/selling plus lease costs if the tenant does not refund the landlord)
- Accounting costs (audit, etc.)
- Local Property Tax may soon be offset against tax liability on your rental income – at least, this was promised, and hope springs eternal!

18. Working from home – if self-employed, be aware of your right to reclaim partial costs, e.g. electricity, heat and telecoms.

19. Save – be aware of the changing deposit interest rates, and keep between three months' and six months' net annual income in a Rainy Day Fund for three reasons:

- Emergencies (your car breaks down)
- Sudden loss of income (a partner loses their job)
- Investment opportunities (buying a rare Arabian oil lamp ...)

20. Rent-a-room relief – Renting a room in your home is tax-free up to a limit of €14,000 per year – no expenses may be deducted and it is not available between connected parties. One bedroom apartments do not comply!

21. Educate yourself – there is no excuse not to better inform yourself on any financial issue under the sun. Seminars, webinars, the printed word, consultations and good old Google – you are not alone.

FOOD, DRINK AND HOUSEHOLD ITEMS

22. Always shop with a pre-written grocery list – Stick to what is on the list. Men in particular are disastrous for impulse buying.

23. Check to see what you need before making out a shopping list – Many shoppers buy items they already have in stock.

24. **Create a daily list for updating** – If you run short of tea, washing-up liquid, kitchen towels, etc., these can be added to your main shopping list.

25. **Look for special sale announcements in your store, newspapers, radio and television** – It may be worth your while buying a month's supply of an item you would normally buy, if you can avail of a huge discount.

26. **Shop only once a month for your non-perishables** – This means you have to plan for the full month and should not overspend by additional visits to your local convenience store.

27. **Keep your shopping receipts** – You should track your spending and compare prices (a little black book might be just the job, or better still, avail of the free Money Doctors app to track your precise spending habits).

28. **Shopping at discount stores should not mean that you ignore generic products in the main supermarkets** – Tesco, Dunnes, Supervalu, Centra, Spar, Lidl and Aldi all produce their own generic goods at considerably cheaper prices than the brand names. Input all your loyalty cards on one app such as STOCARD. It's free and saves you having to carry around all those cards.

29. **Buy direct when you can** – All vegetables and fruit come from the land. If you have access to a local farm, buy directly. Apart from saving money, you will benefit from the fresh produce.

30. **Grow your own** – If you have a garden or a plot, try growing a few vegetables, or you could try growing your tomatoes in the house!

31. **Buy in bulk** – Economies of scale apply, in particular to non-perishables (tins of beans) and toiletries (24-roll tissue packs). You will need to analyse your consumption to evaluate your bulk needs.

32. **Don't buy bulk unnecessarily** – A half-ton of nails at rock bottom prices might be fine if you are a carpenter. Special offers such as '3 for the price of 2' might not suit your palate.

33. **Use vouchers and cut outs** – You will be amazed how all those little discounts add up to big savings on your shopping bill; there is no shame in availing of these offers. You may even have a discount offer on the back of your shopping receipt. Watch out too for 'double coupon' days. Look after the pennies and the pounds will look after themselves!

34. **Avail of in-store discounts and special offers** – You could come across a 'loss leader' at your local store that you might have on your shopping list.

35. **Shop online** – This can be cheaper because impulse buys no longer apply. Delivery charges are negated by the cost of travelling to your supermarket and parking. Not to mention the latté! Check out www.cheapeats.ie, www.coeliac.ie and www.goodfoodireland.ie to name but a few.

36. **Online discount websites** – before you shop, you should spend a few minutes checking out some of the discount websites for economies not just on food, for example www.dealrush.ie and www. groupon.ie.

37. **Check the date on all your purchases** – No point in arriving home with out-of-date food fit for the bin. The same goes with food in stock – ensure that you consume foods that have been stored the longest (that are, of course, still safe to eat).

38. **Avoid buying at the check-out, and never ask for cash back** – You are bombarded with chocolates, batteries, magazines, etc. in that last-ditch attempt to lure the money from your wallet at the check-out before you leave the shop. Resist the temptation! Receiving cash back only increases the cost of your purchases, as the cash back is soon frittered away.

39. **Bring your own bags to the store** – There is a 22 cent charge for every bag bought at the check-out used to carry your purchases. You could kill two birds with the one stone by buying bio-degradable and environmentally friendly bags.

40. **Buy food with balance in mind** – Food and drink should be based on a balanced diet. Eating pizzas and drinking Coca-Cola seven days a week is not going to do a whole lot of good for your diet. Plan your meals to reflect this balance.

41. **Avoid snacks after shopping** – You have been shopping for an hour and you go to the store café for a coffee and a sit down. Instead, go home and put on the kettle.

42. **Don't buy on an empty stomach** – You often end up buying food simply because you are hungry.

43. **Bring your own lunch to work** – Prepare your own roll or baguette and refill your water bottle, as long as the water is fit to drink from the taps. Water will soon be scarce, so use it wisely – never run the tap washing or brushing your teeth.

44. **Review your car** – does it need replacing? Could you upgrade the model for efficiency purposes (e.g. if you are currently achieving 25 miles per gallon or 40 kilometres per 4.55 litres, if you were to change to a car doing 50 miles per gallon or 80 kilometres per 4.55 litres, you would save 50% on fuel costs).

45. **Change your car to an electric model** – apart from the environment support through reduced carbon emissions, you could save hundreds of euro by such a change. Budget 2018 introduced the abolition of Benefit in Kind (BIK) tax on all fully electric company cars up to a value of €50,000. Annual savings of 30% BIK every year as long as you hold the car are not to be sniffed at!

46. **Avoid company cars** – in about 80% of cases and outside of all-electric cars (to avoid BIK, the value of the electric car must be less than €50,000), it does not pay to maintain a company car. BIK on company cars is prohibitive – 30% of the value of the car when first purchased: e.g. a Toyota Avensis (diesel version) at €25,520 means that for as long as you have this company car you will pay BIK each and every year of €7,656, or €638 per month, irrespective of the car's depreciating value. Better to take mileage expenses at €0.6348 per mile.

47. **Buy a classic or vintage car (over 25 years old)** – Apart from the style, it would be cheaper to buy (and if you deem this car a company vehicle, the tax payable will be based on the value of the car at the time of purchase!). Also, they are cheaper to insure, and there is minimal tax payable.

48. **Reduce your dependency on fuel #1 – pool your car** and share it with others going the same way or working in the same company.

49. **Reduce your dependency on fuel #2 – charge your work colleagues** a fuel-sharing fee should they have no car and wish you to drive them to work each day.

50. **Reduce your dependency on fuel #3 – keep your car in top trim** with regular servicing, keeping the correct tyre pressure, driving under the speed limit, driving smoothly, and no unnecessary weights inside the car.

51. **Check your tyres for wear** – new tyres will be more efficient than the worn tyres that currently adorn your car. Over two years old, and under normal annual mileage, your car can be a death trap anyway. Review those tyres!

52. **Shop around for fuel** – take a note of your local stations and their fuel prices. Sometimes, to grab greater market share, stations will run a discount campaign to drive custom through their business. Look out for fuel discount cards and web sites (www.pumps.ie).

53. **Reduce your dependency on cars #1** – if you are a two-car family, review the need for the second car. Work out the practicalities. Would public transport – which is improving all the time – be more appropriate?

54. **Reduce your dependency on cars #2** – would the purchase of a bicycle be practical? Apart from the obvious exercise benefits, the humble bike costs nothing to run and there are even tax breaks for employers to provide same for their staff.

55. **Think regular car maintenance check-ups** – if you look after your car, your car will look after you financially.

56. **Car loans are deterrents** – if you are a person who changes your car every three years and just renews the existing (and expensive) car loan at that point, try saving over a three-year period so that you do not need that car loan.

57. **Car loans** – shop around if you must take out a car loan. Personal Contract Plans are now the most popular form of borrowing. Be sure to read the small print. Some car manufacturers offer 0% finance to buy their cars. Expect to be charged between 6.5% (from some credit unions or if you have a really solid relationship with your bank) and 15% depending on the institution you approach. Avoid moneylenders if at all possible.

58. **Walk** – good for the body, pocket and planet.

59. **Use public transport** – it's great and actually much more economical than maintaining your own car.

60. **Home oil** – shop around through the various home heating companies looking for economies. Paying upfront for the year's oil requirements may reap dividends.

61. **Home heating** – turn your thermostat down just 1% and you can save as much as 10% of the actual cost. Remember to switch off the heating when away – even for weekends, and especially at the onset of summer.

62. **Boiler** – if your boiler is more than ten years old, you could consider replacing it with a new condenser boiler – this is much more energy-efficient and should repay installation costs within two years.

63. **Insulate your house and your pipes** – you will save hundreds of euro through minimising loss.

64. **Avail of the energy grants for improving the efficiency of your home –** there are a number available, check out www.seai.ie/grants.

LIFESTYLE AND MISCELLANEOUS NEEDS

65. **Brush up the CV** – keep your resumé updated. You will never know the day when you may be looking for a job. The most recession-proof employments can be found in education, healthcare, environment, energy and security. If you are not in these industries, you should brush up your skills, go to night classes or online courses. Whatever you do, don't stay in a sector that is in decline.

66. **Buy cloth napkins and nappies, and stick to your annual clothes budget –** limit your spending on clothes to a budget rather than impulse buying for that special party.

67. **Look after your clothes** – change into casual clothing after work. Hang up everything rather than leaving it on the floor or throwing it on a chair.

68. **Charity clothes shops** – it is no shame to buy clothes from these outlets – firstly, you are helping the charity, and secondly, the clothes, often with designer labels, are far cheaper than buying new.

69. **Use eBay to sell unwanted items** – watch out for special offers throughout the year, e.g. 50% off normal advertisement placements. Great for selling unwanted clothes, electrical and electronic goods, concert tickets, etc.

70. **Buy generic medication** – you will always find brand-name medicine more expensive. Ask your doctor to prescribe generic medicine.

71. **Go to your library** – all your magazines, movies and books are there and are free. Soon you will be able to order online and just collect. The good news for authors is royalties are now being paid, albeit miniscule, when books are taken out. You now know! You could even read newspapers online.

72. **Review your health club** – if you enjoy your membership, ensure you are getting value. Monitor your weight and fitness. The same applies to golf clubs, or any sporting or social membership. *If you are not using it, cut it out.*

73. **Entertain at home** – game nights, movie nights, music soirées. As entertainment outside the home becomes more expensive, the simpler life beckons, and it can also be much more fun and much more social.

74. **Plan your annual gifts** – family birthdays and Christmas presents, special friends' gifts. You know you will have to buy them, but why wait until the week before Christmas – the most expensive week of the year?

75. **Review your cable and telecoms** – do you really need the movie channels? You may be a golf buff, but are you really going to spend *that* much time on Sky Sports *and* BT Sports, let alone the Golf Channel?

76. **Subscribe to Skype** (www.skype.com) – especially if you have to make calls from your laptop/PC outside the country. With over 310 million subscribers and 15 million online at any one time, the savings are very significant (Skype to Skype calls are free, while Skype to landlines are 0.017c per minute!). If you have chatterbox children, block all outgoing mobile calls – the savings could be significant while you should always check your telecom bill and review the top 10 most called and top 10 most expensive – this can be very revealing! WhatsApp is equally efficient and no cost.

77. **Check with Com Reg's website** at www.comreg.ie/compare/#/services – This site gives you all the comparison options for operators and various mobile phone, home phone, broadband and TV price plans. The new eurotariff legislation on roaming charges may make it cheaper to phone home than send a text message (which is not covered under the new legislation).

78. **Shop around for your electronic communication handsets** – mobile phones incorporating mp3 players, internet, email, camera, video and radio are becoming cheaper and more sophisticated by the year. Some of the electronic equipment you now have is either out of date or incorporated in new gizmos. Sell it. Also, use rechargeable batteries – even placing batteries in a fridge will prolong their life.

79. **Social networking** – Facebook, Twitter, LinkedIn, YouTube, Pinterest, Instagram – use these websites to your best advantage. Putting your name in front of millions can reap dividends for whatever your purpose.

80. **Friends' holiday homes** – you may find that your friends are under financial pressure and would welcome offers at a discount to rent their foreign holiday homes. A win–win situation for them and you.

81. **Do your own garden and handyman jobs around the house** – you will tone your muscles, become fitter and your garden will positively bloom – not to mention attracting admiring glances from your neighbours.

82. **Take haircuts at longer intervals** – instead of every six weeks, make it ten weeks. Better still, cut your own hair or ask a friend to do it.

83. **Garage sale** – rather than store, hoard or dump your prized possessions, sell them from your garage or car boot.

84. **Wheelie bins** – only leave out your respective bins (general refuse bins, green bins etc.) when they are completely full. Collection charges apply irrespective of weight if you leave the bins out.

85. **Enter competitions** – scratch cards, newspapers, magazines, radio and TV – someone has to win and it could be you. If you're not in, you can't win!

REDUCE YOUR ELECTRICITY AND HEATING BILLS

86. **Review your gas/electricity utility provider** – since the successful Big Switch campaign from Bord Gais, competition is now intense. Electric Ireland are back on the field (they had to wait until 40% of their business had migrated to other providers before being allowed back in the game) and with Airtricity, Flogas and the new kids on the block Energia, the consumer has choice. Keep checking and install a meter (pinergy.ie and prepaypower.ie – the two main prepaid electricity suppliers.)

87. **Changing your bulbs to CFLs** – this will save you up to 20% of your annual bills. They may not look as pretty, but they will put money back in your pocket.

88. **Only use washing machines and dishwashers with full loads** – like your dustbin, it pays to optimise the load.

89. **Never have the immersion on with your central heating** – the immersion should only be used during the summer or when you do not need your central heating. The immersion is like a kettle – it should be switched off when you have heated the water.

90. **Turn your thermostat down by 1°** – you will save 10% of your annual heating bill!

91. **Use timers**, and use dimmers for light switches – also for those washing loads at night. Heavy sleepers never hear the din but count the money! Better still, install Bord Gáis' hivehome.ie or similar technology, a system that allows you to control your heating and hot water through an app for mobile, tablet or PC from anywhere in the world. Simply brilliant.

92. **Use nightlights, especially in the bathroom.** They are cheap to run.

93. **Avoid peak time** use as much as possible (between 5pm and 7pm).

94. **Turn off all lights in rooms not being used.** Children especially should be encouraged to turn off lights in their own bedrooms when they leave for school on winter mornings. Minimise lighting where you can. Think of using candles – it's more romantic!

95. **Only boil water in a kettle for your immediate needs** – no need to put on a full kettle of water when you only want a cup of tea for yourself!

96. **Take short showers** and, if bathing, have all the family use the same water – but not if one of them has just returned from a rugby match!

97. **Ensure your fridge and freezer are full** – if you cannot fill it, place jugs of water inside. It is cheaper to run a full freezer than an empty one.

98. **In summer, use the clothesline to air washing** – it's cheaper than the expensive tumble dryer. Only use that tumble dryer off-peak and preferably at night-time rates.

99. **Switch off all electronic equipment when not in use** – leaving devices on standby mode uses 20% of their normal consumption.

The final tip

100. **Keep in touch with the money doctors** at consultation@moneydoctors.ie or call (+353 1) 278 5555.

     • Buy the *Money Doctors* book each year – it's updated and has all the latest financial tips.

     • Book a 20-minute Money Doctors consultation – only €65 – for a once-a-year financial makeover to blow out your financial cobwebs. Better still, book one for a friend who needs help.

     • Download the Money Doctors app **for free** to track your daily spending.

     • Choose the Money Doctors financial well-being seminar (*Financially Healthy for Life*) for your company – an important yet entertaining hour-and-a-half journey through personal finance including a Q&A presented by John Lowe.

     • Use social networks to keep in touch with Money Doctors via Twitter (@themoneydocs), LinkedIn (27,000+ connections), Pinterest, Instagram and Facebook (The Money Doctors).

• Visit www.moneydoctors.ie or www.independentfinancialadvice.ie and sign up for the free monthly ezine.

APPENDIX 9

MORTGAGES FOR FIRST-TIME BUYERS

We here in Ireland have always had a desire to own our homes. Unlike our neighbours on the European mainland, we have generally regarded renting as a short-term option. The boom of the Celtic Tiger years accelerated this trend, resulting in indiscriminate building, reckless lending, unsustainably high prices and the inevitable crash.

The Central Bank of Ireland introduced stringent new guidelines for mortgage lenders in January 2015, and revised them further in January 2017:

- For first-time buyers, a maximum loan-to-value ratio of 90% applies.
- Home loans are subject to a limit of 3.5 times gross income.

These limits were imposed in order to prevent a new property bubble emerging in the future.

In addition to these limits, mortgage lenders have their own internal guidelines and tests to ensure that borrowers will be able to afford their repayments into the future.

Ability to make the repayments, a key component in approving a loan, is based on a number of factors:

- The maximum percentage of net disposable income (monthly income after tax, PRSI and USC) deemed to be available to meet all loan repayments will range between 35% and 50%, depending on the level of income.
- The proposed mortgage repayments will be stress-tested at 2% above the current lending rate to ensure that repayments can still be afforded if rates rise.
- The potential buyer will have to show that his/her regular monthly savings and/or present rent paid are sufficient to cover the stressed repayments.

SAVING FOR A DEPOSIT

The first thing you should do is complete a budget plan to establish how much you can save each month. Email the Money Doctors (info@moneydoctors.ie) for a budget spreadsheet template, which practically tots itself up. You should also determine where you would like to buy your home and set yourself a price limit based on what you can afford.

In addition to the deposit, you will need to factor in stamp duty (1% up to €1,000,000 purchase price, 2% over this threshold) and legal fees & outlay. Most banks offer regular monthly savings plans at reasonable rates and you should ideally use one of these to start your savings habit, saving between €100 and €1,000 per month per person. As you will probably be unable to save the deposit in one year, you should review your budget annually and increase your monthly savings accordingly.

HELP TO BUY SCHEME

In the 2017 budget, the government introduced a Help to Buy scheme. First-time buyers of new homes with a maximum value of €500,000 can claim a refund of 5% of their tax paid over the previous four years subject to a ceiling of €20,000 (€ 400,000). A further condition is that the purchaser must be availing of a mortgage of at least 70% of the purchase price. The scheme was due to end on 31 December 2019, but was extended in Budget 2020.

WHAT TO CONSIDER WHEN BUYING

When buying a home, you must consider the possibility that this will be where you live for your lifetime. For this reason, the location should be carefully evaluated. If you are young and single, an apartment in a town-centre setting may be an attractive proposition. However, such a home would probably be most unsuitable for family life.

The factors to be considered include:
- Convenience to work
- Availability of public transport
- Proximity to shops, schools, sports facilities and public parks
- The age of the building, its energy efficiency and state of repair
- Any zoning issues in the locality that could impact its future value

For a couple who intend to have children, a major consideration has to be the high cost of childcare and the possibility that they may have to live on one income for a number of years. In either of these scenarios, will they still be able to afford the mortgage repayments?

WHICH LENDER?

At the moment there are 8 institutions offering mortgages, each with a range of plans. Some of these institutions offer incentives such as cash-back, discounted home insurance or a contribution towards solicitors' fees. These can be attractive, but you should remember that they are once-offs; if their lending rates are not the best available, the advantage can be wiped out in the first few years by the higher interest being charged. For the best possible advice, it is essential that you consult an independent mortgage intermediary.

WHICH MORTGAGE?

The decision to be made here is between a fixed interest rate mortgage and a standard variable rate option.

Fixed rate mortgages give you the certainty that your monthly repayments will not increase for the duration of the fixed period. On the other hand, you will not benefit from any overall drop in lending rates during this period, should they occur. Breaking a fixed interest rate can be costly too and usually prohibitively so.

Standard variable interest rates can be higher than fixed, but at a time when standard and fixed rates are at an all-time low, there is only one way they can go – upwards. Repayments can rise suddenly and substantially.

Here again, the advice you get from an independent mortgage intermediary is invaluable. Get in touch with the Money Doctors ((+353 1) 278 5555 or info@moneydoctors.ie) for the latest mortgage interest rates, mortgage news or a one-to-one mortgage consultation.

I have always found it useful to use acronyms to memorise structures or systems. For first-time borrowers, that acronym is **TILE**.

T – TERMS AND RATES

Up to 10 years ago, you could obtain a 40-year term for your home loan or up to age 75, whichever came first. That has now been reduced to 30 to 35 years, while the age threshold has been reduced to age 65 for some lenders. You should **not** be repaying a mortgage after retirement. Over half the working population will only have the state pension to live on when they retire, which is currently €248.30 per week – if the government still has the ability to make these payments at your time of retirement.

Tracker rate mortgages were taken off the mortgage menu in November 2008, leaving only standard variable and fixed interest rates available. The current best standard variable rates at the time of going to press:

- Up to 50% loan-to-value – 2.75%
- 50%–80% – 2.95%
- Over 80% – 3.15%

I – INCOME

All lending is based on the ability to repay, not on the asset. The method used to calculate the mortgage amount you are eligible to borrow is a combination of income multiples and net disposable income (NDI).

Eight years ago, if you were earning over €60,000 with no dependants or debts, you could borrow five times your annual income. Accountants, solicitors and doctors attracted even higher multiples – even up to ten times their annual income. For couples, 4.5 times their combined incomes became the multiples norm. Compare this to the humble building society days, when the rule was 2.5 times the main earner's annual income plus the second earner's annual income (to allow for the female partner to stay at home).

Today, under Central Bank regulations, it is 3.5 times your total income. Affordability is then factored in, which takes account of family circumstances, other borrowings and other commitments.

Job security is also of paramount importance. Contract, temporary or part-time work is in most cases a no-no, while overtime and bonuses are often not fully taken into account by mortgage lenders. For the self-employed, it is the **net** profit, not the gross that counts.

The lender will also check your credit history with the Irish Credit Bureau (ICB) or the new state agency the Central Credit Register (CCR) to ensure your financial past is clean. The ICB, in Clonskeagh, Dublin 14, is made up of over 140 financial institutional members, including credit unions, who record every credit transaction and take note of every missed or late payment and financial judgement on their customers. One missed payment stays on the record for five years; with financial judgements, the record is there forever. All lenders check with the ICB or CCR when they receive loan or credit card applications. For those who want to check their own credit history, you can send €6 to ICB, Newstead, Clonskeagh, Dublin 14, giving details of your address(es) and date of birth or click on www. icb.ie. It takes about 3 to 4 days for the response. Or click on www.ccr. ie to request your report – it is free with them and they report on your finances in greater detail than the ICB.

L – LOAN TO VALUE

At one point in the glory days, 110% mortgages were available. Today some lenders are offering 90% loans (the Central Bank will allow 15% of a lender's mortgage book at this LTV), but only for first-time buyers; the majority offer 80% loan to value, as per the Central Bank guidelines. This means you have to come up with that balance and most lenders prefer that you save it to reinforce repayment capacity rather than inherit or win it!

E – EXPENSES

The main cost in buying a home for first-time buyers is the deposit – the difference between what you are borrowing from a lender and the purchase price. This will be at least 10% of the purchase price – so a €350,000 purchase will require €35,000 savings – and the lender would prefer you to have saved this over a certain period. On top of the deposit, you will also need:

- Stamp duty (1% up to €1,000,000, 2% above this amount)
- Legals (generally 1% of purchase price + VAT and outlay)
- Valuation fees (for you and the lender) – about €130
- Basic furnishings and that lick of paint

So is a night on the TILES all that it is cracked up to be? Get in touch ((+353 1) 278 5555 or info@moneydoctors.ie) and let me know.

APPENDIX 10

THE MONEY DOCTORS' TIPS FOR THE TOP

In this appendix, I am again delighted to introduce five innovative, competitive and market-leading products and services. These have my endorsement and could be useful in your armoury for better managing and protecting your money. As they say, it's your pocket that matters!
Please contact me directly if you want further details. These are not in any particular order:

1. Irish Life – Multi Asset Portfolio funds (MAPS)
2. Initiative Ireland – a secured peer to peer lending opportunity
3. Cantor Fitzgerald – a bespoke private clients' service
4. GoldCore Ltd – Ireland's #1 dealer in gold, an important hedge in a volatile world
5. RebateInsolve.ie – Ireland's #1 personal insolvency practice

1. IRISH LIFE – MULTI ASSET PORTFOLIO FUNDS (MAPS)

Established in 1939, Irish Life is Ireland's leading life and pension company. Since July 2013, Irish Life has been part of the Great-West Lifeco group of companies, one of the world's leading life assurance organisations.

Deposit interest rates are currently close to zero, whereas in 2009 the equivalent household term deposit rate was 4.25%. 'Interest rates on new household term deposits remained in July 2019 at 0.04%' – Central Bank of Ireland report, 13 September 2019.

Investors are looking for greater potential returns, but are cautious and slow to put their toes into the investment market with all the bad news on Brexit. Investors who stayed out of the markets this year because of scary Brexit headlines have missed out on a 15%+ return in global stock markets up to 30 September (source: Bloomberg). Brexit news (despite all the media headlines) has had little or no effect on the global stock market, as the UK only makes up around 4.75% of the global stock market and around 2% of the global economy (worries about potential effects of worst-case scenario Brexit on the Irish economy are completely justified, but worries about effects on global stock markets have not materialised so far).

Each person has different investment needs and goals – some for the short term, while others are looking at the longer term. Some are quite conservative when it comes to investment decisions, while others are happy to take a more adventurous approach. It all comes down to finding the right balance between risk and reward.

Individualising stock market selection can prove a mug's game, but when three features stand out on one particular investment, you can only take note and consider.

Irish Life's Multi Asset Portfolio funds were launched in May 2013. Those three features?

1. Instead of individually selecting stocks, 5 funds were created representing differing levels of risk and return and all you had to do was *stick to your lane*. Choose from these five multi-asset funds, ranging from cautious funds – cash, bonds and a small amount of shares (MAPS 2) – to more risky funds, almost totally made up of shares and including a one-third exposure to emerging markets (MAPS 6). Bear in mind, if you want growth in your investments, there has to be an element of risk.

   The European Securities Marketing Authority (ESMA) categorises every stock, share and company in the world into seven separate risk categories, from 1 to 7 – the lower the number, the lower the risk. All insurance companies have managed funds, and most people would not bother with 1 or 7, as they are seen as too extreme, so essentially you only have 5 funds to choose from – makes life simple ...

2. Buying individual stocks also means that the only way of exiting is to sell those stocks and take the loss/profit. With MAPS you don't have to leave the investment – simply move to more cautious or more aggressive funds with no fund switching charge applying. Therefore you do not crystallise any potential loss or profit.

   There is no DIRT payable on these investments. The gross roll-up (to 8th Anniversaries) exit tax system applies instead – this allows you to accumulate profits, and only pay tax on partial/ full withdrawals or 'exits' and 8th anniversaries. This 'exit tax', applied on any applicable profit, is currently at 41% for personal investments and 25% for corporate investments, despite DIRT currently being at 35%.

3. Dynamic Shares to Cash (DSC) – for those who are not au fait with the ups and downs of the stock market, one of the many risk-management features of MAPS is DSC, which allows Irish Life to reduce the amount of your investment that's held in global shares and move it partially or fully into cash in the event of severe market worsening or turbulence. DSC is designed to look at long-term trends in the market, and not to react to short-term or one-off shocks.

Multi-asset investing

A golden rule of investing is diversification, and this isn't just limited to investing across shares of different companies. It can also mean spreading your money across different types of assets, such as shares, bonds, alternatives and property, while also investing in a range of countries. Each asset responds differently to changes in investment conditions. Some go up in value at the same time as others go down. Of course, even a well-diversified portfolio can still fall in value.

What are the benefits of investing in an Irish Life MAPS fund?

It simplifies your fund choice: With so many funds in the market to choose from, choosing the right one can be daunting. With five distinct funds to choose from, MAPS funds make this choice a lot simpler.

You can choose your risk level: Each of the five MAPS funds is managed on an ongoing basis to make sure it constantly matches the level of risk you've chosen initially. However, if your attitude towards risk or your circumstances change, you can simply switch to another MAPS fund.

Diversification: These multi-asset funds invest in a broad range of assets. This helps to spread your risk and gives you exposure to a wide range of global investment opportunities.

Monitored, reviewed and actively managed for you: The assets in these funds will all perform differently at different times. So, each fund is monitored, reviewed and actively managed by Irish Life's investment managers.

Ease of access: The funds are priced daily and are available across a range of pensions, post-retirement, savings and investment products. Plus, with Irish Life's online services and apps, you can track the performance whenever and wherever you are, and can even switch funds if you want.

A further thought: Irish Life Multi Asset Portfolio funds can help you achieve your investment needs and goals, but is your legacy protected against Capital Acquisitions Tax on death? Through an insurance plan set up under Section 72 CAT Consolidation Act 2003 with a guaranteed price and a guaranteed level of cover, Irish Life can help you protect your legacy into the future. For further information, email me at jlowe@moneydoctors.ie

Be aware that all funds can fall as well as rise in value, and may be worth less than what was paid in. MAPS funds will not be suitable for you if you do not want to take any risk. They may be affected by changes in currency exchange rates. As with all managed funds, there are associated annual management/fund charges, and there may be early exit fees. Please email me for more details.

2. INITIATIVE IRELAND – A SECURED PEER TO PEER LENDING OPPORTUNITY

Founded in 2015 by Padraig W Rushe, Initiative Ireland is an **Impact Finance Platform**, designed to appeal to conservative investors who want to 'earn good and do good', as impact investors.

Initiative Ireland provides finance to experienced property developers, to fund the construction of energy-efficient social and affordable housing projects. These loans are co-funded by the company's online co-funding community, made up of both private and corporate members.

The company is very selective in choosing the residential construction projects it backs. To provide security for its community of investors, Initiative Ireland also takes the first legal charge over the houses being built, requiring a minimum of 133% in expected collateral cover throughout the project.

The interest rates for each loan vary from 6% to 8%. As a co-funder, you can expect opportunities to last from 3 to 24 months, and you get to pick which loans you want to fund, via your secured lending account. The minimum investment amount of €1,000 is also very accessible for a personal investor.

More about Initiative Ireland

Initiative Ireland operate Ireland's largest Secured Lending Marketplace. Unlike other peer to peer or marketplace Lenders, all of their loans are secured against property and the company also puts significant focus on social impact. Initiative Ireland has a very experienced senior management team with impressive finance backgrounds, standing apart from many other platforms in Ireland and the UK. The company also manages the entire process on behalf of its investment community from end to end, working with an impressive panel of solicitors and quantity surveyors.

Reviewing the company's website, it is clear that they take every reasonable precaution in how they manage and structure loans, with well-thought-out contingency plans to address the sorts of issues that can arise on a residential housing project. Each project is also co-funded by one of their Corporate Credit Partners, meaning you are accessing not only secured but institutional-quality opportunities.

What Products do they Offer?

Private Lending Accounts: The company offers Private Lending Accounts for small investors, which you can open online with as little as €1,000 to lend. The application process is quick, and the website has a number of videos and FAQs on risk, returns and protection.

Pension Lending Accounts: If you have or want to open a self-managed pension, the company has partnered with a network of pension trustees and financial advisers who can help you to open a Pension Lending Account. You will have to commit €25,000 to open your account, but this compares favourably to a lot of pension products. Once you've set it up, you can lend funds from your pension into projects that you like. You benefit from the same security and social impact as with a Private Lending Account, but because you're lending from your pension, the interest income you earn is tax-free back into your pension.

Corporate Lending Accounts: At a time when many businesses are charged to hold deposits in the bank, Initiative Ireland offers businesses an opportunity to put their money to good use and earn a fair reward. Apart from making financial sense, this should appeal to Irish businesses who are looking to do their part to help tackle the housing crisis and beat the banks at their own game.

How do they manage risk?

There are risks in investing in any asset, but Initiative Ireland have clearly designed their product to appeal to lower-risk investors and financial advisers. They have taken steps to mitigate many of the risks normally associated with residential housing development, with the central one being their insistence on only offering secured loans. Just like with a mortgage, the loans are secured against the property title deeds from the start, to the benefit of you as a co-funder.

They carefully assess each loan to assure a minimum of €133k in property collateral value is in place for every €100k released to the borrower during the loan. This collateral cover protects you as a lender from market volatility, providing a more predictable return for lenders without the work and risks usually involved with direct property investing. The company also has the right to simply step in and take control of the development to further enhance outcomes for investors.

They go to great lengths to explain these risks, and it is very clear that they understand them and have the experience and resources to manage them for their clients.

What are the key benefits for you as a lender?

A real return: The primary objective of every saver and investor should be to be able to buy more of what they need and/or want in the future as an outcome of not spending their money now. Why would you put your hard-earned cash away for a few years only to find when you take it back that you can buy or afford less of what you need or want? The investment must therefore earn a return greater than the rate of inflation (which erodes value) and net of income tax, i.e. a 'real return'. Initiative Ireland offers such real rates of return to their investors after allowing for inflation and tax liability.

Cost savings: Unlike most investment products, Initiative Ireland's Personal and Corporate Lending Accounts currently do not have any charges for investors, thus enhancing the available return. Pension Lending Accounts do have a one-time setup fee of 0.5%, but this compares well to similar products.

Transparency: Initiative Ireland's website is comprehensive and provides the detail necessary for investors to make informed decisions. As a client you're in the driving seat – you can see each loan and project and decide which ones you want to back.

Diversification: Investments in senior secured property loans of this kind have low volatility historically and are less impacted by traditional markets.

Resilience: Initiative Ireland doesn't finance high-end developments, instead focussing on social and affordable housing. In the event of market volatility or an economic downturn, the demand for social housing is only likely to increase, so this compares favourably to more high-end property investments in terms of market resilience.

For an income: Earning interest from lending is one of the oldest forms of generating an income return. Many investments available currently are struggling to generate worthwhile real income returns.

Access: The investment term of 3 to 24 months (project specific) is considerably shorter than many available with other investment products. With fixed interest rates on offer, it does exactly what it says on the tin.

What are the key benefits for the property developer, compared to bank lending?

Speed of decision: Initiative Ireland have streamlined their online services to enable them to deliver quicker decisions on loan approvals than the banks and many other financial institutions.

Finance reliability: Because of Initiative Ireland's Corporate Credit Partners, they offer borrowers the same surety of funding they get elsewhere, but long term, as new funders enter and leave the market via Initiative Ireland, the borrower can access a broad network of funders while building one trusted relationship with their highly professional team.

Competitive interest rates: Initiative Ireland offer competitive rates compared to other lenders in the market. This is good news for investors, because competitive pricing attracts more experienced developers, which further reduces lending risks.

Social focus: It only makes sense that borrowers feel more comfortable working with impact investment platforms that want to see the homes delivered and are willing to work extra-hard to see that happen. No doubt borrowers also enjoy the idea of their interest repayments directly enriching everyday people instead of bank shareholders.

Why Initiative Ireland is one of my top tips for 2020

Initiative Ireland aim to be 'honest, fair and inclusive', offering investors a real return while delivering badly needed social impact in the Irish residential housing sector, where demand continues to outstrip supply. They could offer their clients lower returns and still compete favourably, but I guess that's yet another benefit of working with a social impact platform.

For further information visit www.initiativeireland.ie. Investors can commit funds online or through their financial advisors.

3. CANTOR FITZGERALD – A BESPOKE PRIVATE CLIENTS' SERVICE

What is a private client? Cantor Fitzgerald Ireland is part of leading global financial services firm Cantor Fitzgerald. Their clients include private investors, business owners, directors, self-employed, families, charities and various corporate and non-profit organisations seeking wealth management advice and investment solutions. Whether a first-time investor or a more experienced client, Cantor Fitzgerald private clients' services have the experience and expertise to guide you through various investment options. Working closely with private clients since 1995 when Cantor Fitzgerald (Cantor) first set up in Ireland, the company fully recognises that clients' goals and requirements will be unique to them.

Cantor private client's services offer a range of wealth management services tailored to investment objectives and risk profile. They specialise in direct investment solutions for individual, pension, corporate and charity clients and believe strongly in the value of personal contact and client relationships. Always encouraging investors and clients to call them or to request a call-back at a time that suits, their service levels are second to none.

Cantor private clients' services have four levels of service. Each can be accessed via an investment account or a pension account.

- Execution Only
- Advisory
- Advisory Managed
- Discretionary

The Execution Only service is for you if:

- you have knowledge of financial markets;
- you are comfortable making your own investment decisions and/or managing your own portfolio;
- you don't require advice or investment recommendations; and
- you fully understand any investment and the associated risks.

With this range of service levels, Cantor take a personalised approach to understanding your needs, wants and aspirations to provide you with long-term, bespoke investment solutions. You should consider either Advisory service if:

- you like to retain control of your own investment decisions/the final decision rests with you;
- you will receive professional advice and recommendations from your broker or portfolio manager – to help you seize the best opportunities;

- Cantor implement the agreed investment decisions on your behalf; and
- you will be required to monitor your investments on an ongoing basis.

Their Advisory service is for clients who like to discuss individual investments on a stand-alone basis, and their Advisory Managed service is for clients who want advice on investments within an overall portfolio.

You should consider a Discretionary service if:

- you would prefer a professional investment manager to manage your investment decisions (within agreed parameters);
- you may not have the time to manage your own investments; or
- you may have limited knowledge of financial markets and the associated risks involved.

You will be regularly updated on the performance of your investments, as frequently as required.

Full details on a Discretionary Portfolio Service can also be accessed on request.

All Wealth Management services involve:

- an initial discussion to get to know the client;
- completion of a full fact find;
- assisting your current financial circumstances;
- understanding your needs and goals; and
- assessing your risk tolerance, capacity for loss and investment time horizon.

Cantor then provide a financial proposal, and review this plan annually to ensure it is aligned with your goals and updated for any changes in your personal or family circumstances.

Establishing the above information allows Cantor to design the most appropriate investment strategy for you. You may have multiple goals with different time horizons attached. It is not uncommon for a Cantor portfolio manager to manage more than one investment strategy in separate portfolios that are based on your different goals. Think of it as a goal-based approach to investing, setting up different investment buckets for your short-, medium- and long-term goals.

- Your short-term goal might be a college fund for children or deposit for a house.
- Your medium-/long-term goal might be to fund your retirement.
- If you have surplus funds and assets, your long-term aspirational goal might be to preserve your wealth to pass onto your children.

Each goal-based portfolio will have a different investment time horizon and often different risk profiles attached due to this investment time horizon. For example, your short-term investments may need to be lower-risk investments, but your medium- to long-term investments may be moderate-risk.

Generally, the longer your money remains invested, the greater the potential for growth, as market trends and fluctuations tend to smooth out over time. Investing for short-term gains can be risky.

Access to your investments is an important consideration when deciding the most suitable option for you. By establishing the time horizon for your investment, you can potentially avoid the panic that comes with short-term market fluctuations and volatility.

Portfolio Construction: A very important decision when constructing your personalised portfolio is asset allocation. Your portfolio manager will work with you to build a portfolio that is allocated to various assets that offer you the best chance of achieving your investment goals within your level of risk tolerance. Cantor offer diversified portfolios that spread your investment across a broad mix of assets, helping to reduce the impact of sudden falls in any individual investment or individual markets.

Depending on your requirements, your Cantor portfolio could contain some of the following:

- Cantor's Merrion Investment Managers (MIM) multi asset funds. MIM offer a full suite of funds across multi-asset, equities, fixed income, cash and absolute return, and specialise in active investment management that follows their proven and robust three-pillar investment process. These funds have an excellent short-, medium- and long-term performance record.
- Cantor's Discretionary Portfolio service, such as their actively managed Equity model portfolios, which aim to generate superior risk-adjusted returns over the medium-long term. Two such examples include:
  - Global Equity Income
  - Cantor Core Portfolio

  These are particularly suited to high-net-worth individuals, non-profit organisations and family offices.
- Cantor's Bespoke Advisory Service offers expert bespoke advice to clients devising short-term and long-term trading strategies. This is a highly client-engaging and interactive level of service, with each adjustment to the portfolio requiring client approval. Your portfolio manager may also provide access to a range of specialist investment

opportunities, tax relief schemes (EIIS), private equity and loan
notes, structured investments and various investment funds and
ETFs.

Once your portfolio is established, the Cantor portfolio managers will
work with you to review and reshape your investments over time. You will
receive regular valuations and have access to their online portal where you
can view your portfolio and documents. The minimum investment amount
for a dedicated Portfolio Manager looking for their Wealth Management
service is €200,000.

If you would like any further information on their Execution Only
service or any of their Wealth Management services, including an
Integrated Financial Advice and Lifestyle Planning service, please email
MoneyDoctor@Cantor.com

4. GOLDCORE LTD – IRELAND'S #1 GOLD DEALER

With many stock and bond markets at all-time record highs after
significant appreciation in recent years, it is a good time for Irish
investors to rebalance investment and pension portfolios.

Uncertain times make gold an increasingly important diversification,
and volatility in stock markets on concerns about Trump, Brexit and the
global economy are seeing investors continue to diversify into gold.

Brexit is a real risk, but it has yet to significantly impact markets,
investments and Irish investors. Property markets in London and Dublin
are, however, beginning to show strains after significant appreciation.

It is important to remember that gold is a hedge and acts as a hedge
when traditional assets fall in value. This was seen classically during the
financial crisis, and again for UK investors when the Brexit process began
in 2016. Gold rose over 40% in 2016 in sterling terms, and thus acted as a
hedge for UK investors and savers.

Gold has performed quite poorly in the short term as most stock, bond
and property markets have seen strong gains – many reaching new record
highs. But over the long term, of 10, 15 and 20 years, gold has performed
strongly. Over a 15-year period, gold has returned 8.9% per annum in euro
terms (see table on next page).

Central banks remain the largest buyers of gold in 2018. They continue
to diversify their foreign exchange reserves into gold bullion due to
concerns about fiat currencies – including the dollar and the euro.

The smart money is diversifying into gold, as seen in gold buying by
Lord Rothschild and billionaire investors such as Rogers, Faber, Singer,
Dalio, Bass, Einhorn, Odey, Druckenmiller, Paulson and Gross.

Gold Price Performance: % Annual Change   Thursday, October 11, 2018

	USD	AUD	CAD	CHF	CNY	EUR	GBP	INR	JPY
2003	19.7%	-9.5%	-0.4%	7.7%	19.7%	0.5%	8.6%	13.6%	7.7%
2004	5.3%	1.8%	-1.9%	-3.4%	5.3%	-2.7%	-2.3%	0.6%	0.7%
2005	20.0%	28.9%	15.4%	37.8%	17.0%	36.8%	33.0%	24.2%	37.6%
2006	23.0%	13.7%	23.0%	14.1%	19.1%	10.6%	8.1%	20.9%	24.3%
2007	30.9%	18.3%	12.1%	21.7%	22.3%	18.4%	29.2%	16.5%	22.9%
2008	5.6%	31.3%	30.1%	-0.1%	-2.4%	10.5%	43.2%	28.8%	-14.4%
2009	23.4%	-3.0%	5.9%	20.1%	23.6%	20.7%	12.7%	19.3%	26.8%
2010	29.5%	13.5%	22.3%	16.7%	24.9%	38.8%	34.3%	23.7%	13.0%
2011	10.1%	10.2%	13.5%	11.2%	5.9%	14.2%	10.5%	31.1%	4.5%
2012	7.0%	5.4%	4.3%	4.2%	6.2%	4.9%	2.2%	10.3%	20.7%
2013	-28.3%	-16.2%	-23.0%	-30.1%	-30.2%	-31.2%	-29.4%	-18.7%	-12.8%
2014	-1.5%	7.7%	7.9%	9.9%	1.2%	12.1%	5.0%	0.8%	12.3%
2015	-10.4%	0.4%	7.5%	-9.9%	-6.2%	-0.3%	-5.2%	-5.9%	-10.1%
2016	9.1%	10.5%	5.9%	10.8%	16.8%	12.4%	30.2%	11.9%	5.8%
2017	13.6%	4.6%	6.0%	8.1%	6.4%	-1.0%	3.2%	6.4%	8.9%
2018	-6.3%	2.8%	-2.8%	-4.8%	-0.8%	-2.8%	-4.1%	8.2%	-6.7%
Average	9.4%	7.5%	7.9%	7.1%	8.0%	8.9%	11.2%	12.0%	8.8%

goldprice.org

There is also buying from institutions such as the world's largest insurer Munich Re, the world's largest asset manager Blackrock Inc. and the increasingly powerful People's Bank of China.

Currency debasement is likely to continue, and now deposit 'bail-ins' and confiscation are quite possible. Irish banks are vulnerable, as seen in the recent stress tests.

Being properly diversified, with the twin Brexit and Trump risks and in an era of negative interest rates and bail-in risks, is paramount. Having an allocation to gold has never been more important for investors, savers and pension owners.

The investment and savings landscape in Ireland is uncertain – as is the outlook for stocks, property and various savings vehicles.

Gold's medium and long-term fundamentals remain positive due to 'MSGM' – which stands for macroeconomic, systemic, geopolitical and monetary risks:

- **Macroeconomic risk** is high, as there is a serious risk of recessions in major industrial nations that are massively debt-laden as the global debt-to-GDP ratio has risen to over 327%. The US national debt continues to surge and has risen another $1.5 trillion as Trump spends money with reckless abandon.

- **Systemic risk** remains high, as little of the trouble in the banking and financial system has been addressed. There is a real risk of another 'Lehman Brothers' moment, or a new 'Grexit' moment, and a seizing up of the global financial system. Deutsche Bank is a risk in this regard, as is Italy.

- **Geopolitical risk** remains elevated. Brexit has created a whole new set of risks to Ireland, the UK and the entire eurozone. The Middle East remains a powder keg, and tensions with Russia remain very real. There is a real risk of conflict and the consequent effect on oil prices, global markets and the global economy.
- **Monetary risk** is high, as the Federal Reserve, the ECB, the Bank of England, the BOJ and the majority of central banks try to move away from the unprecedented quantitative easing of recent years (over $15 trillion worth) toward quantitative tightening. The printing of currency and debasement of currencies on a grand, global scale will likely not end well.

Owning physical gold in the safest vaults in the world will again protect and grow wealth in the coming years.

The wise old Wall Street adage was that one should have 10% of one's assets in physical gold and hope that it does not work. The implication here is that gold is counter-cyclical – if gold rises sharply in price, it usually means that stocks and shares, bonds, property, and indeed one's business, may be losing value. This has been seen throughout history, and was again seen during the financial crisis from 2007 to 2011.

Allocations can range from 5% on the low side to 20% on the high side. Today, respected investment experts internationally are advocating allocations of 20% to gold, given the risks of today.

Placing all of one's wealth in any asset, including gold, is risky, but an allocation to gold is essential financial insurance in these uncertain times.

How to invest in gold

GoldCore Secure Storage: Directly own gold coins or bars as an investment or in your pension in segregated and allocated insured storage in some of the safest private vaults in the world in Dublin, London, Zurich, Singapore and/or Hong Kong. Premiums on gold bars range from 1% to 3.75% and annual insured storage is 0.49% to 1% per annum depending on the size of the investment.

Perth Mint Certificates: This is operated by the Perth Mint of Western Australia, established in 1899, which is wholly-owned and guaranteed by the Government of Western Australia. The PMCP allows Irish investors, savers and pension funds to own investment-grade gold, silver and platinum bullion. Fees on buying certificates range from 2% to 3.9% depending on the amount bought.

Unallocated gold certificates have no storage fee and allocated gold certificates cost 1% per annum. The selling fee is 1.5%.

GoldSaver: GoldSaver is a regular savings account, but instead of saving in euro, one saves in physical gold. GoldSaver account holders buy gold online on a monthly basis with a minimum monthly purchase from as little as €100, paid conveniently by direct debit. Account holders can also make additional lump sum deposits at any time. GoldSaver has a 5% premium to buy and a 1% annual administration plus a charge of 1.5% when you sell.

Gold coins/bars – insured delivery or safety deposit box storage: GoldCore make a market in all popular gold bullion coins and bars for delivery and insured storage in specialist vaults or safety deposit boxes. They offer competitive pricing for gold bars (1 ounce, 10 ounce and 1 kilo), British Gold Sovereigns, Austrian Philharmonics, Canadian Maple Leaves, American Eagles, South African Krugerrands, Silver Eagles, Silver Maples and all major bullion products. Volume discounts are applied to large lump sum investments.

5. REBATEINSOLVE.IE – IRELAND'S #1 PERSONAL INSOLVENCY PRACTICE

Although I am a Personal Insolvency Practitioner (PIP) myself, Rebate Insolvency Solutions of Newbridge, County Kildare, are considered the best in the country when it comes to finding debt solutions for their clients. They are authorised and regulated by the Insolvency Service of Ireland for personal insolvency and the Central Bank of Ireland for debt management. This dual regulation allows for far wider resolves.

Getting out of debt or resolving a debt issue is like a game of snakes and ladders. The key thing is that you must start somewhere and, at some stage, move along to a resolution. Some moves you make will bring you on and some will bring you back, but everyone will eventually get a resolution if they choose to engage with the game.

Those working in financial institutions are generally nice and good people, doing a job. Those in the Arrears Support Units and Personal Insolvency Units report to a Credit Committee that remain faceless, and the Committee makes the call on whether to direct their solicitors to write nasty letters or write directly themselves – it is all directed by policy. So debtors should be nice and relaxed too in the process. Always take the call and never ignore them. It may be painful, but these people are trying to help.

If you can't face the call, seek help from a PIP. There are 114 of them around the country, acting as arbitrators between debtors and creditors or MABS (Money Advice & Budgeting Services – with offices all over Ireland), or Debt Managers regulated by the Central Bank of Ireland.

Always remember there *is* a solution, no matter how bleak your situation may seem. RebateInsolve.ie have had €millions written off in many of their personal insolvency cases, attracting great media attention. However, they always seek to find a fair and balanced resolution to keep their clients in their family home and allow them to contribute to the economy and the growth of the country.

Understanding the creditor and the debtor owner

This is key to knowing who you are dealing with – their credit policy; how they are regulated; their long-term goals; their business plan; how they operated in the past; and how they are dealing with debts at present.

This is the first look at the cards they are holding and what type of a game needs to be played for a resolution. Some mortgage providers that might have a bad name are the ones RebateInsolve.ie prefer to deal with – don't listen to pub talk.

The Maths

The maths are the maths, and cannot be argued away. You earn X amount; you spend Y amount to live day to day; and you have Z amount left over for mortgage and bills. If there is No Z amount, then you have reduced options in dealing with your debt, and the bankruptcy option comes to the forefront, or mortgage-to-rent on the family home. If you have Z amount, maybe a restructuring of the mortgage, with some allowance for unsecured debts, and then a Personal Insolvency Arrangement (PIA) is your resolution.

Insolvency and bankruptcy

If the structure of an insolvency arrangement gives a better return to the creditors than the return if the same person was made bankrupt; if the insolvency arrangement is fair and balanced and the actions of the debtors are good; then in all probability the Court will see merit in this. The court review process is enacted when a personal insolvency arrangement fails at the meeting of creditors. It's a safety net for a resolution.

The Central Bank and regulation

The lenders or creditors, and some of the funds involved, are regulated by the Central Bank of Ireland, and some opt to use companies under this regulation as the debt owner. The interpretation of regulations and rights fall under the MARP process and the CCMA (see Chapter 35).

The Law, courts and judgements

Judgements have been made by the High Court over the last number of years by different justices. These judgements have come to define the insolvency law and resolves, and the structure of these resolves. So, your case could already have a precedent in insolvency law.

The family and the family home

Protecting the family home is the key priority in most debt cases. Very few people lose their family home if they make an effort to hold on to it. Insolvency legislation; the land and conveyancing act; Central Bank regulations; children in primary, secondary or college – all of these factors are taken into account when considering an application. All items of expenditure are looked at in detail.

Investment properties and commercial and business debt

Non-core assets should all be sold to bring down the debts, unless it's your business and it is required to maintain your income. The PIA should deal with the residual amount from these sales and at the end of the term.

Solicitors' letters from creditors, and court dates

Never fear such a letter, and never fear a court date. The State has put help in place, and all you need to do is go and talk and set out the situation in full. There is legal aid, the Abhaile scheme (which pays for PIPs, accountants and legal services) and duty solicitors, all there to assist you and support you.

Summary

There is a resolution for all, and there is a solution for all. The worst thing you can do is nothing at all. If you have a money issue, if it worries you or affects your sleep, call someone. There is help available to resolve it. Always make sure you find a very active PIP with a good record of results. Ask that question.

Always take action and never believe that your situation has no resolve – they all do. The best feeling people in RebateInsolve.ie get is seeing clients leaving their office after the first free consultation with hope and belief.

Time can sometimes be the resolution, as it can bring change – new job, inheritances, bank debt sale to new creditors, change in bank policy, new regulation, a new judgement. No one knows the future. Take control and sort it out today.

www.isi.gov.ie
www.backontrack.ie
www.rebateinsolve.ie
www.mabs.ie

John Mc Cormack is a PIP, QFA, Dip in Law, CMAR, APA debt management.
Rebate House, No 1 Moorefield Terrace, Newbridge, County Kildare
Tel: (045) 394014
Email: jmccormack@rebate.ie or www.rebateinsolve.ie

APPENDIX 11

BUDGET 2020

One word that encapsulates Budget 2020 is 'Brexit' ...

Paschal Donohoe, Minister for Finance and Minister for Public Expenditure and Reform, delivered his fourth budget speech at 1pm on Tuesday, 8 October 2019, and stated that his decisions were influenced by the increasing likelihood of a no-deal Brexit.

A €1.2 billion package has been announced, excluding EU funding, to respond to Brexit, if it happens. €200 million in Brexit expenditure will be available next year, to increase staffing and upgrade infrastructure across a number of departments and agencies.

With €2.1 billion already committed to expenditure measures as per the Summer Economic Statement, the balance of €700 million has a 2 to 1 loading in favour of increased spending:
- €233.3 million for tax reductions.
- €466.7 million on extra spending.

HIGHLIGHTS AT A GLANCE

- Stamp Duty on non-residential property to increase by 1.5% to 7.5%.
- Free medical cards for 56,000 additional people over the age of 70.
- Free GP visits for children under 8 and free dental care for children under 6.
- Climate change:
  - Carbon tax has increased by €6 per tonne.
  - Petrol and diesel up 2 cents per litre.
- Christmas bonus: 100% bonus will again be paid to those qualified – 1.2 million for December 2019
- Housing:
  - €2.5 billion allocated as per previous announcements, including another 11,000 new social homes in 2020 and 12,000 in 2021.
  - An additional €80 million for the Housing Assistance Payment scheme.
  - Help to Buy Scheme for first-time buyers on new and self-build homes is extended for another 2 years to 2021.
  - €20 million additional funding (totalling €166 million in 2020) to homeless services.

INCOME AND OTHER TAXES

Income tax
The Earned Income tax credit provided to the self-employed and to proprietary directors will be increased by €150 to €1,500. This will mean a tax saving of €150pa for most self-employed people and proprietary directors.

Universal Social Charge
No change in this tax (though it had been promised ...):

2019			2020	
First €12,012	0.5%		First €12,012	0.5%
Next € 7,360	2%		Next € 7,862	2%
Next €50,672	4.75%		Next €50,170	4.5%
Balance	8%		Balance	8%

For the self-employed only when income exceeds €100,000, the rate continues to attract 3% additionally to 11% (8% for employees).

Corporation Tax
- Remains unchanged at 12.5%.

Capital Gains Tax
- Remains at 33%.

Capital Acquisition Tax (inheritance tax)
- The threshold for Group A category (parent to child) increases by €15,000 to €335,000.
- Categories B & C thresholds remain unchanged.
- Rate remains at 33% over the thresholds.

Dividend Withholding Tax increases to 25%
- Dividend Withholding Tax (DWT) is currently levied at standard rate, 20%, on dividends paid by Irish resident companies, with exemption for pension and ARF investors.

Deposit Interest Retention Tax (DIRT)
- The DIRT rate has been being reduced in stages from 41% in 2016. This means the DIRT rate in 2020 will reduce from its current 35%

rate to 33%, which will be the same as the Capital Gains Tax and Capital Acquisitions Tax rate.

- No change in the exit tax rate of 41% on investments.

Stamp Duty

- 1.5% increase on all non-residential (commercial) property, to 7.5%.

Electric cars

- 0% BIK (Benefit In Kind) charge on electric vehicles extended to 2022, if they qualify:
  - Under €50,000 price.
  - All electric (not hybrid).
- VRT relief on hybrids extended to 2020.

Small and medium-sized businesses

- Earned Income Tax Credit for self-employed increased by €150 to €1500. This will benefit over 147,000 people.
- Increase in employer's PRSI rates:
  - Because of a 0.1% increase in the National Training Fund Levy (which is collected with PRSI) the employer's PRSI Class A rate will increase from its current 10.95% to 11.05% in 2020, for employees earning more than €386 pw. For lower earners, the employer's PRSI Class A rate will increase from 8.7% to 8.8% in 2020.
  - For income up to €20,072 the new rate is 8.8%.
  - For income exceeding €20,072 the new rate is 11.05% (0.1% increase).
  - Income threshold for higher rate employer PRSI increasing to €386pw (€20,072 a year).

SOCIAL WELFARE BENEFITS

- Free medical cards to qualifying pensioners over age 70.
  - Income thresholds raised by €500 for a single applicant, and by €1,050 for a couple.
  - An additional 56,000 people will now qualify for a medical card.
- State pensions increased in Budget 2019 by €5 to €248.50 per week from March 2019, but there was no increase in Budget 2020.

  It meant that those forced to invest in AMRFs because they did not reach the threshold of an annual income of €12,700 attain that mark, and their AMRFs will become ARFs (this is automatic –

no paperwork). Should they wish to encash the entire fund, they may do so now, but it will be fully taxable.

- Home Carer Tax Credit – €100 increase to €1,600 per annum.
- The Living Alone Allowance will increase by €5 to €14 per week from March 2020.
- One Parent Allowance – earnings disregard increased by €15 to €165 per week, without affecting the One Parent Family Payment.
- Job Seeker Transition Allowance – earnings disregard also increased by €15 to €165 per week.
- Jobseekers Allowance for those aged 25 will increase by €45.20 to €203 per week from January 2020.
- Jobseeker's Allowance payment for those aged under 25 will increase to the maximum rate where they are living independently and in receipt of State housing support.

CHILDREN

- The Qualified Child Payment paid to parents on social welfare increases by €2 to €36 per week in respect of under 12s, and by €3 to €40 per week in respect of over 12s.
- Children under 8 to get free GP visits.
- Children under 6 to get free dental care.

HOUSING, THE HOMELESS AND OTHER SOCIAL HOUSING BENEFITS

- Help to Buy Scheme retained for first-time buyers of new homes by way of a 5% income tax refund. Maximum payment is €20,000, and maximum purchase price is €500,000. The rebate will be of income tax paid over the previous four years and only purchases of new homes will qualify. The applicants must also take out a mortgage of 70% of the purchase price to qualify. In 2019, 15,000 first time buyers availed of this grant. This scheme is retained to December 2021.
- Mortgage Interest Relief due to end 2017 for those who took out mortgages between 2004 and 2012 is extended but will be phased out by 2020 – 25% in 2020.
- Homeless services budget increased by €20m to €166m.
- €2.5bn in funding for housing, with 11,000 new social housing units by 2020 still the target, and 12,000 of them built in 2021 by the local authorities and approved housing bodies.

- An extra €80m provided for the Housing Assistance Payment (HAP) to support existing tenants and also provide an additional 50,750 new tenancies next year.
- Fuel Allowance increases by €2 to € 24.50 per week.
- Household Benefits Package extended – gas/electricity allowance and free TV licence to qualifying people under 70 who have another adult living with them (currently only single adults under 70 can avail of the household benefits package).

INDIRECT TAXES, EXCISE AND OTHER DUTIES

- Tobacco – up 50 cents per pack of 20, now costing €13.50 per pack, and 30g packet of rolling tobacco will now be more than €16, effective from midnight, 9 October 2019. If you smoke a pack of cigarettes a day and you are on the 40% tax rate, you will need to earn about €872 every month to maintain your habit!
- Petrol/diesel – up 2 cents per litre (or €1 for a 50-litre fill) from midnight, 8 October 2019. This is the first of 10 planned annual increases. Home heating oil will only increase next May, after winter has passed. A tank of oil will cost you an additional €15 from next May.
- Alcohol – no increases on beer, spirits or wines.
- Nitrogen oxide tax – the 1% diesel surcharge introduced on VRT last year is being replaced by a nitrogen oxide tax that will be applied to all new cars and used imports from January 2020.

OTHER ITEMS

EII scheme limit increased

The Employment and Investment Incentive (EII) scheme relief is one of the few remaining 'all income' tax relief schemes, where investors can get full income tax relief (subject to certain conditions) for investment in qualifying small and medium-sized trading companies.

The current €150,000 limit on investment in the EII scheme increases to €250,000 from 8 October 2019 and tax relief will now be available in the year of investment rather than splitting it over two instalments as at present.

The annual limit increases to €500,000 for investors who are prepared to invest in EII for ten years or more.

Paid parental leave

A new paid parental leave scheme, announced in Budget 2019, will be introduced in November 2019 to provide two extra weeks' leave to every parent of a child in their first year. The Government intends to increase this to seven extra weeks over time.

Prescription charges

- €1.50 prescription charge reduced to €1.00 for those over 70 years of age with a medical card.
- Threshold for the drugs payment scheme falls from €124 to €114 per month.

For farmers, farming and the agri-food sector

- Farm restructuring relief will be extended until 2022.
- The Government is investing €2 billion in rural Ireland in 2020, including €51 million more for the Department of Agriculture.
- €3 million will go to pilot new agri-environmental schemes in 2020, to reduce emissions in the sector.

INDEX